Political Violence and the Imagination

Using a variety of theoretical reflections and empirically grounded case studies, this book examines how certain kinds of imagination – political, artistic, historical, philosophical – help us tackle the challenge of comprehending and responding to various forms of political violence.

Understanding political violence is a complex task, which involves a variety of operations, from examining the social macro-structures within which actors engage in violence, to investigating the motives and drives of individual perpetrators. This book focuses on the faculty of imagination and its role in facilitating our normative and critical engagement with political violence. It interrogates how the imagination can help us deal with past as well as ongoing instances of political violence. Several questions, which have thus far received too little attention from political theorists, motivate this project: Can certain forms of imagination – artistic, historical, philosophical – help us tackle the challenge of comprehending and responding to unprecedented forms of violence? What is the ethical and political value of artworks depicting human rights violations in the aftermath of conflicts? What about the use of thought experiments in justifying policy measures with regard to violence? What forms of political imagination can foster solidarity and catalyse political action?

This book opens up a forum for an inclusive and reflexive debate on the role that the imagination can play in unpacking complex issues of political violence.

The chapters in this book were originally published in a special issue of the journal, *Critical Review of International Social and Political Philosophy*.

Mathias Thaler is Senior Lecturer in Political Theory at the University of Edinburgh. His main research interest is in contemporary political theory. He is currently working on a project analysing the utopian dimensions in current debates around climate change.

Mihaela Mihai is Senior Lecturer in Political Theory at the University of Edinburgh. Her research interests cut across political and social theory, history and aesthetics. More precisely, she has written on political emotions, political judgment, the politics of memory, art and politics.

Political Violence and the Imagination
Complicity, Memory and Resistance

Edited by
Mathias Thaler and Mihaela Mihai

LONDON AND NEW YORK

First published 2020
by Routledge
2 Park Square, Milton Park, Abingdon, Oxon, OX14 4RN

and by Routledge
52 Vanderbilt Avenue, New York, NY 10017

Routledge is an imprint of the Taylor & Francis Group, an informa business

© 2020 Taylor & Francis

All rights reserved. No part of this book may be reprinted or reproduced or utilised in any form or by any electronic, mechanical, or other means, now known or hereafter invented, including photocopying and recording, or in any information storage or retrieval system, without permission in writing from the publishers.

Trademark notice: Product or corporate names may be trademarks or registered trademarks, and are used only for identification and explanation without intent to infringe.

British Library Cataloguing in Publication Data
A catalogue record for this book is available from the British Library

ISBN13: 978-0-367-51517-1

Typeset in Myriad Pro
by Newgen Publishing UK

Publisher's Note
The publisher accepts responsibility for any inconsistencies that may have arisen during the conversion of this book from journal articles to book chapters, namely the inclusion of journal terminology.

Disclaimer
Every effort has been made to contact copyright holders for their permission to reprint material in this book. The publishers would be grateful to hear from any copyright holder who is not here acknowledged and will undertake to rectify any errors or omissions in future editions of this book.

Contents

Citation Information vii
Notes on Contributors ix

Political violence and the imagination: an introduction 1
Mihaela Mihai and Mathias Thaler

1 Understanding complicity: memory, hope and the imagination 8
  Mihaela Mihai

2 The arts of refusal: tragic unreconciliation, pariah humour, and haunting laughter 27
  Bronwyn Anne Leebaw

3 How America disguises its violence: colonialism, mass incarceration, and the need for resistant imagination 46
  Shari Stone-Mediatore

4 The subversive potential of Leo Tolstoy's 'defamiliarisation': a case study in drawing on the imagination to denounce violence 66
  Alexandre Christoyannopoulos

5 Our wildest imagination: violence, narrative, and sympathetic identification 85
  Jade Schiff

6 On representation(s): art, violence and the political imaginary of South Africa 102
  Eliza Garnsey

7 The art and politics of imagination: remembering mass violence against women 122
Maria Alina Asavei

Index 141

Citation Information

The chapters in this book were originally published in the *Critical Review of International Social and Political Philosophy*, volume 22, issue 5 (June 2019). When citing this material, please use the original page numbering for each article, as follows:

Introduction
Political violence and the imagination: an introduction
Mihaela Mihai and Mathias Thaler
Critical Review of International Social and Political Philosophy, volume 22, issue 5 (June 2019), pp. 497–503

Chapter 1
Understanding complicity: memory, hope and the imagination
Mihaela Mihai
Critical Review of International Social and Political Philosophy, volume 22, issue 5 (June 2019), pp. 504–522

Chapter 2
The arts of refusal: tragic unreconciliation, pariah humour, and haunting laughter
Bronwyn Anne Leebaw
Critical Review of International Social and Political Philosophy, volume 22, issue 5 (June 2019), pp. 523–541

Chapter 3
How America disguises its violence: colonialism, mass incarceration, and the need for resistant imagination
Shari Stone-Mediatore
Critical Review of International Social and Political Philosophy, volume 22, issue 5 (June 2019), pp. 542–561

Chapter 4
The subversive potential of Leo Tolstoy's 'defamiliarisation': a case study in drawing on the imagination to denounce violence
Alexandre Christoyannopoulos
Critical Review of International Social and Political Philosophy, volume 22, issue 5 (June 2019), pp. 562–580

Chapter 5
Our wildest imagination: violence, narrative, and sympathetic identification
Jade Schiff
Critical Review of International Social and Political Philosophy, volume 22, issue 5 (June 2019), pp. 581–597

Chapter 6
On representation(s): art, violence and the political imaginary of South Africa
Eliza Garnsey
Critical Review of International Social and Political Philosophy, volume 22, issue 5 (June 2019), pp. 598–617

Chapter 7
The art and politics of imagination: remembering mass violence against women
Maria Alina Asavei
Critical Review of International Social and Political Philosophy, volume 22, issue 5 (June 2019), pp. 618–636

For any permission-related enquiries please visit:
www.tandfonline.com/page/help/permissions

Notes on Contributors

Maria Alina Asavei, Institute of International Studies, Charles University, Prague, Czech Republic

Alexandre Christoyannopoulos, Politics and International Relations, Loughborough University, Loughborough, UK

Eliza Garnsey, Department of Politics and International Studies, University of Cambridge, Cambridge, UK

Bronwyn Anne Leebaw, Department of Political Science, University of California–Riverside, Riverside, CA, USA

Mihaela Mihai, Politics and International Relations, School of Social and Political Science, University of Edinburgh, Edinburgh, UK

Jade Schiff, Department of Politics, Oberlin College, Oberlin, OH, USA

Shari Stone-Mediatore, Philosophy Department, Ohio Wesleyan University, Delaware, OH, USA

Mathias Thaler, Politics and International Relations, School of Social and Political Science, University of Edinburgh, Edinburgh, UK

Political violence and the imagination: an introduction

Mihaela Mihai and Mathias Thaler

Grappling with political violence is a complex task, involving several operations, from examining the social macro-structures within which actors engage in violence, to investigating their concrete motives as perpetrators, collaborators and bystanders. This issue focuses on the faculty of imagination and its role in facilitating our critical and political engagement with violence. It interrogates how the imagination can help address past and present instances, practices and structures of violence. Several questions guide the following contributions: How does the imagination restrict or enable the ways in which we respond to political violence? What is the relationship between the individual imagination and the shared pool of meanings – the social imaginary – we tap into when we act in the world, including when we act violently or when we react to violence? What elements in a social imaginary fuel, and what elements thwart, political violence? How can we destabilise dominant, violence-generating narratives within social imaginaries? What role do victims' testimonies play in this process? Can we envisage a role for artworks as well, and if so, what kind of artworks are suitable? How exactly can artworks foster solidarity, catalyse resistance and nurture habits of denouncing violence within a community, but also beyond its boundaries and trans-generationally?

Building on insights from political thought, social theory, history, aesthetics, literature and visual arts, this issue provides a forum for an inclusive and reflexive debate on these questions. The papers combine theoretical reflection with in-depth analysis of case studies, ranging from ideologically and economically motivated violence in Vichy France, mass incarceration in the United States, sexual violence against women in the Former Yugoslavia and Egypt, colonial violence and violence against animals.

Complicity with systemic, institutionalised violence is a central theme for all contributors. While a vast literature in political and legal philosophy offers rich conceptualisations of complicity, Mihai kick-starts the issue by arguing that we need to leave behind mainstream philosophy's methodological individualism, its time-slice approach to wrong-doing and its implausible account of human agency. She proposes that the interplay between individuals' socially mediated memories, the scope of their political imagination and the intensity of their hopes and fears influence their position on a spectrum of involvement in systemic violence. Moreover, this position should be understood relationally, dynamically and temporally. Mihai's paper envisages individuals as socially embedded beings, located within a temporally and intersubjectively experienced social world, with which, in a deep sense, they are inescapably complicit. This embeddedness influences their participation in practices and patterns of complicity with political violence. An individual's positionality in the social world (at the intersection of class, gender, religion, among others) influences her horizon of expectations, her views of her own agency and the others', her memories and the memories she shares collectively through the social imaginary, the type of social relations she inhabits, her level of social trust, as well as the extent of her political imagination. Most importantly, this position changes over time, reflecting transformations in both context and the agent herself. A temporally sensitive analysis of several forms of complicity in Vichy France – ideological collaboration, working for repressive police institutions and *délation* (the systemic practice of denouncing Jews, communists, masons and other 'undesirables' to the authorities) – gives concreteness to these theoretical proposals.

Leebaw, too, is interested in complicity with violence, which she captures through the language of reconciliation in three different ways: 'reconciliation to one's role as a participant in, or bystander to abuse, reconciliation as self-abnegating assimilation, and reconciliation as compromise, scapegoating, or denial.' (p. 524)The first form of reconciliation/complicity is exemplified by Adolf Eichmann, the second by assimilationist refugees, and the third by soldiers who participate in war crimes. Like Mihai, Leebaw thinks of complicity temporally: 'If people feel that action is futile, they begin to make compromises that can grow larger over time.' (p. 528)Trying to understand why people 'become reconciled to what they should refuse or resist' (p. 526), she is particularly puzzled by the deadening of emotions, thoughtlessness and the failure of the imagination to inspire options beyond those that one is faced with. Building on Hannah Arendt's work, Leebaw reflects on how we can awaken emotional responsiveness and get the imagination moving to avoid problematic reconciliations to a violent and unjust reality. Against Eichmann's cog-like mentality, Leebaw argues that tragic accounts of resistance can combat resignation and despair, by inviting critical thinking and pushing our imagination to conjure alternative courses of action. Against those who internalise the role of the pariah in order to assimilate to the very communities that reject them, she proposes the antidote of pariah humour – Heine's and Chaplin's – which invites the affective identification with the marginalised 'little man'. While precariously successful, pariah humour exposes the absurdity of all human hierarchies and assimilationist aspirations that require the marginalised to renounce their identity just to be recognised as human and equal. Against the tendency to reconcile with the 'fact' of war atrocities – and the myths of heroism that obscure them – Leebaw introduces anti-war veterans' haunting testimonies of being actively trained to disregard the other's humanity. Veterans who refuse to resign themselves to their role as participants in atrocities – 'winter soldiers' – thematise the meaninglessness of violence, thus destabilising social imaginaries of wartime heroism. Implicitly, they mobilise public shame and invite civilian bystanders to confront their own complicity in the reproduction of such mythologies.

Stone-Mediatore tackles the issue of complicity by investigating how a society's imaginary – and especially its resilient narratives about various categories of human beings – sustains and reproduces systemic violence. She is particularly interested in the US's 'common sense' about criminal justice and traces its similarities to the colonial imaginary, as problematised by Enrique Dussel, Aníbal Quijano, and Roberto Rodriguez. Her intention is not, however, merely interpretive. Like Mihai and Leebaw, Stone-Mediatore aims to reveal how communities become insensitive to the victims of systemic violence, accept and self-righteously exalt such violence, thus becoming complicit with it. The link between insensitivity and complicity is central to her drawing of parallels between the colonial and the criminal justice imaginaries. Within both these frames, violence is justified as having a noble end that would justify the means. It targets an unworthy, dehumanised subject, and is applied pedagogically. While colonisers invoked 'progress', supporters of mass incarceration invoke 'security' – hollow categories with no grounding in historical or contemporary reality. Both imaginaries 'contribute to an ensemble of institutional practices that regularise the abuse of people defined as violable subjects.' (p. 552) The colonised and the incarcerated are silenced and, should they dare speak, presented as threats. The coloniser's imagination – as much as that of the tough-on-crime politician – is stunted as no identification with the colonised or the inmates seems possible. Not all hope is lost, though, and Stone-Mediatore argues for recuperating imagination's power to help us see what we have been trained to ignore. Like Leebaw, she trusts stories' capacity to dislocate reified ideas about the other. Building on Hannah Arendt's account of world-travelling through the imagination, Stone-Mediatore argues for 'close engagement with the work of incarcerated writers and artists, reaching out through letters to incarcerated individuals, or joining practical struggles with incarcerated people or their families.' (p. 556) By training our imagination to take the perspective of demonised inmates, we can end up productively 'destabilising the divisions between "good" and "bad" people, and between law and violence, around which many of us have oriented our lives.' (p. 556)

Stone-Mediatore's suggestion that storytelling and art produced in prisons can help those on the outside see what the world looks like from the inmates' perspective opens up the space for Christoyannopoulos's and Schiff's contributions. Both examine literature for its capacity to move complicit readers towards potentially progressive political action. Christoyannopoulos invites us to engage with one of the giants of Western literature, Leo Tolstoy, not as a novelist, but as a Christian anarcho-pacifist. Christoyannopoulos asks a pressing question: How can our imagination be engaged critically in order to come to terms and resist our own complicity with systemic violence and oppression? The answer is through 'defamiliarisation' or *ostranenie* – an artistic device meant 'to shake readers into recognising the absurdity of common justifications of violence, admitting their implicit complicity in it, and noticing the process which numbed them into accepting such complicity' (p. 562). Theorised by Viktor Shklovsky as a tool to disturb our naturalised, automatic perceptions of social reality, defamiliarisation refuses to name the familiar by its name, breaks it down into its components and re-assembles it again, as if perceived through the eyes of a child who sees it for the first time. Tolstoy successfully deployed defamiliarisation to denounce entrenched practices of violence (flogging, deportations to Siberia, imprisonment) and their central, unquestioned place in Russia's imaginary. The social, conventional acceptance of norms that reproduce violence – the institutions of war, criminal law and conscription, or the practice of decorating military 'heroes' responsible for mass atrocities – is rendered questionable through *ostranenie*. Thus, those who, 'hypnotised by habit' (p. 566), are complicit with state-sponsored and ideologically-sanctioned violence, are encouraged to reflect on how they implicitly authorise it. Along similar lines as Leebaw's 'pariah humour', *ostranenie* can disrupt routine thinking, using laughter to prompt a recognition of routinised violence, subverting hierarchies and facilitating empathy.

Schiff is equally interested in literature's power to build solidarity through the imagination, but she aims to expand the range of beings with whom solidarity should be felt and cultivated. Motivated by the polarisation of US society in the wake of Trump's election, Schiff argues that 'there are no bounds to our capacities for sympathetic identification' (p. 581) – and that, though we may resist it, we can identify with those we share a world with, even with those we fundamentally disagree with. Through a discussion of Coetzee's *Waiting for the Barbarians*, she invites us to ponder how encounters with narratives can push readers to identify with those who inflict cruel violence on their victims. Carefully reading *Animal Farm*, Schiff proposes that we can even identify with animals, provided we let go of our attachment to the idea of human distinctiveness and control over nature. Such processes of complex identification presuppose the reader's overcoming her psychological resistance to accepting her own capacity for inflicting violence. This also involves accepting what is animal-like in humans: not just our embodied fragility, but also aggressive instincts. Through these new ways of seeing ourselves, we learn something about our imbrication in institutionalised practices of violence, such as torture or factory farming. Just as Tolstoy's defamiliarisation and Heine's humour enlightens us about our complicity with systemic violence, Coetzee's and Orwell's novels illuminate how we also have, within us, the capacity for cruelty and aggressiveness. Yet, whereas for Tolstoy the public's ignorance of their own complicity in violence was a matter of automated, habituated perception, for Schiff this is a *willed* ignorance – a deliberate reigning in of our imagination – that renders us complicit in the very cruelty we wish to deny, lest our sense of the self be endangered. If, however, we soberly reckon with the cruelty and aggressiveness that lie in us, Schiff suggests, we might hope to attenuate them, rather than unleash their destructive power on others.

While Schiff, Leebaw and Christoyannopoulos examine single-authored literary works and their capacity to trigger individual and collective processes of transformation, Asavei and Garnsey shift the focus to visual art and its role in politicising received ideas about colonial, postcolonial and war-time violence. While Garnsey follows into Schiff's, Leebaw's and Christoyannopoulos's steps by focusing on single artists, Asavei examines the critical potential of collaborative-participatory art projects that tackle political violence.

Garnsey makes theories of political and aesthetic representation to bear on ethnographic work done at the Venice Biennale, where she explored how South Africa's pavilion engaged with the issue of political violence. She examines three artworks – David Koloane's *The Journey*, Sue Williamson's *For Thirty Years Next to His Heart* and Zanele Muholi's *Faces and Phases* – to show that, first, at the Biennale, artistic representation is enmeshed with political representation: the artists were enlisted by the state to become its cultural ambassadors. Second, the artists' representations of violence challenged the national imaginary and its entrenched myths about the past, thus undermining the representative role the state had assigned them. Koloane's *The Journey* chronicles Steve Biko's death at the hands of the police, and was created while the Truth and Reconciliation Commission (TRC) was hearing his murderers' application for amnesty. Although their application was rejected, Biko's murderers were never prosecuted due to lack of evidence and expired statutes of limitations. Thus, the painting 'complicates the progressive narrative of the TRC by drawing attention to its limitations.' In contrast to Koloane's engagement with brutal violence, Williamson's *For Thirty Years Next to His Heart* tackles institutional violence. It depicts a *dompas* – an identity document that, during Apartheid, every black South African over 16 had to carry at all times. It contained private information including the bearer's work situation, and had to be endorsed by the employer. The *dompas* was the instrument through which the government legally enforced spatial segregation. Williamson's piece reveals and denounces violence in its structural guise – as law that regulates and restricts access to space and work – but also as a web of complicity in which many who upheld the system of Apartheid participated: the *dompas* features various administrators' and employers' signatures, not all of them in official capacity, thus highlighting the implication of large swathes of the white population in the institutionalised violence of Apartheid. Muholi's *Faces and Phases* completes Garnsey's analysis by directing attention to a specific category of victims of violence: LGBTI victims of hate crime. The artwork consists of several rows of portraits, from which those of hate crime victims have been removed: 'The simultaneous presence and absence of the portraits draws attention to this violence.' (p. 611) Black queer identities are thus rendered visible through a mix of 'celebration and bereavement' (p. 611) in a way that does not relegate violence to the past of Apartheid, but reveals its continuation into the present.

Asavei's article further deepens Garnsey's interest in the power of visual art to call upon the spectator's imagination to unsettle social imaginaries. However, she expands the framework of reference (the nation) and steers our attention to collaborative and participatory artworks that can, through a productive interplay between memory and the imagination, foster transnational, collective political memories. Asavei focuses on violence against women perpetrated during war or by repressive political regimes. This emphasis is important since women's voices tend to be silenced in the national imaginaries that frame processes of memory-making and redress. It is the nation, and not the various groups within and beyond it, that is usually the locus of political remembering. Violence against women often escapes the national framework – it traverses frontiers, as Asavei's examples poignantly demonstrate. In looking at collaborative artworks, she argues that 'the focus is not on the relationship art object–art spectator, but on a communal experience of co-authoring, which prepares the ground for a dialogue'. (p. 620) Building on Augusto Boal's ideas, Asavei argues that certain collective artistic practices can transform passive spectators into engaged 'spect-actors', who, even though they have not experienced the violence first-hand and thus are only 'post-witnesses', can nonetheless build solidarity with victims of violence across national borders. Spect-actors participate in new forms of grassroots politics through the very act of co-authoring an artwork. The use of the imagination in these artistic collaborations culturally mediates the collective memory of those who have not themselves directly witnessed the violence, helping them learn about it, but simultaneously fueling their hope for a different world without violence. Imagination hence interacts with memory in instructive ways: it assists spect-actors in acquiring knowledge about the victims' experience but also enables them to develop a hopeful vision of the future. A close reading of Alketa Xhafa-Mripa's *Thinking of You* (2015) and *The Blue Bra* (2011) substantiates Asavei's theoretical claims.

To those looking for unambiguous, clear guidelines about how political violence should be engaged with, the articles in this issue will fall short of bullet-proof solutions. As all the authors show, political violence is always underpinned by institutionalised patterns of exclusion and recalcitrant hierarchical social imaginaries, relationally embedded and emotionally anchored. We cannot put all our trust in the sheer power of testimonies, artistic encounters or co-production of artworks to dislocate all forms of collusion with cruelty and marginalisation. Moreover, we know that exposure to artworks and testimonies is not uniform, nor do people experience them in the same way. And of course, defamiliarisation, pariah humour, identification, engagement with testimonies by perpetrators and victims, and spect-actorship will not of necessity lead to progressive action and solidarity. There is no guarantee that our proposals for kick-starting the imagination will be successful. However, they can contribute – and have historically contributed – to expanding our sense of justice to include various victimised beings, human and non-human. It is from these precedents that we draw hope and learn how to cultivate political solidarity.

Acknowledgments

We warmly thank our contributors for their papers. Some of them participated in a workshop on political violence and the imagination which we convened at the ECPR Joint Sessions 2016 in Pisa. We are grateful to all the workshop participants for the valuable discussion. Special thanks are owed to Alex Livingston, Verena Erlenbusch, Yves Winter and to the anonymous reviewers, who offered their views on the submitted manuscripts. The ECPR workshop and this issue were supported financially by two research grants: an ERC Starting Grant (637709 GREYZONE – PI: Mihaela Mihai) and a Marie Curie Career Integration Grant (618277 JUDGEPOL – PI: Mathias Thaler). We wish to express our gratitude to the funders, and to Richard Bellamy for endorsing our idea for this special issue.

Disclosure statement

No potential conflict of interest was reported by the authors.

Funding

This work was supported by two research grants: an ERC Starting Grant [637709 GREYZONE – PI: Mihaela Mihai]; and a Marie Curie Career Integration Grant [618277 JUDGEPOL – PI: Mathias Thaler].

ORCID

Mathias Thaler http://orcid.org/0000-0001-7045-6159

Understanding complicity: memory, hope and the imagination

Mihaela Mihai

ABSTRACT
This paper addresses the thorny issue of complicity with wrongdoing under conditions of systemic political violence, such as authoritarianism, totalitarianism or military occupation. The challenge of dealing with collaborators – those who colluded with the apparatus of repression or who benefitted from its existence – is central to subsequent processes of justice and memory-making. This paper proposes several arguments. Firstly, it claims we need to think about complicity and resistance not dichotomically, but as a continuum of locations individuals can occupy. Secondly, these locations are influenced by the agents' positionality within the social world, each agent being situated at the intersection of several axes of distinction: class, gender, racialisation, and religion, among others. Thirdly, to understand complicity we also need to draw a connection between individual's experience of time and their actions: temporality is experienced from within a social position, through the interplay between memory, imagination and hope. Positionality thus affects one's memories and self-understanding, the scope of one's imagination, as well as the type and intensity of one's hopes. Therefore, individuals' capacity to build on the past to imagine a future, to invest emotionally in the future and act accordingly are interrelated aspects of their experience, which will influence how they navigate the muddy waters of systemic wrongdoing, more or less complicitly. To give concreteness to these three theoretical arguments, the paper discusses several forms of complicity with violence during the Vichy Regime in France.

Introduction

This paper addresses the thorny issue of complicity with wrongdoing under conditions of systemic political repression, such as authoritarianism, totalitarianism or military occupation. The challenge of dealing with collaborators – those who colluded with the apparatus of repression or who benefitted from its existence – is central to subsequent processes of justice and memory-making. France's purges of Vichy supporters or the lustration laws unmasking secret police informers in Eastern Europe after 1989 are just two examples of official attempts to illuminate the 'grey zone' beyond the victim-perpetrator binary. This paper proposes several arguments. Firstly, it claims we need to think about complicity and resistance not dichotomically, but as a continuum of positions individuals can occupy. Secondly, these positions can only be accounted for by reflecting on agents' positionality within the social world, each agent being located at the intersection of several axes of distinction, such as class, gender, racialisation, or religion. These axes make possible different forms of intersubjective relationality. Third, to account for complicity we need to understand the temporal nature of human beings: temporality is experienced from within a social position, through the interplay between memory, imagination and hope. Positionality affects one's memories and self-understanding, the scope of one's imagination, as well as the nature and intensity of one's hopes. Individuals' sense of time, their capacity to build on the past to imagine a future and to invest emotionally in that future are interrelated aspects of their socially embedded experience, which have repercussions on how they act and navigate the muddy waters of systemic wrongdoing, in more or less complicit ways.

The first section reviews existing theories of complicity, criticising the dominant moral-legal philosophical account. The second section invites us to calibrate our assessments of practices of complicity by considering the relationship between positionality and one's temporal horizon of expectations and hopes, as well as the socially situated reach of one's imagination, given the fragility of trust and the uncertainty of the future under repressive circumstances. The third section substantiates these theoretical claims by sketching three forms of complicity in Vichy France.

Before delving in the argument, one clarification. This is a critical-hermeneutical exercise, reflecting on *how* we need to think about complicity. The aim is to invite the scholar of complicity to embrace a broader perspective on a complex, slippery phenomenon, with a view to imagining a different political future. Thus, the paper is not motivated by a search for the guilty, but by the challenge of taking political responsibility for the future, given the unsavoury past and given that most people are not heroes. It is with the non-heroes that this paper concerns itself: with how they responded and positioned themselves in relation to human rights violations, from within their own social island and temporal horizon. This exercise is crucial for understanding how we can collectively prevent the emergence of socio-political conditions of systemic violence and, should we fail, how we can stimulate habits of solidarity with its victims.

Complicity/resistance: from dyad to continuum

Complicity as a concept makes the object of two – relatively isolated – literatures. On the one hand, ample conceptual work focuses on levels of human responsibility for injustice in moral and legal philosophy. On the other hand, political theorists have reflected on the structural circumstances within which uncoordinated yet mutually reinforcing acts of complicity take place unimpeded. This paper leans towards the structural perspectives, shying away from the individualism and intransigent moralism of legal and moral philosophers. It does not, however, fall prey to structural reductionism: just as there is no perfectly unencumbered agency, no order is ever so totalising as to annihilate all resistance. Acknowledging the constraining force of institutions, forms of sociality and power constellations over individuals, it contributes to the literature by problematising the relationship between complicity on the one hand, and temporal expectations, imagination and hope, on the other. To outline my contribution, I now turn to a critical engagement with these two existing bodies of work.

Moral and legal philosophy converge in their aim to provide a universal set of sharp analytical tools for differentiating between different levels of *individual* complicity in wrongdoing, thereby enabling legal reasoning and ascription of moral guilt.[1] Philosophers disagree about the conditions for counting somebody complicit: debates focus on the type and role of intent, the existence of a causal contribution, the degree of autonomy necessary, among others.[2] Depending on one's level of involvement, complicity covers connivance, contiguity, collusion, collaboration, condoning, consorting, conspiring, and full joint wrongdoing.[3] These precise, distinct categories can illuminate the many faces occupying the *grey zone* for the purpose of legal accountability, according to the wrongdoer's relative degree of blameworthiness. Moreover, they help identify those instances when individuals cannot be held legally liable.

Thus deployed, methodological individualism produces a sophisticated account of complicity. However, because of the collapse of moral (and political) philosophy into legal reasoning, this literature embraces a rather simplistic notion of subjectivity and agency.[4] The criminal law paradigm colonises the imagination of the moral-political philosopher, whose object of study exceeds criminal law's blunt categories. This paper proposes to understand complicity as always enmeshed in complex social relations and influenced – though not fully determined – by one's location within those relations, as well as the temporal horizons opened by that location. While useful for ascertaining legal liability, moral-legal philosophical frames fail to capture diffuse, temporally enduring patterns of often unconscious complicity. To understand this complexity – in general and under circumstances of political repression – we need to leave behind the philosopher's and lawyer's *ceteris paribus* and explore the temporal, positional and relational nature of human subjectivity.[5]

First, complicity is mediated by power structures that normalise wrongdoing and render complicity invisible. Moral-legal philosophers focus on obvious, discrete, and intentional individual acts of implication in wrongdoing. The purpose is to determine the level of blameworthiness and/or the existing legal category under which to subsume such acts. They are not preoccupied with routinised, often unreflective, patterns of complicity or *series* of complicitous acts in temporally stable, structural violence.

Social and political theorists are more sensitive to how power relations shape *both* the contexts *and* the agents of wrongdoing. Mobilising historical and sociological knowledge, they give preponderant weight to the social, legal, political and cultural background against which practices and patterns (rather than acts) of complicity emerge, in often uncoordinated but mutually reinforcing fashion.[6] Reflection on the historical conditions that render abuses against certain groups habitual and permissible, part of the everyday repertoire of social interaction, paves the way for explaining first, how violations often go on unhindered for long periods[7] and second, why official mechanisms of redress are frequently met with societal resistance. The absence of reflection on facilitating conditions makes the moral-legal perspective only surgically effective – rather than politically transformative.

Therefore, second, we need a more sophisticated understanding of agency and subjectification to replace the highly individualised and temporally circumscribed account of intent. Moral-legal philosophers do not assume accomplices are persons with a history, occupying a certain position within the hierarchy of human worth that a society is structured by at a certain moment in time.[8] They work with a time slice that begins just before the commission of a wrong act and ends after its completion. The ways in which processes of subject constitution inform an actor's behaviour do not enter moral-legal philosophers' reasoning. Consequently, the individual's subjectification through the internalisation of certain ideas about the social world which she helps reproduce – the coordinates of her positionality – is left out from standard accounts of complicity.

Thirdly and relatedly, most moral-legal philosophers assume the subject is essentially rational and transparent to herself and that different levels of intent – from full intent, to encouragement and ratification – can be parsed out easily.[9] This paper argues that any attempt to redress wrongs and think politically (rather than merely legally) about the future must rely on a moderately sceptical account of the possibility of reflexivity in the face of violence. The analysis of the social, political and cultural context can help us understand that collaborators, beneficiaries of violence and bystanders often have mixed motives for action, that long-term, indifferent collective passivity frequently elides reflexive intent, and that the effects of complicity are often ambiguous and difficult to isolate.

Fourth, this paper argues that complicity is a matter of degree, not one of dichotomic choice. The 'moral purity/legal innocence versus unambiguous guilt' paradigm does not capture the myriad of positions one can occupy on a temporally dynamic continuum between complicity and resistance.[10] Where an individual finds herself on this continuum is a function of her social position, which influences – but never fully determines – the horizon of expectations regarding her own agency and the others', the type of sociality she inhabits, her level of social trust, the scope of her political imagination, as well as the content and intensity of her hopes and fears. Most importantly, this position is not fixed, but changes over time, reflecting changes in both the context and the agent herself.[11]

To sum up, any evaluation of complicity must recognise individuals as socially embedded, located within a temporally and intersubjectively experienced social world, with which, in a deep sense, they are inescapably complicit.[12] This embeddedness influences their participation in more or less complicit practices and patterns of behaviour, in ways that can only be partially captured by the moral-legal paradigm.[13] In what follows, I focus on the relationship between positionality – which is always relational – and complicity, via a discussion of other interrelated aspects of individuals' socio-temporal experience: memory, imagination, hope.

Situated complicity: memory, imagination, hope

As temporal creatures, with sophisticated cognitive abilities to understand ourselves and others as temporally enduring beings (Calhoun, 2008), we build on past experiences – captured in our memories – to project ourselves in a hoped-for future, which we know to be uncertain and not fully within our control. The faculty of the imagination intervenes in the twin process of building a coherent narrative of our past (Keightley & Pickering, 2012) and of experimenting with strategies and potential trajectories into the future we hope for (Bovens, 1999). Thus, hope mediates our relationship with our future, in light of our past, though not straightforwardly or manifestly. In hoping, we explore imaginatively what we might achieve through our actions, notwithstanding our limitations, our fears and the negative evidence available.[14]

We continue to have hopes for as long as we believe in the possibility of a future (Fletcher, 1999): hope provides us with 'a sturdy enough bridge to the future in this life.' (Urban Walker, 2006, pp. 40–41)[15] When we fail, imagination helps us refocus our hopes on alternative objects. These processes of orientation to the future do not happen in a vacuum: hope is always situated. I have already pointed to how memory influences hope, both in terms of the objects it latches on and its intensity. Memories are themselves underpinned by ongoing processes of intersubjective self-constitution, which influence the kind and range of objects the imagination conjures in hoping. Our social embeddedness impacts the scope of our imagination, i.e. the type of things we fear and hope for. Therefore, visions of the future will be informed by past experiences that constitute the self, by the types of sociality it encounters and cultivates, the norms constituting it and the levels of social trust it enjoys: situated memory and experience provide the imagination with an anchorage and delimit the content and strength of our hopes.[16]

Depending on what future we can imaginatively project ourselves into, we act differently in relation to personal and political goals. Both psychological (Miceli & Castelfranchi, 2010; Snyder, 2002) and philosophical texts (Bovens, 1999; Calhoun, 2008; Downie, 1963; McGeer, 2004, 2008; Meirav, 2009; Pettit, 2004) have highlighted the effect hope has on the assessment of one's agency in relation to one's future. Hope can kindle our trust in our own capacities to achieve our goals – whatever they might be – even when the odds are measly (Pettit, 2004; Urban Walker, 2006). They can mobilise our attention, emotional and rational faculties, pushing us to devise effective, flexible strategies. Hope fortifies and sustains us through adversity, fuelling our resilience and ability to act, sharpening perceptions and helping us adjust our plans in response to obstacles. The pleasure we get from imaginatively anticipating the hoped-for state of affairs energises us when facing set-backs (Bovens, 1999).

Hope does not have this effect on agency only self-referentially: our hopes about others can facilitate their engaging in actions that can contribute to success. Our hopes about others' actions encourage and sustain *them* in their endeavour to live up to our expectations. Thus, our hope provides a scaffold for their actions (McGeer, 2008). Conversely, *their* hopes about us sustain *us*. Because of this dynamising tendency, hope feeds trust and solidarity. There is a strong connection between hope and the very possibility of collective action (Pettit, 2004), whatever its goals. This connection has important repercussions wherever individuals and groups position themselves politically on the complicity-resistance spectrum in the contexts of interest to this paper.

However, to thrive, hope needs a responsive world that at least partially supports our efforts (McGeer, 2004). Otherwise, its dynamic tendencies fail to nurture individuals' and collectives' agency. In hoping, we take 'an agential interest in the world' (McGeer, 2008, p. 246) in our own – but also others' – future. Losing hope can be dramatic – through war, famine and genocide – or gradual, through the slow erosion of the capacity to imagine a future – through resilient poverty, social marginalisation, or encroaching dehumanization.[17] When a future is not imaginable, whether because of physical or social death, hope has no place: 'To find oneself utterly unable to imagine a desirable, possible future, is to lose the basis for taking an interest in one's own agency.' (Calhoun, 2008, p. 29)

How does this all bear on the issue of complicity with systematic wrongdoing? I have so far argued that, to comprehend the complex dynamics of complicity, we must account for the agent's social and temporal positionality, a function of processes of subjectification that influence her experiences and their sedimentation in memory, her hopes for the future and the role she ascribes to her own agency in bringing about that future. Under circumstances of political repression, visions of the future will vary in their hopefulness, but all will be affected by the historical context, some in enabling, others in constraining ways. No context is experienced uniformly. In what follows, I sketch a few points on the relationship between memory, imagination, hope and agency for several positions on the spectrum of involvement.

For willing collaborators – informers, propagandists or *délateurs*[18] – the future looks promising as various hoped-for benefits feed their moral disengagement from the victims. Ideological commitment ranges from zealotry to mere opportunism, depending on past political experience, socio-economic status and one's immediate community: political views, religious beliefs, personal ambition or greed animate their hopes and the actions they undertake in their pursuit. Physical and economic safety, career boosts, access to scarce material goods, a higher life quality are just some of the benefits derived from willing collaboration.[19]

For by-standers who do not directly collaborate, various futures are imaginable, depending on their social capital, access to resources, prior political engagement, the sense of their own agency and capacity to navigate circumstances, as well as the availability of opportunities to maintain or form new relationships of trust.[20] Some navigate along the continuum, becoming collaborators or even perpetrators, especially if they share – more or less consciously – the repressive regime's ideology. One could simultaneously be a by-stander in one area of social interaction, and a resister or a collaborator in another. During long periods of intense political violence, in the absence of a credible temporal horizon for change, bystanders become collaborators to fulfil some personal or professional hopes. Under such circumstances, solidarity in resistance remains improbable. For example, to understand everyday life in totalitarian Romania (1945–1989), Pârvulescu asks us to 'borrow the psyche of someone who knows that it is highly likely that her entire life will go *like this*, moment by moment and year by year, till the end. And that, after her death, the life of her own children will also be, moment by moment, and year by year, *like this*.' (2015, my translation) In a stable climate of fear, refusing all compromises requires a doubly heroic attitude of courage and endurance.

Consequently, many remain passively compliant, muddling through everyday hardships. *Attentisme* (Rousso, 1987) – waiting to see how things develop before occupying the most advantageous position – is often initially embraced. As change becomes unimaginable, people adjust their hopes and actions to the situation[21]: hope sometimes attaches to a future that does not get worse, while the imagination fails to conjure a vision of solidarity with victims. And since societal wrongs grow in communities that tolerate them, adjustment and accommodation feed repression.

Avoiding complicity need not require irrational or heroic hopes. In a climate of terror and generalised suspicion, individuals tend to anxiously exaggerate the danger triggered by modest – yet crucial – resistances, short of armed struggle and sabotage. This is not to say that risks are always overestimated, but only to point out that passively standing by cannot always be justified by invoking risks to oneself.[22]

Some by-standers slide towards the other end of the spectrum, resistance. Resistance can be motivated by various hopes, whose objects translate personal, political or ethical commitments, all of which, however, are inextricably related – more or less directly – to an orientation towards the political world. Resistance ranges from armed struggle and sabotage to protest, clandestine publishing, refusals to collaborate, pay taxes and obey laws. For example, the Madres de Plaza de Mayo marched against the Argentine juntas in the hope of burying their disappeared children, the French *maquis* fought for national sovereignty, communist ideals[23] and redeeming French masculinity, while intellectual dissidents worldwide invoke the harm silence inflicts on their integrity.[24] Just like complicity, different forms of resistance correspond to different positionalities within a community's lifeworld, influenced by structures such as gender, class, profession and religion.

Which brings us to the intersubjective dimension of hoping, imagining and acting. A responsive social world is a precondition for hope and '...shared hopes become collective when individuals see themselves as hoping and so acting in concert for ends that they communally endorse.' (McGeer, 2004, p. 125) This is valid for both wrongdoing and resistance against wrongdoing. As will emerge from the case study, perpetrators and collaborators offer each other the necessary scaffolding for their hopes, mobilising to act more efficiently in pursuit of their vision. On the other hand, while no two repressive regimes are alike, social trust is usually eroded. Fear of violent reprisals for dissent, anxieties about potential betrayal and general hardships usually have an atomising effect.[25] The social scaffolding that hopes for a different future need to flourish is often unavailable. The opportunities for solidarity – which depend on cultivating hope in others' capacity to act in concert – are diminished, and with them the possibility of effective resistance. Invoking the earlier examples, without the mutual support that their shared hope made possible, the Argentine Madres may have caved in. Without the Allies' aid, the moral and concrete support by local populations or communist comrades, the *maquis* would not have contributed to the France's liberation. Without friends' and families' trust and faith, many dissidents would not have found the strength to sustain their struggle.[26]

To substantiate these theoretical ideas about complicity, I analyse certain complicitous practices in relation to time, positionality, relationality, memory and hope in a complex context of collaboration: France under the German Occupation (1940–1944). The last section does not provide an exhaustive account of collaboration, only a discussion of three forms thereof, highlighting the socially embedded nature of action.

Complicity during the 'Black Years'

France was partially, then fully occupied by Germany between 1940–1944. This section analyses three forms of complicity: collaborationism, seeking employment with repressive institutions and denunciations. My analysis is organised around the temporal and structural (legal, economic, ideological, gendered and religious) vectors that frame the French population's response to the occupation.

Temporally, several elements need mentioning. The painful memory of WWI – which killed almost 1.5 million Frenchmen – made pacifism widespread before 1939. (Rousso, 1992) Pacifism paradoxically motivated various collaborators, who hoped for an enduring reconciliation between France and Germany (Joly, 2011, p. 14). *La drôle de guerre* – the short, quiet period between September 1939 and May 1940 – blunted the spirits and made the shock of the defeat worse. Following the defeat, everyday pressures and relief that 'the war was over' made most people acquiescent supporters of Vichy, incapable of imagining a way out (Diamond, 1999, p. 72). Finally, 1942 brought a major shift in French people's horizon of hope as it marked both the occupation of France's entire territory and the moment Germany's defeat became imaginable. These temporal vectors affected the scope of individuals' imagination and the courage of their aspirations, as well as the relationships they entertained and the practices they participated in to pursue their goals.

Several structures framed individuals' locations on the spectrum of involvement: gender, the socio-economic and professional profile, anti-Semitism, religion, the split ideological horizon that predated the war, the political memory of WWI, and the laws and policies passed by Vichy and the Occupier. As I show below, these temporally dynamic structures *incited, elicited, inspired* or *facilitated* various forms of collaboration that cannot be reduced to discrete, intentional, fully reflexive acts.

Immediately after the defeat, general Pétain launched the doctrine of 'state collaboration' with Germany, kick-starting the 'National Revolution' in the free zone: a fascist cultural revolution replacing 'Liberty, Equality,

Fraternity' with 'Work, Family, Motherland.' 'Motherland' excluded 'groups that, due to their "race" or convictions, could not or would not subscribe to the primacy of the French nation: foreigners, Jews, masons, communists, internationalists of all origins and loyalties' (R. Gillouin cited in Rousso, 1992, my translation). Anti-Semitic laws were passed, mostly (not exclusively) by the Occupier, unequivocally tapping in a history of French anti-Semitism (Joly, 2006, 2007b, 2012b, 2015; Joly & Passera, 2016).[27] In adopting administrative and economic collaborationism and embracing the Occupier's cause, Pétain hoped to maintain French sovereignty.

The first form of complicity, collaborationism, was rare. Few individuals were true collaborationists,[28] or *collabos*, supporting the institutionalisation of anti-Semitism without scruples (Joly, 2011): Jacques Doriot's Le parti populaire français, Marcel Déat's Rassemblement national populaire and Eugène Deloncle's Mouvement social révolutionnaire were virulent vehicles for anti-Semitic, anti-Communist and anti-Masonic propaganda, tapping into a history of extreme right politics and militarism. They printed newspapers – *Le Francisme, Le cri du people* and *Au pilori*. Intellectuals were not immune: some collaborated out of interest or conviction, promoting racist propaganda (Joly, 2011). Thus, Le Groupe Collaboration assembled writers, scientists, clerics, artists aspiring to get famous, while the newly-founded Institute for the Study of Jewish Questions organised the anti-Semitic exhibition 'The Jew and France': 200,000 French citizens, including pupils, paid the entry ticket in 1941 (Rousso, 1992, p. 98). These institutions provided the necessary scaffolding for *collabos'* collective contribution to the Occupier's mission.

Moving along the spectrum, we find those who applied for jobs within the repressive state apparatus, an important target of post-war purges: the *milice* (the 80,000-strong institution that transformed Vichy into a police-state) and the General Commissariat for Jewish Questions (controlling Jewish persons and the spoliation of their property). 'Economic aryanisation' required an army of clerks (Bruttmann, 2013). Two categories of employees emerge from the archives. First, those recommended by personal contacts in Vichy's bureaucracy. One's political connections and belonging to certain political and professional networks – one's relational positionality – framed one's image of professional success and the means for achieving it: working as a public servant. The second category is the 'bureaucratic proletariat' developing after 1940, stuck on temporary, underpaid jobs: secretaries, accountants, office personnel of businesses and publications discontinued after 1940. Many applied to the commissariat – seen as an ordinary institution – to secure financial stability (Joly, 2016). Thus, a different positionality, of economic vulnerability, pushed especially older unemployed and underqualified men and women – some of them war refugees or repatriated POWs – to apply for salaries above average before 1942. (2016, p. 170) The number of fervent anti-Semites among the applicants was low, around 10%.[29] After 1942, the change in public opinion, the general hope in an Allied victory, budgetary cuts as well as a dramatic decrease in unemployment, led to a recruitment crisis. The commissariat started hiring unqualified personnel, even with criminal records (2016, p. 172).

Women too joined anti-Semitic organisations and repressive institutions (including *la milice*) for political, religious, economic and personal reasons. Imagined political futures animated some *miliciennes*: a 'new French order, national and socialist' made an ideologically zealous young woman join the *milice* as 'the only guarantor of the French order, the only hope for a brighter future,' for which she was ready 'to dedicate all her forces' (Simonin, 2010, p. 19). In general, however, women's political hopes and the scope of their imagination was filtered through the matrix of gender, but also that of Catholicism. The post-WWI pacifism mentioned above pushed them to join the *milice*: 'the end of all wars between France and Germany' rendered collaboration natural. Religious duties of charity – often combined with *maréchalisme* (attachment to Pétain's heroic past and fatherly image) – were yet another factor. Building on a tradition of 'social citizenship' going back at least to WWI, Catholic women joined repressive institutions to do social work for the wounded or the displaced, thus simultaneously adhering to their Catholic faith and serving Pétain (Fageot, 2008). They became 'universal mothers' (Simonin, 2010, p. 22). Gendered notions of work and citizenship informed their positioning on the complicity spectrum: their collaboration perversely enfranchised them, fuelling emancipatory hopes for public engagement, at a time when they could not vote.

Regarding their socio-economic status, statistics show *la milicienne* is a young, single, economically vulnerable woman with limited education, a secretary, dactylographer, or telephone operator.[30] The socio-professional status determines women's economic options, whose precarious situation is often manipulated. For example, Déat's RNP recruited many women by promising to help bring back family members who were POWs.

These examples highlight gender, class and religion as important structures of the war experiences and their role in shaping the hopes and relations one could cultivate. Illuminating the structural factors is not meant to exculpate these applicants. Many were favourable to the agenda of the Vichy regime. Archives do show, however, that few were rabid anti-Semites: for most, economic gain came before ideology (Joly, 2016, pp. 183–184).

Anti-Semitic legislation served as a propitious framework for a third, insidious form of collaboration: uncoordinated denunciations of Jews, communists, freemasons to the French police, the Gestapo or the General Commissariat for Jewish Questions (*délations*). The anti-Semitic press had dedicated rubrics for *délations*. The practice went back to the 19th Century: Édouard Drumont's newspaper *La Libre Parole*, launched in 1892, contained 'revelations' about Jewish interference in French affairs – a clear precursor to the practices of the 1940s (Joly, 2007c). Revealing this lineage simultaneously highlights the role of institutional and political memory in shaping patterns of behaviour, and the limits of the individualistic, act-based paradigm. Most *délations* – oral or written, signed or anonymous – were motivated by personal reasons: a neighbourly conflict, jealousy, greed,[31] bitterness and frustration linked to deprivation, a professional rivalry, excessive respect for the law, or duress (Joly, 2013), always tainted by anti-Semitism – visceral or circumstantial, militant and cultivated or rough, normalised by legislation and the general atmosphere (Joly, 2007c).

Temporally speaking, the numbers of denunciations spiked around the main round-ups, when Jews went into clandestinity. Emboldened by the official policy, which legitimised hate and scaffolded the hope for a Jew-and-communist-free France, some French citizens used this well-tested instrument to settle personal and professional scores, but also to feed their political aspirations, often with bravado or self-righteous outrage. Writing, finding the address and mailing the letters presupposed a strong personal investment in the matter, especially since few were remunerated (Joly, 2012a). The world was responsive to the *délateur's* hopes: Jews were arrested and deported, thus encouraging repetition. Spouses, neighbours, in-laws, friends and colleagues are denounced in response to numerous public campaigns soliciting information in the name of justice or the law, with deadly consequences for victims.

More diffuse, non-official acts of collaboration took place in the occupied zone: the occupant was omnipotent. Servility was normal, and the occupation was initially seen, by many, to be less terrible than expected. Terror only affected few, mostly communists and Jews. The occupiers became the biggest consumers of French goods (Sebba, 2016). While men were deported, POWs or working in Germany, women did not experience the occupation homogenously. Poor urban women bore the brunt of food shortages.[32] Economic interest kept them employed in German-run factories: giving up such a job was no easy decision under the circumstances (Diamond, 1999, p. 77). Bonds of solidarity formed in response to shared hardship: women's organisations emerged, scaffolding each other's hopes, but the objective was mere survival. The much talked-about 'sexual collaboration' – less widespread than assumed (Simonin, 2010) – was also often motivated by imperious economic needs. Lastly, the term 'larval collaboration' refers to the flourishing cultural life: cinemas, theatres, libraries were always full (Rousso, 1992). No single explanation suffices: cultural life could have simultaneously been a coping, escapist mechanism, a sign of political blindness, or a means to support French intellectual traditions. Many, therefore, adjusted to the situation, for psychological and economic rather than ideological reasons, and mostly for want of a better alternative: the Germans appeared to be there to stay, making the horizon of hope and the scope of the imagination contract.

1942 is a breaking point for French perceptions of political time and hopes: it marked an important shift in public perceptions of the Occupation and Vichy. Germans' exploitation of the French economy led to massive shortages, which mobilised the population against Vichy, the Occupier and black-market profiteers. (Diamond, 1999, p. 75) Supported by communists, women organised protests against the rationing policy in 1942 (Schwartz, 1999). The establishment of the *Service du Travail Obligatoire* – the regimented recruitment of French citizens to work in Germany – fuelled a dramatic change in public opinion that made it difficult for the institutions of repression to recruit French personnel (Joly, 2013, 2016; Simonin, 2010). November marked the beginning of the Allied 'Operation Torch' in North Africa, which emboldened the population's imagination about the possibility of freedom, simultaneously worrying collaborationists who proceeded to calibrate their hopes and rethink their political alliances.[33] Parisians reportedly exhausted the stocks of USSR maps, feverishly following the successes of the Red Army. This coincided with Germans occupying the whole French territory, revealing Vichy's shambolic pretence of sovereignty, further driving public Germanophobia and hope in an Allied victory (Drake, 2015, pp. 291–294). From then onward, the structural and temporal coordinates change and, while collaboration practices continued, motivations and strategies adjusted to the plausibility of liberation.

Conclusion

This paper sought to illuminate complicity as embedded in its temporally and structurally complex constellations. It departed from moral-legal accounts, highlighting the limited notions of causality, temporality and agency they presupposed. It proposed to expand our perspective and conceptualise complicity in terms of the agent's relational positionality, which affects the resources her memory can summon, the scope of her imagination, the courage of her hopes and the direction of her engagement with the world. The contextual analysis of three types of complicity in occupied France has shown the salience of the change in conceptual and methodological perspective this paper advocates. Accounting for temporal and structural vectors has thus opened the path for a more nuanced account of complicity in systemic wrongdoing. Based on this diagnosis, more capacious visions of political responsibility and solidarity become thinkable.

Notes

1. See Kutz (2000, 2007)), Gardner (2007), May (2010), Ciurria (2011), Lepora and Goodin (2013).

2. For example, recent contributors to the debate, Kutz, Goodin and Lepora disagree about the criteria for being complicit. Kutz emphasises participatory intent, whereas Goodin and Lepora argue that knowledge of the wrongdoing and knowledge of the fact that one's actions contribute to wrongdoing are sufficient (Kutz, 2000; Lepora & Goodin, 2013). For disagreements over causation see Gardner (2007), Kutz (2007).
3. Discussed extensively in Lepora and Goodin (2013).
4. For fresh critiques of methodological individualism see Afxentiou, Dunford, and Neu (2017).
5. Most moral and legal philosophers still work with what Galtung called the traditional ways of thinking about injustice, characterised by the individualisation of the actors, its visibility, and the concern with intention (Galtung, 1969). Kutz (2000) departs to a certain extent from this description: he acknowledges the collective nature of wrongdoing. He proposes accountability should be understood relationally, from the perspective of the agents involved, and reflects on the challenge posed by cases where we do not intend to be complicit in wrongs, but are nonetheless, by virtue of participating in a way of life that fosters them. His understanding of participation in a culture is, however, problematic: he does not account for the role that culture plays in subjectification. Thus, he unduly assumes a high capacity of individual reflexivity about one's intentional participation in that way of life, a capacity that grounds individual responsibility for unstructured harms. Kutz argues that, fundamentally, participatory intent – however remote – is the crucial marker of complicity.
6. See, for example, Kissell (1999), Celermajer (2009), Applebaum (2010).
7. See Crawford (2007), Miller (2008), Pankhurst (2008).
8. Lawford-Smith (2015) somewhat accounts for subjectification, but only to justify the possibility of collective agency and action. She proposes socialising more mutually responsive people and more coordinated groups to address complex ills like global poverty and climate change. I value her contribution but resist the idea that the solution lies with character formation.
9. For a good example of this, see Kutz's discussion (2007) of the legal categories for subsuming the authors of the memos on 'torture lite' after 9/11. For an alternative, more convincing position, see Brecher and Neu (2017).
10. Social psychologists propose a 'spectrum of acquiescence' or 'spectrum of involvement' ranging from bystanders to perpetrators (Edgren, 2012).
11. Lepora and Goodin (2013) introduces a sliding scale of degrees of complicity and claims to go beyond the legal paradigm. And yet, it is the individuals' intent and level of contribution to a one-off act of wrongdoing that determines their culpability.
12. Analysing the role intellectuals played in apartheid South Africa, Sanders (2002) distinguishes two senses of complicity. First, the inescapable complicity inherent in sociality, which apartheid destroys by separating people – setting them *apart*. Then, discrete acts of complicity, for which individuals can be held accountable. While the distinction is useful, there are forms of sociability that we can be held responsible for because they cumulatively and insidiously contribute to violence.
13. While not within this paper's remit, one can plausibly argue that these shortcomings affect the usefulness of our notion of complicity, whether we discuss complicity by western citizens with post-colonial, systemic poverty, racialised

wealth distribution and climate change or say, by passive witnesses to genocide or mass murders.
14. A wealth of research developed regarding the 'standard account of hope', associated with J. P. Day's work (1969). This account, simply put, conceptualises hope as composed of a desire for an outcome and a less than zero probability that it might obtain. Debates focus on whether hope is an emotion (Drahos, 2004), an attitude (Govier, 2011), an emotional attitude (Calhoun, 2008), a state of mind (Urban Walker, 2006), a socially mediated human capacity (Webb, 2007), a syndrome (Martin, 2014) or an intellectual virtue (Cobb, 2015). Other scholars have added more components to the analysis: mental imaging (Bovens, 1999; Calhoun, 2008), futurity and efficacy (Urban Walker, 2006) or a generic 'third factor', be it God, another agent, fate, nature, or one's community (Meirav, 2009). Various typologies of hope exist: superficial and substantial (Pettit, 2004), general and constitutive (Bovens, 1999) specific/general, ground level/latent, high/faint, conscious/unconscious, individual/social and active/passive (Govier, 2011; McGeer, 2004; Miceli & Castelfranchi, 2010) or patient, critical, estimative, resolute and utopian hopes (Webb, 2007). Hope can be valued instrumentally (Calhoun, 2008), in itself (McGeer, 2008) or both (Bovens, 1999). Rational and irrational hopes, as well as good and bad hopes motivate yet another set of inquiries (McGeer, 2004; Pettit, 2004; Webb, 2007).
15. Contra Walker, this future can also correspond to a belief in the after-(physical) life.
16. I discuss the breaks positionality puts on imagination's freedom in Mihai (2016).
17. Urban-Walker poignantly writes '[N]ot all lives are so thickly or uniformly threaded with hopes. In some lives at some times the threads fray to breaking, are cut by violence, or are snapped by deprivation.' (Urban Walker, 2006, pp. 40–41).
18. *Délation* refers to (often anonymous) letters sent by 'good' citizens to the authorities, informing on their peers' belonging to undesirable groups, illegal activities or violations of rules and regulations. France under the German Occupation is a frequently studied example. See, for example (Joly, 2012a).
19. The access to 'benefits' differ according to the context. There is a large literature on the Holocaust: e.g. Hilberg (1992) and Goldhagen (1996). For accounts of forms of collaboration in Paris in the 1940s, see Virgili (2002), Joly (2007a), Sebba (2016). For profiles of French *collabos* see Joly (2011). For a historical approach to complicity in totalitarian Romania, see Vasile, Vasilecu, and Urs (2016).
20. For psycho-social accounts of by-standers, see Edgren (2012).
21. Interviewed by Angelika Klammer, Herta Müller cogently declared that, to remain a decent human being under totalitarianism one had to fail miserably in the public domain (Müller, 2016). Not many assumed such cost.
22. In France after the Liberation, we find an imbrication of structural, rationalising myths of *résitencialisme* – Rousso's term (1987) for the Gaullist myth of a unified Resistance against Germany – and individual practices of *résistentialisme*, i.e. exaggerated, post-factum narratives of individual resistance, denounced by Desgranges (Desgranges, 1948).

23. On the communist party's flexible ideology and hopes in relation to Britain before and after Germany's invasion of USSR, see Pike (1993).
24. 'Bram" Fisher, the Rivonia trial defence attorney, pleaded when tried for belonging to the underground communist party: "When a man is on trial for his political beliefs and actions, two courses are open to him. He can either confess to his transgressions and plead for mercy. Or he can justify his beliefs and explain why he acted as he did. Were I to ask for forgiveness today, I would betray my cause. That course is not open to me.' (Bould, 1991, p. 151).
25. For the atomising effect of fear in France under the occupation see Joly (2012a, pp. 23–24). For totalitarian Romania: Mihâilescu (1993), Pârvulescu (2015), Müller (2016).
26. For an account of friendship's role in sustaining hope when facing the Romanian political police, see Lovinescu (2010), Müller (2016). Manea (2016) reveals the hopeless loneliness of the lucid analyst of duplicity. For a global selection of testimonies about the various sources of hope and the intersubjective scaffolding that sustain resisters see (Bould, 1991).
27. Rousso argues that, in the first stage of anti-Semitic legislation (1940–41), France took the initiative as the Germans had not yet formulated the Final Solution (1992, pp. 86–92). According to Rousso, the 'application' of anti-Semitic measures was meant to prove Vichy's capacity to govern.
28. In French 'collaborationist' – as opposed to 'collaborator' – is the term reserved for the 'ultra' ideologically motivated collaborator (Joly, 2011, p. 6).
29. Building on archival work, Joly speculates that office work was not appealing for the collabos (2016).
30. Unsurprisingly, during the post-war legal purges, *miliciens* received much harder punishments than *miliciennes*, once again affirming gendered notions of responsibility (Simonin, 2010).
31. Spoliation is an important motivator: denunciations catalyse 'economic aryanisation.' (Bruttmann, 2013).
32. Sebba (2016) offers an insight into the classed experience of women in Occupied Paris. Rich French women did not feel the effect of penury.
33. For an account of the *collabos*' political manoeuvring in response to November 1942, their repositioning regarding Pétain and Laval, and the way they adjusted to developments in Eastern Europe and North Africa, see Joly (2011), Drake (2015).

Acknowledgments

I would like to thank the members of the political theory research group at the University of Edinburgh. Special thanks are owed to Mathias Thaler, Richard Bellamy and the journal's anonymous reviewers.

Disclosure statement

No potential conflict of interest was reported by the author.

References

Afxentiou, A., Dunford, R., & Neu, M. (2017). *Exploring complicity: Concept, cases and critique*. London: Rowman & Littlefield International.

Applebaum, B. (2010). *Being white, being good: White complicity, white moral responsibility, and social justice pedagogy*. Lanham, MD: Lexington Books.

Bould, G. (1991). *Conscience be my guide*. London: Zed Books.

Bovens, L. (1999). The value of hope. *Philosophy and Phenomenological Research, 59*(3), 667–681.

Brecher, B., & Neu, M. (2017). Intellectual complicity in torture. In Afxentiou A., Dunford R. and Neu, M. eds. *Exploring complicity: Concept, cases and critique*. London: Rowman and Littlefield, pp. 143–160.

Bruttmann, T. (2013). La délation, un instrument au service de l'"aryanisation"? *Archives Juives, 46*(1), 35–44.

Calhoun, C. (2008, March 28). *Hope matters*. Vanderbilt University.

Celermajer, D. (2009). *The sins of the nation and the ritual of apologies*. Cambridge: Cambridge University Press.

Ciurria, M. (2011). Complicity and criminal liability in Rwanda: A situationist critique. *Res publica, 17*(4), 411–419.

Cobb, A. D. (2015). Hope as an intellectual virtue? *The Southern Journal of Philosophy, 53*(3), 269–285.

Crawford, N. C. (2007). Individual and collective moral responsibility for systemic military atrocity. *Journal of Political Philosophy, 15*(2), 187–212.

Day, J. P. (1969). Hope. *American Philosophical Quarterly, 6*(2), 89–102.

Desgranges, J.-M. (1948). *Les crimes masqués du résistantialisme*. Paris: Éditions de l'Élan.

Diamond, H. (1999). *Women and the Second World War in France, 1939–48: Choices and constraints*. Harlow: Longman.

Downie, R. S. (1963). Hope. *Philosophy and Phenomenological Research, 24*(2), 248–251.

Drahos, P. (2004). Trading in public hope. *Annals of the American Academy of Political and Social Science, 592*, 18–38.

Drake, D. (2015). *Paris at war, 1939–1944*. Cambridge, MA: The Belknap Press of Harvard University Press.

Edgren, H. (2012). *Looking at the onlookers and bystanders*. Stockholm: Living history forum.

Fageot, C. (2008). *La Milice en Vaucluse, 1943–1945*. Mazan: Études comtadines.

Fletcher, A. (1999). The place of despair and hope. *Social Research, 66*(2), 521–529.

Galtung, J. (1969). Violence, peace, and peace research. *Journal of Peace Research, 6*(3), 167–191.

Gardner, J. (2007). Complicity and causality. *Criminal Law and Philosophy, 1*(2), 127–141.

Goldhagen, D. J. (1996). *Hitler's willing executioners: Ordinary Germans and the Holocaust* (1st ed.). New York: Knopf : Distributed by Random House.
Govier, T. (2011). Hope and its opposites. *Journal of Social Philosophy, 42*(3), 239–253.
Hilberg, R. (1992). *Perpetrators, victims, bystanders: The Jewish catastrophe, 1933–1945* (1st ed.). New York, NY: Aaron Asher Books.
Joly, L. (2006). Les débuts de l'Action française (1899–1914) ou l'élaboration d'un nationalisme antisémite. *Revue historique, 639*, 695–718.
Joly, L. (2007a). La délation anti-sémite sous l'Occupation. *Vingtième Siècle. Revue d'histoire, 96*(4), 137–149.
Joly, L. (2007b). Antisémites et antisémitisme à la Chambre des députés sous la IIIe République. *Revue d'histoire moderne et contemporaine, 54–3*, 63–90.
Joly, L. (2007c). La délation antisémite sous l'Occupation. *Vingtième Siècle. Revue d'histoire, 96*, 137–149.
Joly, L. (2011). *Les Collabos. Treize portraits d'après les archives des services secrets de Vichy, des Renseignements Généraux et de l'Épuration*. Paris: Éditions Les Échappés.
Joly, L. (ed.). (2012a). *La délation dans la France des années noires*. Paris: Perrin.
Joly, L. (2012b). D'une guerre l'autre. L'Action française et les Juifs, de l'Union sacrée à la Révolution nationale (1914–1944). *Revue d'histoire moderne et contemporaine, 59–4*, 97–124.
Joly, L. (2013). Contextes sociaux de la dénonciation des Juifs sous l'Occupation. *Archives Juives, 46*(1), 12–34.
Joly, L. (2015). Fascisme et antisémitisme dans la France des années 1930 : Une irrésistible convergence? *Revue d'histoire moderne et contemporaine, 62–2/3*, 115–136.
Joly, L. (2016). Postuler un emploi auprès du commissariat général aux Questions juives (1941–1944). Antisémitisme d'État et crise de recrutement dans la fonction publique des années noires. *Revue d'histoire moderne et contemporaine, 63–3*, 163–185.
Joly, L., & Passera, F. (2016). Se souvenir, accuser, se justifier : Les premiers témoignages sur la France et les Français des années noires (1944–1949). *Guerres mondiales et conflits contemporains, 263*(3), 5–34.
Keightley, E., & Pickering, M. (2012). *The mnemonic imagination: Remembering as creative practice*. Basingstoke: Palgrave Macmillan.
Kissell, J. (1999). Complicity in thought and language: Toleration of wrong. *Journal of Medical Humanities, 20*(1), 49–60.
Kutz, C. (2000). *Complicity: Ethics and law for a collective age*. Cambridge: Cambridge University Press.
Kutz, C. (2007). Causeless complicity. *Criminal Law and Philosophy, 1*(3), 289–305.
Lawford-Smith, H. (2015). What 'we'? *Journal of Social Ontology, 1*(2), 225–249.
Lepora, C., & Goodin, R. E. (2013). *On complicity and compromise*. Oxford: Oxford University Press.
Lovinescu, M. (2010). *Jurnal esențial*. Bucharest: Humanitas.
Manea, N. (2016). *Întoarcerea huliganului*. Bucharest: Polirom.
Martin, A. M. (2014). *How we hope: A moral psychology*. Princeton: Princeton University Press.
May, L. (2010). Complicity and the Rwandan genocide. *Res publica, 16*(2), 135–152.
McGeer, V. (2004). The art of good hope. *The ANNALS of the American Academy of Political and Social Science, 592*(1), 100–127.
McGeer, V. (2008). Trust, hope and empowerment. *Australasian Journal of Philosophy, 86*(2), 237–254.

Meirav, A. (2009). The nature of hope. *Ratio, 22*(2), 216–233.
Miceli, M., & Castelfranchi, C. (2010). Hope: The power of wish and possibility. *Theory and Psychology, 20*(2), 251–276.
Mihai, M. (2016). Theorizing change: Between reflective judgment and the inertia of political habitus. *European Journal of Political Theory, 15*(1), 22–42.
Mihăilescu, I. (1993). Mental stereotypes in the first years of post-totalitarian Romania. *Government and Opposition, 28*(3), 315–324.
Miller, Z. (2008). Effects of invisibility: In search of the 'economic' in transitional justice. *The International Journal of Transitional Justice, 2*, 266–291.
Müller, H. (2016). *Patria mea era un sâmbure de măr*. Bucuresti: Humanitas.
Pankhurst, D. (2008). *Gendered peace: Women's struggles for post-war justice and reconciliation*. Abingdon: Routledge.
Pârvulescu, I. (2015). *Și eu am trăit în comunism*. Bucharest: Humanitas.
Pettit, P. (2004). Hope and its place in mind. *Annals of the American Academy of Political and Social Science, 1*, 152–165.
Pike, D. W. (1993). Between the Junes: The French communists from the collapse of France to the invasion of Russia. *Journal of Contemporary History, 28*(3), 465–485.
Rousso, H. (1987). *Le syndrome de Vichy*. Paris: Éditions du Seuil.
Rousso, H. (1992). *Les années noires: Vivre sous l'Occupation*. Paris: Gallimard.
Sanders, M. (2002). *Complicities*. Durham: Duke University Press.
Schwartz, P. (1999). The politics of food and gender in occupied Paris. *Modern & Contemporary France, 7*(1), 35–45.
Sebba, A. (2016). *Les Parisiennes: How the women of Paris lived, loved and died in the 1940s*. London: Weidenfeld & Nicolson.
Simonin, A. (2010). La femme invisible: La collaboratrice politique. *Histoire@politique, 9*, 96.
Snyder, C. R. (2002). Hope theory: Rainbows in the mind. *Psychological Inquiry, 13*(4), 249–275.
Urban Walker, M. (2006). *Moral repair*. New York, NY: Cambridge University Press.
Vasile, L., Vasilecu, C., & Urs, A. (2016). *Traversând comunismul. Conviețuire, conformism, compromis*. Bucharest: Poliron.
Virgili, F. (2002). *Shorn women: Gender and punishment in liberation France* (English ed.). Oxford: Berg.
Webb, D. (2007). Modes of hoping. *History of the Human Sciences, 20*(3), 65–83.

The arts of refusal: tragic unreconciliation, pariah humour, and haunting laughter

Bronwyn Anne Leebaw

ABSTRACT
This paper investigates Hannah Arendt's writings on tragic unreconciliation and pariah humour as offering creative strategies for confronting the deadening of emotion that enables people to become reconciled to what they should refuse or resist. She offers a distinctive contribution to debates on reconciliation and justice, I suggest, by articulating a tragic approach to *unreconciliation*. Yet Arendt recognised that tragic accounts of violence can reinforce denial and resignation. In writings on the 'hidden tradition' of the 'Jew as pariah,' Arendt suggests that humour can be an important response to tragic accounts of political violence and a strategy for awakening an emotional response in those who cannot perceive tragedies to which they have become reconciled. As arts of refusal, tragic unreconciliation and pariah humour invoke and subvert the tragic imagination to reveal possibilities for solidarity, responsibility, and transformation that challenge problematic forms of reconciliation – reconciliation to one's role as a participant in, or bystander to abuse, reconciliation as self-abnegating assimilation, and reconciliation as compromise, scapegoating, or denial.

Introduction

How do people become *unreconciled* to the political violence that they have accepted or failed to recognise *as* violence? Debates on political reconciliation are generally framed in response to the problem of 'hot' or intense emotional responses to violence that lead people to seek a 'cooling of hearts' (Anyeko et al., 2011). Somewhat less attention has been paid to the problem of hearts that are *too* cool. The deadening of emotion is not as provocative as the expression of intense emotions, yet it is arguably more dangerous as a response to violence. Emotional indifference and desensitization can empower abusive authorities by enabling people to condone atrocities, to participate in organised abuses, and to avoid a sense of responsibility for political violence and its legacies.

This paper investigates Hannah Arendt's writings on tragic unreconciliation and pariah humour as creative strategies for confronting the deadening of emotion that enables people to become reconciled to what they should refuse or resist. In the tragic imagination, several scholars have located an approach to political reconciliation premised on the transformative mediation of intense emotions. Arendt offers a distinctive contribution to such debates, I suggest, by articulating a tragic approach to *unreconciliation*. Yet Arendt recognised that tragic accounts of violence can reinforce denial and resignation. In writings on the 'hidden tradition' of the 'Jew as pariah,' Arendt suggests that humour can respond to tragic accounts of political violence and constitute a strategy for awakening an emotional response in those who cannot perceive tragedies to which they have become reconciled. As arts of refusal, tragic unreconciliation and pariah humour subvert the tragic imagination to reveal possibilities for solidarity, responsibility, and transformation, thus challenging problematic forms of reconciliation – reconciliation to one's role as a participant in or bystander to abuse, reconciliation as self-abnegating assimilation, and reconciliation premised on scapegoating or denial.

The first section of the paper locates a challenge to the minimalism of contemporary approaches to transitional justice and human rights in Arendt's writings on tragic reconciliation and unreconciliation. Tragic accounts of resistance, Arendt suggests, can aid people in reconciling 'with reality' and in accepting political responsibility for authorised abuses, while refuting the perception that it is futile to confront the systemic logics of abuse. The second section discusses Arendt's writings on pariah humour, exemplified in the works of Chaplin and Heine, as a basis for contesting reconciliation as assimilation. Pariah humour, as Arendt analyses it, expresses a tragic refusal to reconcile, yet invokes comedy to reveal absurdities and particularities that are distorted by tragic abstractions. The third section locates a very different form of pariah humour in accounts of cruel jokes and laughter that are repeatedly shared in narratives of atrocity gathered by anti-war veteran associations. Reviewing testimonies from the 1971 Winter Soldier hearings on the Vietnam War and those gathered by Winter Soldier in Iraq, I consider how veterans publicly identify themselves as social pariahs by sharing memories of transgressive laughter. Whereas Arendt frames pariah humour as a strategy of refusal expressed by the persecuted, anti-war veterans invoke it to renounce their own persecution of others and to awaken a sense of responsibility in civilian spectators. The two forms of pariah humour share a common logic, however, in the mockery of tragic abstractions that divert attention from the materialities, particularities, and absurdities of violence. Both forms of pariah humour summon laughter to sustain tensions between a commitment to tragic unreconciliation and an assertion of radical responsibility for the world.

Tragic unreconciliation

Human rights and transitional justice institutions have not entirely ignored the problem of emotional indifference to violence. A major goal of these institutions has been to mobilise shame in response to human rights abuses. By gathering information, publicising testimony, and sharing victims' stories, they aim to shame perpetrators of abuse and urge audiences not to be passive bystanders. However, human rights institutions have strategically minimised their challenge to problematic forms of reconciliation in an effort to mitigate concerns regarding emotional volatility and disruptive backlash. By framing reports in accordance with a melodramatic logic that pits the goodness and innocence of victims against the shameful villainy of individual perpetrators, human rights institutions enable bystanders and beneficiaries to experience compassion without having to reflect on their own responsibilities (Clarke, 2009, pp. 89–117; Meister, 2011; Anker, 2014). By identifying accountability and justice with individual criminal guilt, human rights institutions seek to neutralise vengeful anger, while averting the backlash that might result from a broader framing of responsibility.

As chair of South Africa's Truth and Reconciliation Commission, Desmond Tutu (1999) analogised political reconciliation to therapy, suggesting that victims, perpetrators, and witnesses might pursue a 'healing' closure by talking through traumatic experiences associated with apartheid-era violence. This therapeutic approach to reconciliation influenced the framing and design of subsequent truth commissions and theoretical debates on transitional justice and reconciliation (Minow, 2009). Therapeutic reconciliation treats rage and grief as pathological, reactive, responses to systematic abuse (Brudholm, 2008; Chakravarti, 2014). The emphasis on therapeutic 'closure' suggests that a political break with past abuses has been achieved and that emotional trauma is a response to past abuses, rather than their continuities or legacies (Meister, 2011). An emphasis on therapeutic closure communicates, then, that the refusal to reconcile might have been appropriate in the *past*, but is no longer an appropriate in the *present*.

The tragic imagination, as many scholars have argued, offers an alternative avenue for conceptualising political reconciliation that does not dismiss the voices of the unreconciled. Like therapeutic closure, tragic reconciliation implies a cathartic engagement with painfully intense emotions. However, tragic catharsis is animated by a confrontation with the tensions inherent in human endeavours and the fragility of reconciliation. (Euben, 1986, p. 11) The tragic imagination subverts the idea of a clean break between present and past by depicting reconciliation as a provisional political achievement given meaning through voices that express rage, grief, and dissonant experiences of time by those who remain unreconciled.

Tragic approaches to reconciliation offer a basis for pursuing the insight that transitional justice institutions would do better to engage and transform, rather than avoid, volatile emotional responses to political violence (Mihai, 2016). In tragic drama, the voices of the unreconciled expose the limitations of tragic closure, yet remind audiences of its value (Brendese, 2014; Chakravarti, 2014).

Arendt asserts that it is through the 'unending activity' of understanding that we 'come to terms with and reconcile ourselves with reality, that is, try to be at home in the world' (1994, p. 308). Reconciliation 'with reality' is not the same thing as reconciliation with one's enemies or abusers and does not entail pragmatic accommodation. Rather, Arendt characterises reconciliation as a form of political solidarity and responsibility for the world predicated on the acceptance of tragic realities. Drawing on the logic of tragedy, she asserts that stories can aid people come to terms with reality through a cathartic response to intense emotions. 'All sorrows can be borne if you put them into a story,' writes Arendt, quoting Isak Dinesen (1958, p. 311). Tragic narrative can mediate and transform the intense emotions that prevent us from coming to terms with reality, she suggests, and channel painful emotions into political expression.

For Arendt, the tragic imagination is also useful in confronting the *deadening* of emotions that leads people to become reconciled to what they should refuse. Whether or not Eichmann was lying when he said that he did not 'intend' to carry out mass killings of Jews, Arendt concludes, it would not be appropriate to reconcile with him (see Berkowitz, 2011). 'Just as you supported and carried out a policy of not wanting to share the earth with the Jewish people and the people of a number of other nations,' she writes, in an imagined response to his defence, 'we find that no one, that is, no member of the human race, can be expected to share the world with you' (1963, p. 279). Arendt's insistence on unreconciliation as a response to Eichmann is not simply a response to the gravity of his crimes, but also what she took to be the pernicious logic animating his defence – that as a mere 'cog,' Eichmann could not be held responsible for atrocities that he carried out. She articulates her refusal to reconcile with Eichmann as a refutation of this logic. People should refuse to reconcile with institutionalised atrocity, she contends, and to the very idea of themselves as 'cogs' in an institutional order.

Eichmann told the court that everyone around him had 'looked forward to his own death with indifference' and had come to feel the same about their role in persecution. 'As the months and years went by,' writes Arendt, Eichmann had 'lost the need to feel anything at all' (1963, p. 135). His indifference exemplified, for Arendt, a more pervasive logic of denial resulting from the acceptance of one's role as 'cog' in a machinery that obfuscates the destruction it reproduces and maintains (Pitkin, 1998). The logics of 'administrative massacre,' as she put it, enable those with the greatest responsibility to remain physically detached from the violence they authorise, while those who carry out abuses can remain emotionally detached by casting themselves as mere instruments in a system that they cannot alter. 'He was not stupid,' Arendt wrote of Eichmann, yet his 'remoteness from reality' was, as she put it, a manifestation of 'thoughtlessness' and evidence of a 'lack of imagination' (1963, pp. 287–8). People become desensitised to violence when they cannot imagine alternatives to the choices they are given or the roles that they are assigned. By likening himself to a helpless 'cog,' Eichmann also represented himself as a kind of tragic figure, caught up in logics that he could not master and did not intend. By asserting that Eichmann was guilty because he was a mastermind and not a cog, she suggests, the court implicitly condoned the denial and resignation of those who see themselves as mere 'cogs.'

If the inability to *feel* is bound up in a refusal to *think* or to imagine alternatives, then changing the way that we think must be an important response to desensitisation. To challenge the desensitisation that enables people to condone and participate in atrocity, Arendt contends, it is important to challenge the logic that enables people to think of themselves as 'cogs.' The very idea of government as mastery, premised on the 'Platonic separation of knowing and doing,' she suggests, implies the violent suppression of plurality and political agency (1958, p. 225). Against Plato and others who liken the art of politics to fabrication, Arendt proposes that 'the theater is the political art par excellence,' because it dramatises human action, interaction, and conflict (1958, p. 188). As displayed in tragic drama, 'action almost never achieves its purpose,' she observes, due to the 'existing web of human relationships, with its innumerable, conflicting wills and intentions' (1958, p. 184).

To accept the tragic reality of political action, Arendt suggests, means that instead of identifying responsibility with authorities that can assert mastery and control, people must be responsible for thinking critically about authorities. If they did so, she suggests, people could not remain emotionally detached from their role in authorised abuse. Arendt develops this idea with a discussion of critical thought as identified, in the Socratic dialogues, with the gadfly that stings people awake and the stingray that paralyses. Critical thought is both provocative and paralysing, Arendt writes, adding that what appears to be paralysing can be 'felt as the highest state of being alive' (1971, p. 432). When we stop to think, she suggests, we are compelled to interrupt our routine activities and when stung awake by the impact of thinking, we may no longer be able to continue doing what we have been doing.

To accept responsibility for actions within a 'web of human relationships,' Arendt acknowledges, is to feel 'guilty' of consequences that we never intended, yet to accept that cannot undo them (1958, p. 233). 'All of this is a reason to turn away with despair from the realm of human affairs,' she writes, 'which entangles people in ways that can make us feel like we are 'the victim and sufferer,' rather than 'the author and doer' of what we have done (1958, p. 233). Even those who are outraged by systematic atrocity can become reconciled if they feel that resistance is futile. It was this kind of resignation that Arendt saw in the memoir of Peter Bamm, a German physician who served on the Russian Front. 'Everyone who had seriously protested or acted against the killing unit would have been arrested,' wrote Bamm, 'and would have disappeared.' (1963, p. 231). The sense that resistance is 'practically useless' is reinforced, Arendt thought, by the belief that public officials will succeed in burying all evidence of resistance in 'holes of oblivion' (1958, p. 459). If people feel that action is futile, they begin to make compromises that can grow larger over time. The care taken to bury accounts of resistance, however, is evidence of the power in such accounts.

In response those who become resigned to systematic abuse, despairing about the possibility of meaningful resistance, Arendt asserts, 'holes of oblivion do not exist' because 'one person will always be left alive to tell the story' (1963, p. 212). This cannot be factually correct unless we interpret 'the story' very abstractly, yet Arendt presents it as a kind 'self-evident truth' that people should seek to realise and enact. Sharing tragic accounts of resistance, then, can counter resignation by acting against 'holes of oblivion.' Arendt observes that testimony shared during the Eichmann trial regarding Anton Schmidt's story, an Austrian officer who aided the partisan resistance, had a profound impact on the audience. The story, Arendt writes, was 'like a sudden burst of light' in the midst of 'impenetrable darkness' that caused a 'single thought' to be 'irrefutably beyond question': 'How different everything would be ... if only more such stories could have been told!' (1963, pp. 230–231). His story is tragic, rather than triumphal, and can tell us little about when or why resistance will succeed. However, it reveals possibilities for agency, solidarity, and responsibility that are obscured by the emphasis on Eichmann's criminality. By emphasising how Schmidt's story electrified the audience and illuminated insights that were 'irrefutably beyond question,' Arendt suggests that tragic accounts of resistance might aid restore the shared sense of reality. Even when our actions appear futile, then, it is possible that they matter more than we think – not only in their direct and indirect effects, but also in the stories that might one day be told about us and in the ideas, insights, and judgments that could be drawn from such stories.

Arendt's tragic approach to unreconciliation contains a challenge for those who invoke the threat of intense emotions to defend minimalist responses to political violence. Reconciliation 'with reality,' as she frames it, not only requires a response to intense anger and grief, but also to emotional detachment. Tragic unreconciliation entails a refusal to accept the role of 'cog' by thinking critically about our role in systems that we did not create and cannot control. Critical thinking, Arendt suggests, might awaken feeling in those that have become emotionally detached from what they are doing, yet it might also reinforce the despair and resignation that lead people to reconcile to what they should resist. Tragic accounts of resistance, she suggests, challenge problematic forms of reconciliation by recovering critical insight and transformative meaning in acts that might otherwise be dismissed as futile.

Although tragic accounts of violence can challenge desensitisation, they can also be highly effective in reinforcing denial and emotional detachment. Contemporary truth commissions follow colonial commissions of inquiry, writes Adam Sitze, by invoking the logics of tragedy to frame atrocities as simultaneously 'intolerable and unavoidable' (2016, p. 165). The 1923 Bondelzwort Commission Report, Sitze observes, deployed a tragic framework in presenting its report on violence committed by the South African mandatory administration in response to an uprising of a group of Khoi-Khoi known as the Bondelzworts. The killing and wounding of hundreds, declared Jan Smuts responding to the report, was a 'tragic inevitability' resulting from a 'tragic misunderstanding' (2016, p. 165). By depicting Eichmann as a monstrous villain, Arendt worried, the court imbued his actions with a kind of tragic greatness. In a 1974 interview, Arendt recalled that in writing *Eichmann in Jerusalem* she sought to 'take away from people the admiration they have for evil doers like Richard III' and followed Brecht's assertion that 'great political criminals must be exposed and especially to laughter' (Errera 2013, p. 60). No matter what he did, she added, 'he is still a clown' (Ererra 2013, p.60). Many commentators interpreted such statements as evidence of an unseemly coldness in Arendt's own response to suffering. An alternative interpretation can be drawn from Arendt's earlier writings, which elaborate on the political role of humour as a strategy for confronting emotional detachment and challenging the distortions of tragic abstractions.

Pariah humour

In 'We Refugees' Arendt recalls a speech given by the leader of a society of Jewish refugees in France. 'We have been good Germans in Germany,' he declared, 'and therefore we shall be good Frenchmen in France' (2007, p. 272). 'The public applauded enthusiastically,' reports Arendt, drily, 'and nobody laughed.' Ironic laughter would have been a more appropriate response, she suggests, to the denial of reality in his framing of reconciliation as assimilation. 'We Refugees' is written in the first-person plural, yet emphasises the privatising and isolating dimensions of assimilation. 'We fight like madmen for private existences, individual destinies,' she writes.

'We don't feel entitled to Jewish solidarity' (2007, p. 269). The self-erasure and denial of violence associated with assimilation, Arendt suggests, is literally and metaphorically suicidal (2007, p. 267). However, Jewish solidarity premised on a refusal to reconcile with the world was, in her view, equally destructive and absurd. 'Some of the Zionist leaders pretend to believe that Jews can maintain themselves in Palestine against the whole world and that they themselves can persevere in claiming everything or nothing against everybody and everything,' she wrote. 'However, behind this spurious optimism lurks a despair of everything and a genuine readiness for suicide' (2007, p. 387).

In reflections on the theme of the 'conscious pariah,' Arendt elaborates on humour as a response to the self-erasure of reconciliation as assimilation and the destructiveness of unreconciliation as pariah politics. The 'conscious pariah,' writes Arendt, embraces the qualities and values of Jewish life that have been associated with a pariah existence, including humour and the cultivation of a kind of 'disinterested intelligence.' As Hanna Pitkin observes, Arendt characterises the conscious pariah as a figure that refuses to internalise the disparaging status of the pariah and rejects that status consciously, openly, and in solidarity with others (1998, p. 64). Arendt develop this theme in, 'The Jew as Pariah: A Hidden Tradition,' by reflecting on four exemplars of the pariah tradition, including Heine and Chaplin, as well as Franz Kafka and Bernard Lazare, and by analysing assimilationism as the path of the 'parvenu.' What distinguishes exemplars of the pariah tradition, she writes, is their pursuit of an imaginative 'emancipation of their own hearts and brains' under conditions of repression, exclusion, and isolation (2007, p. 276). Arendt identifies limitations in the work of each pariah exemplar, writes Bonnie Honig, yet each contributes to a 'repertoire of resilience' including rebellion, visionary poetry, and humour, as well as an appeal for basic rights (2015, p. 481). Arendt's reflections on Heine and Chaplin stress the centrality of humour as a pariah quality and as a response to injustice.

The classic theories of humour as an expression of superiority, a mechanism for relief of tension, and as a vehicle for the recognition of incongruity, offer useful insight in thinking about the role of pariah humour as a response to political violence. The superiority theory offers insight into the role of humour in asserting dominance, delineating social boundaries and establishing emotional distance from suffering and abuse. Humour reinforces community boundaries by distinguishing insiders, who 'get' the joke, from outsiders, who do not (Kuipers, 2006). Humour may ratify and perpetuate racism, white supremacy, and male dominance in ways that are overt, yet also indirect and therefore challenging to address. Sara Ahmed contends that humour is a 'crucial technique for reproducing inequality and injustice.' Humour creates 'the appearance of distance,' she observes, 'by laughing about what they repeat, they repeat what they laugh about. It is no laughing matter' (2017, p. 261). Thus, Ahmed's 'Killjoy Manifesto' includes, as a central principle, a commitment to act as 'killjoy' in response to jokes that hurt and offend, by refusing to laugh.

Humour can also be mobilised to contest the boundaries of political community and various forms of dominance and hierarchy by revealing incongruities that expose hypocrisy, cruelty, and injustices. The satirical ridicule of authorities can circumvent the risks of direct political commentary and disrupt the political rhetoric of legitimation (Freud, Strachey & Richards 1977, McKegney, 2007). Socrates is depicted as using ironic humour to draw his interlocutors into the kind of critical thinking that would sting them awake (Seery, 1990). Lawrence Langer identifies irony as a narrative strategy for the expression of unreconciliation among those who testified as Holocaust 'survivors' but did not feel that they had survived (1991).

The experience of laughing with others not only relieves tension, but can also reinforce a sense of connection and intimacy that is felt, rather than demonstrated through promises or verbal consensus. Like tears and rage, laughter may be involuntary, disruptive, and difficult to control. It can be contagious in ways that are unexpected and in ways that shatter distancing abstractions. In that sense, laughter has the kind of kinetic energy that Sonali Chakarvarti has associated with anger – the capacity to electrify and circulate, to affect how people see their past and their present, and shift the terms of debate (Chakravarti, 2014). Solitary laughter, laughter at the wrong time, and humour that is not considered funny or appropriate, on the other hand, may be cited as evidence of inhumanity, insanity, or radical disconnect.

Heine's poetry exemplifies the expressive power of pariah humour, Arendt suggests, by invoking comic incongruity to reveal absurdities in social hierarchy, exclusion, and assimilation. Heine humorously situates the figure of the *schlemiel* alongside the divine and tragic heroes of Greek and German literature. In his poem, 'The God Apollo,' Heine depicts a nun who falls in love with a divine figure who can play the lyre, only to discover that the 'Apollo of her dreams' exists in reality as Rabbi Faibusch – a humble cantor from Amsterdam whose mother sells sour pickles and whose son performs as a clown (Arendt 2007). Through this comic incongruity, Arendt observes, Heine turns away from abstract symbolism that might appeal to the privileged by celebrating the everyday humour of the ostracised. Heine's poetry directs readers to the 'true realities' that 'all men are essentially equal,' writes Arendt, by unmasking the absurdity of 'pomp and circumstance' (2007, p. 280). 'Confronted with the natural order of things, in which all is equally good,' writes Arendt, 'the fabricated order of society, with its manifold classes and ranks, must appear a comic, hopeless attempt of creation to throw down the gauntlet to its creator' (2007, p. 279).

Heine also deploys comic incongruities to expose the absurdity and tragedy of assimilation. At a time when Jews were hiding their knowledge of Jewish culture, writes Arendt, Heine wrote, 'as pure German verse,' a poem in praise of a distinctively Jewish dish: 'Schalet, ray of light immortal/Schalet, daughter of Elysium!' With his reference to the 'homespun Judaism' of everyday life, Arendt suggests, Heine mocks those who mask their Jewish identity by embracing German culture, as well as those who seek dignity in proving that they are 'descendants of an especially exalted people' (2007, p. 282). Heine's mocking incongruities also repudiate the ideal of a universalism that denies the particularity of peoples, their material desires, their tastes, and the dishes that they share day to day. 'He was not deceived by this nonsense of 'world citizenship,'' writes Arendt, 'and had no time for academic pipe dreams' (2007, p. 282). He 'simply ignored' the message that 'the Jew might only become a man when he ceased to be a Jew' (2007, p. 283).

In contrast with the parvenu, the pariah remains aloof, writes Arendt. 'It is this aloofness,' she adds, 'that accounts for the divine laughter and the absence of bitterness in his verses' (2007, p. 280). Heine's humour avoids bitterness not by letting go of anger, but by expressing it. Heine 'vents his anger not only at tyrants, but equally at those who put up with them,' she writes (2007, p. 280). However, Heine's aloofness is emblematic of the double-edged character of pariah humour and the transience of its power. '[L]aughter does not kill...neither slaves nor tyrants are extinguished by mere amusement,' writes Arendt (2007, p. 280). The position of the pariah, 'who stands outside the real world and attacks it from without' is always 'remote and unreal,' she adds. Arendt suggests that Heine could transform the 'nonexistence and unreality' of the pariah life into a politically effective identity because he 'sought nothing more than to hold a mirror up to the political world' and because he was able to draw upon art, creativity and humour in order to avoid doctrinaire utopianism and dogma.

If Heine was a schlemiel 'of the visionary type,' writes Arendt, Charlie Chaplin used the figure of the schlemiel to depict a 'grotesquely caricatured' reality, revealing 'a world from which neither nature nor art can provide escape' (2007, p. 286). Like Heine's schlemiel, Chaplin's 'little man' displays a comic innocence to awaken an emotional response to the absurdities and cruelties of social exclusion. Chaplin's schlemiel is always suspect, always on the run, and incessantly harried by the 'guardians of law and order' (p. 286). In contrast with Heine's carefree, impudent schlemiel, Chaplin's is anxious and worried. He 'does not recognise the class order of the world because he sees in it neither order nor justice for himself.' In the figure of Chaplin's 'suspect,' writes Arendt, the poor and economically dispossessed within American society could recognise their affinities with the figure of the persecuted refugee, perpetually 'on the run' (2007, p. 288).

What is comical about Chaplin's films is the incongruity between the innocence and smallness of his schlemiel and the intensity with which he is pursued by the police. Through this comic incongruity, Chaplin depicts the absurdities of persecution, yet repudiates the idea that the persecuted must be defended with reference to their virtues or heroic character. '[F]or the man who is in any case suspect,' writes Arendt, 'there is no relation between the offense he commits and the price he pays' (2007, p. 287). To protest persecution by highlighting the supposed virtues of the persecuted, Arendt suggests, is to reinforce the logics by which racism, anti-Semitism, and class hierarchy characterize whole groups as 'inherently suspect.' Chaplin also conveyed a critique of legalism – an 'expression of the dangerous incompatibility between general laws and individual misdeeds' (p. 287). Although this incompatibility is 'in itself tragic,' Arendt writes, it is made manifest through Chaplin's effective use of comedy.

Arendt stresses that both Chaplin and Heine compelled audiences to fall in love with the schlemiel. 'If they laughed at the way he was falling in love at first sight,' she writes of Chaplin's audiences, 'they realised that the kind of love he evinced was their kind of love' (2007, p. 287). She suggests that Chaplin was able, though affection generated by his humour, to convey a critique that might have appeared 'incredible and untenable' if presented as 'high flown talk about the persecution of the guiltless' and conveyed harsh realities in a manner that was 'warm and convincing' (2007, p. 287). Because he is 'beyond the pale, unhampered by the trammels of society,' writes Arendt, Chaplin's *schlemiel* can 'get away with a great deal' (2007, p. 287).

Arendt's comic pariah expresses a refusal to reconcile that is premised on a reconciliation. That is, her comic pariah articulates a refusal to reconcile with the logics of persecution by reconciling with a disavowed collective identity and recovering its nurturing dimensions. The comic pariah resists annihilation and affirms plurality by playfully unmasking the violence embedded in purportedly universal principles and tragic themes. At the same time, Arendt's comic pariah recovers meaningful generalities by intimately engaging with the particularities of material, sensual, social, everyday life. Pariah humour elicits joy and the connective energy of shared laughter to confront the despair, loneliness and internalised shame that prevent people from acting in solidarity against persecution.

Arendt characterises pariah humour as a limited response to oppression – a creative strategy for mediating tensions between estrangement and political engagement that lacks significance in contexts where estrangement cannot serve as a meaningful avenue for engagement. Bernard Lazare, a Jewish literary critic and political journalist, exemplifies the 'conscious pariah' for Arendt because he translated the pariah status into more explicitly political terms: as a demand for rebellion. However, he failed, she suggests, because he could not persuade others to pursue the pariah identity as a basis for political engagement. The posture of the pariah also ceases to be politically meaningful, Arendt adds, in a context where 'there is no protection in heaven or earth against bare murder, and a man can be driven at any moment from the streets' (2007, p. 296). In such times, she writes, 'you cannot stand aloof from society' and it is only 'when a people functions in consort with other peoples,' that it becomes possible to respond meaningfully to persecution (2007, p. 297).

In contrast with Ahmed's 'killjoy,' who refuses laughter in ways that elicit discomfort, Arendt's comic pariahs transform stigmatising, distancing laughter into the laughter of affection. Yet affective identification is a limited and ambiguous basis for appealing to bystanders or spectators for solidarity. Chaplin's humour fell out of fashion, Arendt observes (2007, p. 288), when people stopped being able to laugh at their own misfortunes. Premised on a stance of unreconciliation to the logics of anti-Semitism, this approach does little to confront the logics of anti-black racism and other forms of white supremacist exclusion. And as Eric Lott and Michael Rogin have demonstrated, desire and love were never straightforward responses to the comic figure of the pariah in blackface, but mingled with exploitation, and anxiety in response to the destabilisation of racial hierarchies (Lott, 2013; Rogin, 1998). To the extent that pariah humour *does* succeed in eliciting affective identification or love for those targeted for persecution, it also extends a degree of reassurance to participants, bystanders and beneficiaries, making it easier to avoid the kind of shame that might inspire responsibility.

Haunting pariah laughter

In 1971, a group of Vietnam veterans gathered in Detroit to share their war stories. These were not the classic war stories of military heroism, but stories about the atrocities of war, told by those who committed or witnessed them. The event was organised by an activist group, Vietnam Veterans Against the War (VVAW), who hoped to demonstrate that the My Lai atrocities were not an aberration from, but result of, standard policies in Vietnam. Referring to themselves as 'winter soldiers,' they inverted Thomas Paine's reference to the 'summer soldier and the sunshine patriot,' who 'will, in crisis, shrink from the service of their country' to position dissent as demanding moral obligation (VVAW, 1972, p. 5). The 1971 Winter Soldier hearings inspired the organization of Iraq Veterans Against the War to host a similar event aimed at demonstrating that the torture and abuses that were documented at Abu Ghraib had not been exceptional, but part of a systematic pattern of abuse (IVAW, 2008).

Humour is an important dimension of these accounts. Anti-war veteran accounts include details about jokes and laughter shared among soldiers as they carried out abuses against civilians and prisoners of war, as well as acts of violence carried out 'for laughs' or 'to get a laugh.' They do so, not to inspire warmth, but to awaken revulsion and to reveal why veterans continue to feel like ghostly pariahs. Like Arendt's comic pariahs, anti-war veterans use humour to sustain tensions inherent in the embrace of radical unreconciliation as a path to engagement and responsibility for the world. Like Arendt's comic pariahs, anti-war veterans use humour to dismantle tragic abstractions by compelling audiences to confront the particularities of material, physical, and emotional experiences of violence in everyday lives. Whereas Arendt's comic pariahs express unreconciliation from the perspective of the persecuted, however, anti-war veterans express a refusal to reconcile with their role as participants in atrocities and as a demand for responsibility from political leaders and civilian bystanders. Like Ahmed's 'killjoy,' Winter Soldier testimonies summon haunting memories of transgressive humour to repudiate offensive laughter by eliciting discomfort and shame.

'It was more or less like a joke,' reported one veteran after describing how his unit had cut off the whiskers of an elderly man in front of his family (VVAW, 1972, p. 28). 'We all laughed about it. And then we forgot about it,' reported another Vietnam veteran describing how his unit had killed a three-year-old boy. By including details regarding their own laughter and the laughter of those around them, veterans reject the individualisation of guilt as an exercise in scapegoating. In anti-war veteran accounts, details regarding joking and laughter in the context of abuse convey the collective nature of this sense of guilt. These stories are not accounts of solitary soldiers laughing silently to themselves. They do not say, 'I laughed,' but 'we laughed.' The 'we' in such stories is a reference to their unit, but also a way of amplifying their message about the more pervasive normalisation of abuse.

Lifton observes that dehumanising jokes were incorporated into military training as part of a strategy of desensitisation that would reinforce logics of superiority and inferiority through humiliation. (1985) Narratives gathered by VVAW and IVAW converge on the role of dehumanisation, sexual humiliation, and racism in training, to expose and condemn the logics by which they became reconciled to what they would later resist. '[O]nce the military has got the idea implanted in your mind that these people are not human, they are subhuman, it makes it a little bit easier to kill 'em,' reflected one Vietnam veteran (VVAW, 1972, p. 45). 'It's a very racist war,' concluded another. 'There's no difference between a good one and a bad one,' said another, 'except that the good one at the time is carrying no weapon, but he is still fair game' (VVAW, 1972, p. 27). IVAW accounts also address the role of racism in training soldiers to kill without thinking too much about the civilian-combatant distinction (IVAW, 2008, p. 64).

In outlining the impact of the desensitisation, veterans elaborate on several factors that undermined their capacity for critical thinking and moral judgment. 'You're not to question. You're not to ask why,' recalled one veteran in his testimony for IVAW (2008, p. 5). 'They make you lose your entire sense of identity,' observed another (VVAW, 1972, p. 151). Such comments resonate with the 'cog defence,' yet by recalling their memories of transgressive humour as a strategy, veterans also challenge the logic animating the 'cog' theory by revealing the extent to which soldiers *could* perceive the criminality and gratuitous nature of their own participation in abuse as they were carrying it out. Anti-war veterans also challenge the idea of themselves as 'cogs' by problematising what they take to be most shameful and irredeemable about their own participation in war. In so doing, they use their memories of laughter as a strategy for channelling their own feelings of shame into a politically meaningful expression of resistance.

Winter Soldier narratives repudiate what many refer to as 'John Wayne syndrome,' as well as heroic mythologies that present violence as inevitable and meaningful by asserting that the violence they committed was just a 'joke' – shockingly absurd and devoid of meaning. Numerous accounts shared with the VVAW include details about soldiers casually harming or killing children for sport without any reason or provocation.'[A]s you drive through the ville you take the cans of C-rats and the cases and you peg 'em at the kids; you try to belt them over the head,' recalled Jack Smith' (VVAW, 1972, p. 37). These are not tales of 'collateral damage' or the tragic stories of soldiers who felt compelled to do regrettable things for duty. By including such details in their stories, soldiers challenge official explanations of violence, while repudiating efforts to derive meaning from violence. By modelling the refusal of solace afforded by legal and tragic abstractions and the acceptance of irredeemable shame, these accounts demonstrate how civilian bystanders might accept responsibility by confronting their own displaced shame.

Details regarding transgressive humour are a uniquely haunting feature of these accounts: they are depicted as haunting to veterans but also meant to haunt audiences. The idea of combatants and veterans as ghosts is a familiar trope in the literature on the war in Vietnam. 'We called the enemy ghosts,' writes Tim O'Brien in 'Ghost Soldiers.' The idea of the ghost-like enemy was a way of coping with the terror of combat, he suggests (O'Brien, 2011). At the same time, O'Brien characterises the ghostly enemy as a projection of the way that fear, violence, and the anticipation of death can make combatants feel like living ghosts. 'Eyes closed, I seemed to rise up out of my own body,' he writes, 'and float through the dark...I was invisible, I had no shape, no substance, I weighed less than nothing. I just drifted...I was atrocity.' War ghosts are often conceptualised as the antithesis of war heroes. 'You're a shadow,' writes O'Brien, 'shedding your own history and your own future...And it's not a movie and you aren't a hero and all you can do is whimper and wait.' (2011, p. 211) If commemorating war heroes is a basis for patriotic inspiration or tragic resolution, acknowledging the ghosts of war compels people to see what remains unresolved, unknowable, indecipherable, and irredeemable.

Veterans, along with many victims and survivors of violence, have also likened their experience of returning home to the feeling of being ghosts among the living. Lifton writes that the 'death guilt' expressed by veterans commonly invoked a sense of responsibility for the 'homeless dead' as well as in the perception of themselves as living ghosts (VVAW, 1972, p. 107). This idea of living ghosts is a visceral expression of estrangement similar to that of the pariah. Living ghosts can no longer be at home in the world as a result of what they have experienced or what they have done, yet remain among the living. They convey a radical dissonance, a being torn between the present and the haunting past, between the desire to communicate and the sense that it is impossible to be heard and understood.

'How shall we remember rather than just appropriate the dead for our own agenda, precluding what the dead tell us?' The haunting accounts of anti-war veterans are limited as a response to this question, posed by Nguyên-Vo Thu-Huong (cited in Nguyen, 2006, p. 8). And accounts gathered by VVAW do little to address the erasure of Vietnamese agency that characterised American representations of the war. However, they haunt in the sense that notifies us, as Avery Gordon puts it, that 'what's been suppressed or concealed is very much alive in the present' (Gordon, 2011, p. 2). The haunting laughter included in anti-war veteran accounts offers a rejoinder to Arendt's insistence that someone will always be left alive to tell the story. These accounts alert audiences to the fact that there are many stories that survivors do not tell or cannot tell, that there are many massacres with no survivors, save those that carried them out. They alert us to the ghostly presence of voices and experiences that are never recorded in the archives and oral histories of war and atrocity.

Haunting accounts of cruel humour and laughter are also a way for veterans to rattle audiences into accepting the burden of work that remains undone. Anti-war veterans use details about transgressive laughter to mark their own shift from what Lifton calls 'static guilt,' to 'animating guilt.' *Static guilt*, writes Lifton, is characterised by a 'closed universe of transgression and expected punishment' and contributes to the deadening of emotional responses to violence (Lifton, 1985, p. 127). In contrast, *animating guilt* draws energy from a 'sustained and formative dissatisfaction with both self and world' and responds to the 'anxiety of responsibility' with active emotional engagement that can awaken suppressed shame and restore a capacity for joy and connection (1985, p. 128). Animating guilt, then, is an avenue for mobilising the role of shame, as Chris LeBron puts it, as the 'moral response that we should tend to have when we fail to uphold principles we affirm' by 'prompting an assessment of our failings as a society' (2015, p. 7). By including details regarding haunting laughter in their accounts, veterans model the acceptance of animating guilt by dramatising the transformation from a former self that laughed at the suffering of others to the self that now recognises such laughter as grotesque and inhuman.

In one account shared with IVAW, one veteran recalls that as his unit was 'constantly struggling to justify our existence' they came up with a joke that captured their frustrations: 'We care so that you don't have to' (IVAW, 2008, p. 46). The slogan uses humour to repudiate mythologies that mask the absurdities of war, including those that elevate the soldier as hero and those that scapegoat individual soldiers for war crimes that were authorised by leaders or predictable outcomes of war policy. 'We care so that Paul Bremer doesn't have to ... so that Congress doesn't have to,' asserted the veteran, 'so the American people don't have to, so that these things can go on in our names and they can just go back to the mall and their daily lives and pretend like nothing's wrong' (IVAW, 2008, p. 46). In her introduction to IVAW's Winter Soldier volume, Kelly Dougherty acknowledged that 'many people ... would rather not be made uncomfortable by being confronted with the grim reality of warfare and occupation.' Publicising such stories, Dougherty writes, is a way to 'pressure our fellow Americans to acknowledge their own responsibility for these occupations, which is a necessary part of bringing them to an end' (IVAW, 2008, p. 5).

Like Arendt's comic pariahs, anti-war veterans invoke humour to shift attention away from legal fictions and tragic abstractions and to reveal the logics of systematic violence through a confrontation with particularities and materialities. However, instead of soliciting laughter and warmth, anti-war veterans invoke memories of transgressive humour to reveal their own shame and to disturb the peace of civilian audiences. By invoking memories of haunting laughter, anti-war veterans position themselves as pariahs, irredeemably estranged from the world; however, they do so as a strategy for accepting political responsibility for what they have done and suffered, while challenging civilian audiences to take up their own political responsibilities and share the burden of shame.

Out of time

As arts of refusal, tragic unreconciliation and pariah humour draw upon and subvert the tragic imagination to confront the emotional indifference that leads people to remain reconciled to what they should resist. They creatively mediate tensions between reconciliation and unreconciliation to imagine novel critical and transformative responses to violence. Tragic unreconciliation and pariah humour are limited in important ways, yet significant as responses, not only to desensitisation and detachment, but to the nihilism and resignation inherent in minimalist responses to political violence. Arendt's tragic account of unreconciliation and her discussion of pariah humour respond to the persistent worry that it is too late to redeem our own shameful actions, to pursue transformative responses to the systematic logics enabling atrocity, too late to contemplate reparative justice or to prevent the catastrophic destruction that is coming. We cannot predict the outcomes of our actions or erase what we have done, yet by the same logic, actions that seem impossible or futile now may become possible one day or meaningful in ways that we cannot predict. Tragic unreconciliation and pariah humour are creative strategies for converting this insight into a political response to the desensitised, the detached, and the resigned, by demonstrating that although it is always too late for actions that redeem, it is never too late for actions that matter.

Acknowledgments

The author wishes to acknowledge the ACLS Foundation for support provided to this project, and is grateful to those who reviewed the paper anonymously, as well as Alex Livingston, Mihaela Mihai, Mathias Thaler, David Wiens and the UCSD Theory Colloquium, for comments on earlier versions of this article.

Disclosure statement

No potential conflict of interest was reported by the author.

References

Ahmed, S. (2017). *Leading a feminist life*. Durham: Duke University Press.
Anker, E. R. (2014). *Orgies of feeling: Melodrama and the politics of freedom*. Durham: Duke University Press.
Anyeko, K., Baines, E., Komakech, E., Ojok, B., Owor Ogora, L., & Victor, L. (2011). 'The cooling of hearts': Community truth-telling in Northern Uganda. *Human Rights Review, 13*(1), 107–124.

Arendt, H. (1958). *The human condition.* Chicago: University of Chicago Press.
Arendt, H. (1963). *Eichmann in Jerusalem: A report on the banality of evil.* New York: Viking Press.
Arendt, H. (1971). Thinking and moral considerations. *Social Research, 38*(3), 417–446.
Arendt, H. (2013). We refuges. In Arendt, H. (Eds.), *The jewish writings* (pp. 264–75). New York: Schocken Books.
Arendt, H., & Kohn, J. (1994). *Essays in understanding, 1930–1954.* San Diego: Harcourt, Brace & Co.
Berkowitz, R. (2011). Bearing logs on our shoulders: Reconciliation, non-reconciliation, and the building of a common world. *Theory & Event, 14*(1). doi:10.1353/tae.2011.0001
Brendese, P. J. (2014). *The power of memory in democratic politics.* Rochester: University of Rochester Press.
Brudholm, T. (2008). *Resentment's virtue: Jean Améry and the refusal to forgive.* Philadelphia: Temple University Press.
Chakravarti, S. (2014). *Sing the rage: Listening to anger after mass violence.* Chicago: Chicago University Press.
Clarke, K. M. (2009). *Fictions of justice: The international criminal court and the challenge of legal pluralism in Sub-Saharan Africa.* Cambridge: Cambridge University Press.
Euben, J. P. (1986). *Greek tragedy and political theory.* Berkeley: University of California Press.
Iraq Veterans Against the War and Glantz, A. (2008). *Winter soldier, Iraq and Afghanistan eyewitness accounts of the occupations.* Chicago: Haymarket Books.
Gordon, A. (2011). *Ghostly matters: Haunting and the sociological imagination.* Minneapolis: University of Minnesota Press.
Honig, B. (2015). The laws of the Sabbath (poetry): Arendt, Heine, and the politics of debt. *UC Irvine Law Review, 5,* 463–482.
Kuipers, G. (2006). *Good humour, bad taste: A sociology of the joke.* Berlin: Mouton de Gruyter.
Langer, L. L. (1991). *Holocaust testimonies: The ruins of memory.* New Haven: Yale University Press.
Lebron, C. J. (2015). *The colour of our shame: Race and justice in our time.* Oxford: Oxford University Press.
Lifton, R. J. (1985). *Home from the war: Vietnam veterans: Neither victims nor executioners.* New York: Basic Books.
Lott, E. J. (2013). *Love and theft: Blackface minstrelsy and the American working class.* Oxford: Oxford University Press.
McKegney, S. (2007). *Magic weapons: Aboriginal writers remaking community after residential school.* Winnipeg: University of Manitoba Press.
Meister, R. (2011). *After evil: A politics of human rights.* New York: Columbia University Press.
Mihai, M. (2016). *Negative emotions and transitional justice.* New York: Columbia University Press.
Minow, M. (2009). *Between vengeance and forgiveness: Facing history after genocide and mass violence.* Boston: Beacon Press.
Nguyen, V. T. (2006). Speak of the dead, dpeak of Vietnam. *CR: The New Centennial Review, 6*(2), 7–37.

O'Brien, T. (2011). *The things they carried: In the lake of the woods: 2 works*. Boston: Houghton Mifflin Harcourt.
Pitkin, H. F. (1998). *The attack of the blob: Hannah Arendt's concept of the social*. Chicago: University of Chicago Press.
Rogin, M. (1998). *Blackface, white noise: Jewish immigrants in the hollywood melting pot*. Berkeley: University of California Press.
Seery, J. E. (1990). *Political returns: Irony in politics and theory from Plato to the antinuclear movement*. Boulder: Westview Press.
Sitze, A. (2016). *The impossible machine: A genealogy of South Africa's truth and reconciliation commission*. Ann Arbor: University of Michigan Press.
Tutu, D. (1999). *No future without forgiveness*. London: Doubleday.
Vietnam Veterans Against the War. (1972). *The winter soldier investigation: an inquiry into american war crimes*. Boston: Beacon Press.

How America disguises its violence: colonialism, mass incarceration, and the need for resistant imagination

Shari Stone-Mediatore

ABSTRACT
This paper examines how a delusive social imaginary of criminal-justice has underpinned contemporary U.S. mass incarceration and encouraged widespread indifference to its violence. I trace the complicity of this criminal-justice imaginary with state-organized violence by comparing it to an imaginary that supported colonial violence. I conclude by discussing how those of us outside of prison can begin to resist the entrenched images and institutions of mass incarceration by engaging the work and imagining the perspective of incarcerated people.

We Americans have perfected the art of being both sanctimonious and deliberately indifferent to the plight of others.
                        Joseph Dole, 'Abolish long-term solitary confinement'

For many Americans, state-organised violence is a problem for other countries but not our own. America is imagined to be ruled by law, which is viewed as a counterforce to violence and brutality. And yet, as part of its criminal-legal system, the United States currently incarcerates a greater percentage of its citizens than any other nation. The 2 million individuals held in prisons and jails across the country have little protection against rampant physical, sexual, and psychological abuse in facilities that operate with little public oversight. Nearly 200,000 men and women are sentenced to spend their entire lives behind bars, many for convictions as juveniles or young adults. Over 80,000 individuals are confined to solitary units, where they spend 23 to 24 hours a day alone in cells no larger than 8 by 10 feet, sometimes for years or even decades, in conditions that the United Nations considers torture (ACLU, 2011, Everest, 2013, Mayeux 2015, Rovner, 2016, Ghandnoosh, 2017, Solitary Watch, n.d., The Sentencing Project, n.d.).

This paper brings critical attention to the violence of mass incarceration by examining how it has been masked and facilitated by a delusive social imaginary of criminal justice. I sketch this imaginary's contours by comparing it to an imaginary underpinning colonialism. This investigation accords with recent work by critical race theorists, who have traced continuities between mass incarceration and systems of racialised violence, forced labor, and legal inequality that constituted U.S. slavery (Alexander 2011, Dilts, 2014, Peláez, 2016). However, while much of the literature views mass incarceration in the context of slavery, I draw on recent scholars of colonialism, including Dussel (1995), Quijano (2000), and Rodriguez (2014, 2015)), to trace recurring colonialist patterns of state-violence-disguised-as-righteousness. Colonialism is not the only form of institutionalised violence that reverberates in mass incarceration; however, recent studies of colonialism offer particularly illuminating insight into the cultural processes that allow 'civilised' people to accept and even exalt barbaric violence.

In tracing analogies between a colonial imaginary of righteous violence and a contemporary criminal-justice imaginary, I elucidate several mechanisms that disguise and support the violence of mass incarceration. I conclude by examining how the faculty of imagination can help destabilise these mechanisms and contribute to honest and responsible engagement with the U.S. criminal-legal system. I argue that, while empirical documentation of the violence of mass incarceration is crucial, we can resist the hold of an imaginary that abets high-minded indifference only when those of us outside prison walls begin to imagine the perspective of those held within.[1]

Colonialism and the disguising of violence

Critics describe colonialism primarily as a vast system of violence. In his classic study of European colonialism, Frantz Fanon argued that 'the conquest of a national territory and the oppression of a people' that constitute colonialism could be achieved only with multi-pronged and systemic violence (1967, p. 81). 'The colonialist structure,' Fanon stressed, 'rests on the necessity of torturing, raping, and committing massacres' as well as imposing European values and customs through 'cannons and sabers,' to maintain the 'through and through' subjugation of the colonised people (1967, pp. 34, 40, 72). Aimé Césaire confirms that colonial rule was maintained only by extreme brutality, including mutilation, massacres of whole cities, forcible transport of millions of men to labour camps, burning of homes, land-theft, and cultural destruction (1972, pp. 18–22).

Colonialism in the Americas was equally violent. The Spanish conquistadores pillaged 185,000 kilograms of gold and 16,000,000 kilograms of silver while killing millions of indigenous Americans through military aggression, land-theft, famine, rape, forced labour, and deprivation-exacerbated diseases

(Dussel, 1995, pp. 38–45, Todorov, 1984, pp. 132–42). Colonisers sabotaged indigenous knowledge-production (Quijano, 2000, p. 541, Rodriguez, 2014). They also inflicted sexual violence on indigenous women, using women's bodies to disempower indigenous men and destroy the social fabric (Dussel, 1995, pp. 45–47, Smith, 2005, pp. 15–33).

A colonial imaginary of righteous violence

As scholars of colonialism show, colonial institutions could be maintained only through an ensemble of coercive military, socio-political, and cultural mechanisms. I focus here on one component of this machinery: a social imaginary that allowed Europeans to interpret colonialism as a noble endeavour. European politicians and intellectuals alike presented colonialism in various kinds of edifying rhetoric; it was presented as salvation for savages, a civilizing mission, a gifting of material progress, and a productive use of idle land (Césaire 1972, pp. 13–22, Dussel, 1995, pp. 64–71). Walter Mignolo describes the basic ruse by which colonial brutality was refashioned in noble clothes as *the logic of coloniality*. This logic appears, Mignolo says, whenever 'control, domination, and exploitation' are cloaked 'in the language of salvation, progress, modernization, and being good for everyone' (2005, p. 6). If this logic made sense to ordinary Europeans, however, it is because the logic was animated by what I call *an imaginary of righteous violence*: a set of culturally transmitted myths of social identities and the social world that allowed Europeans to make sense of the outrageous claim that colonialism was 'for the good of all' (Juan Ginés de Sepúlveda cited Dussel, 1995, p. 63). Below, I describe how key elements of the colonial imaginary sustained this deception.

'The Indian' as violable subject

'Indian,' of course, was the name that Columbus gave to the inhabitants of the western Atlantic islands, which he thought was India. From the beginning, the European image of 'the Indian' was developed – not through close attention to, or communicative interaction with, indigenous people – but through colonisers imposing their perspective and interests on the people whose land they occupied. As ruling-class Europeans sought to present themselves as authoritative knowers, rightful settlers, and world rulers, 'Indians' were invented as people who had no culture, no diligence, no laws, no morals, and no reason; in effect, creatures whom Europeans could dominate and exploit while attributing their aggression to the subjugated people's 'vices'.

Colonial-era scholars betray the European interests behind the construction of 'the Indian.' For instance, while Spain was invading the Americas, the Spanish philosopher Juan Ginés de Sepúlveda argued in his famous Valladolid debate with Bartolomé de Las Casas that 'the Indian' was naturally servile and Spaniards naturally suited to rule (Todorov, 1984, p. 153). As Western European nations began to appropriate American land, the lazy and unruly 'Indian' served as a foil for the supposedly disciplined and productive (male, upper-class) European. For instance, in the mid-17th century, Thomas Hobbes (1968, p. 187) contrasted his proposed law-based government to the 'brutish' conditions of 'the savage people' in the Americas. Half a century later, John Locke (1980, pp. 21, 24) contrasted 'the industrious and rational' landholders of England to both 'the quarrelsome and contentious' people living on the English commons and 'the needy and wretched' people of the Americas, both of whom were supposedly unfit for land ownership. In the 19th century, Georg Wilhelm Hegel contrasted the strong-spirited people of 'the West' to 'the Indians' of South America, who were supposedly so slothful that 'at midnight a bell had to remind them even of their matrimonial duties' (1956, p. 82).

'Progress' as 'good for all'

If 'the Indian' represented an innately defective subject whose vices justified the violence inflicted on him, then invocations of higher ideals allowed the violence to be lauded as noble. Early colonisers claimed to bring 'civilisation' to 'savages.' Later colonisers increasingly appealed to socio-economic ideals of 'progress' and 'modernisation.' In all its permutations, the idealised form of life was conceived from a European perspective but presented as universal. 'Progress,' for instance, was cast in European liberal-capitalist terms but regarded as the supreme aim of all human communities (Césaire 1972, pp. 11–17, Dussel, 1995, pp. 64–67).

Eurocentric images of 'progress' compounded a myth of human advancement that found expression in thinkers from Hobbes to Hegel. In this myth, 'progress' was construed as 'a trajectory that departed from a state of nature and culminated in Europe' (Quijano, 2000, p. 542). Even when the 19th century brought greater attention to history, the same basic myth of the West as the apex of humanity became further elaborated. For instance, Hegel (1956, p. 99) claimed that Africans were so incapable of development that their enslavement by Europeans constituted 'a phase of education' by 'a higher morality and the culture connected with it.' Ultimately, images of 'progress' and 'the Indian' did not so much deny colonial violence as cast it as 'pedagogic violence,' for which colonisers considered themselves 'not only *innocent*, but meritorious for inflicting' (Dussel, 1995, p. 66).

The colonial imaginary and the institutionalising of violence

The colonial imaginary not only dressed colonial violence in edifying clothes but provided visions for organising colonial institutions. In particular, images of 'the backward Indian' and 'the modern Westerner' gave force to the modern logic of 'race,' around which colonial society was organised. 'Race' logic both organised colonial hierarchies and disguised them as a function of 'natural (racial) differences and not consequences of a history of power' (Quijano, 2000, p. 541). In effect, as 'race' differences were codified in law and materialised in divisions of labour, colonial hierarchies gained a veneer of normalcy. The racially organised society 'confirmed' that indigenous people were unfit for the polity and 'naturally obliged to work for the profit' of Europeans (Quijano, 2000, p. 539).

The imaginary of righteous violence also demanded violent tactics to maintain its own credibility. Since the Conquest, indigenous people have resisted European cultural hegemony and continued to live by their own values and narratives (Rodriguez, 2014). Thus, European colonizers could maintain the presumed universality of their cultural frameworks only by force. The early conquistadores tore down temples, set fire to eight centuries of Mayan codices, and burned alive indigenous spiritual leaders (Dussel, 1995, pp. 42–54, Quijano, 2000, pp. 540–542, Rodriguez, 2014, pp. 28–37). In the 19th and 20th centuries, the U.S. and Canadian governments outlawed Native American spiritual practices and forced Native American children into boarding schools, where their languages and rituals were forbidden (Smith, 2005, pp. 35–53). More recently, in continued efforts to suppress challenges to colonialist interpretations of the world, the Arizona state legislature has outlawed popular Raza Studies programs in Tucson, fired teachers, and banned books (Rodriguez, 2015).

The colonial imaginary and the thwarted imagination
Finally, colonialist myths discouraged Europeans from imagining colonialism from the standpoint of indigenous Americans. The philosopher Hannah Arendt explained the role that the faculty of imagination plays in our understanding of political phenomena. Following Kant, Arendt explained that the imagination is 'an important tool of cognition' by which we represent to ourselves in our mind a phenomenon that is not directly present (Arendt, 1953a, p. 79). Arendt's insight is that the imagination is especially vital to political thinking. This is because political phenomena cannot be reduced to preconceived categories or logics but can be adequately understood only when approached as humanly initiated and humanly endured phenomena that appear under 'innumerable perspectives and aspects' (Arendt, 1958, p. 57). With the imagination, Arendt explained, we can approach a political phenomenon in its uniqueness and existential richness, even while exceeding our immediate experience of that phenomenon; for we can imaginatively 'visit' the standpoint of others and thereby engage the phenomenon in its human depth but from new angles (1953b, pp. 391–392, 1982, p. 43). In effect: If a *social imaginary* guides us in making sense of the

world in terms of received cultural logics, then *the imagination* (as a faculty) keeps us responsive to aspects of the living world that exceed familiar logics.

Feminist critics have raised questions about the adequacy of the imagination for engaging radical otherness. For instance, how can we ensure that our imaginative 'visiting' of another's standpoint is true to the other's very different way of seeing the world? How do we ensure that we do not bring so much baggage on our 'visit' that our own biases burden our imagination of the other's perspective? In light of such concerns, feminist scholars have emphasized the need for interaction and solidarity with concrete others, or close engagement with others' stories, which can be challenging and discomfiting (Ortega, 2006, Stone-Mediatore, 2003, pp. 74–78, Taylor, 1993). Still, these concerns do not so much devalue the imagination as they underscore the need to pursue imaginative 'visiting' with humility, diligence, and attentiveness to concrete others.

In the context of colonialism, the myth of 'the Indian' thwarted precisely the kind of work necessary for Europeans to imagine indigenous perspectives with any adequacy. Granted, many Europeans had political, economic, and psychological interests that deterred them from considering indigenous perspectives. Still, the myth of 'the Indian' abetted such self-interested myopia by suggesting that the indigenous people had no perspective of their own for Europeans to consider. As Dussel put it (1995, p. 33), 'the Indian' was an 'aesthetic and contemplative fantasy' of Europeans that 'covered over' actual indigenous people with an image of Europe's projection. Moreover, the myth of 'the backward Indian' boosted European attitudes of superiority and authority, thereby derailing precisely the kind of humility and listening skills that would have been necessary for meaningful 'visiting' of indigenous standpoints. In effect, the myth facilitated a situation in which colonisers did not try to learn the indigenous people's language, listen to them, or understand their cultures but viewed the indigenous people as mere objects to analyse or bodies to exploit. '[I]n the best of cases,' says Todorov, referring to the Spaniards' fascination with the Aztecs, the colonisers 'speak well of the Indians, but with very few exceptions they do not speak to the Indians' (1984, p. 132).

Mass incarceration as disguised violence

Critics have increasingly recognised mass incarceration as state-organised violence. Many have documented severe and systemic physical and psychological abuses against people who are incarcerated. Some also describe how aggressive incarceration of marginalised populations decimates families and communities. Others analyse how a multi-million-dollar prison industry benefits prison-related industries and gentrification, while bleeding schools and social services (Hamilton, 2015, 2017, Irwin, 2005, Kilgore, 2017, Peláez, 2016).

Despite the critical analysis, however, U.S. prisons continue to be viewed by many as a mainstay of the U.S. justice system. Multiple factors conceal the brutality of mass incarceration from those of us who remain sheltered from it. A two-tiered system of justice for people of different social classes, the geographic isolation of prisons, prison practices that obstruct communication across prison walls, a mainstream media that tends to cover prison violence only in terms of threats to 'staff security,' and a culture of disdain for people who are less fortunate all contribute to keeping many Americans oblivious to the systemic violence of our criminal-legal system (Davis, 2009, Dole, 2014, Van Cleve 2016, p. xii).

Supporting all these processes of concealment and attitudes of aloofness, I argue, is an imaginary of criminal justice that functions similarly to the colonial imaginary of righteous violence. The ruses of our own institutions are more difficult to discern than those of the past; however, by tracing structural and functional analogies between the colonial imaginary and today's criminal-justice imaginary, I excavate some of the mechanisms that have underpinned widespread indifference to the violence of mass incarceration.

Early expressions of the imaginary of criminal justice

The images that animate today's imaginary of criminal justice can be traced to classic theories of the modern state. These theories articulate the modern concern with security as well as the identification of security with punishment of lawbreakers. Viewed in historical context, they betray how common notions of 'security' and 'the criminal,' not unlike colonialist myths of 'progress' and 'the Indian,' have been complicit with state-organised violence.

While Spanish, French, Dutch, and English colonisers were invading the Americas, Hobbes and Locke wrote their classic treatises of consent-based government. Notwithstanding their differences, both philosophers describe security as a central purpose of the modern state and both identify security with punishment of lawbreakers. For instance, Hobbes (1968, p. 205) argues that anyone who defies the laws of the state threatens the system of law and 'cannot be received into any Society.' Hobbes (1968, pp. 92, 93) also identifies 'witches' as 'justly punished' for threatening the social order. Locke (1980, p. 12) holds the government to higher standards but he, too, stresses that the government (and, in some cases for Locke, citizens) can punish lawbreakers to safeguard the public and restore justice. As examples of appropriate punishment, Locke explains that someone who has been the victim of a crime that is punishable by death can enslave the alleged criminal, for the accused can always take his own life, if he prefers (1980, p. 17). Locke also allows for a victim of robbery, or even intended robbery, to defend himself by killing the offender, if law enforcement is not immediately on the scene (1980, p. 15).

In the abstract, the identification of security with punishing lawbreakers has a compelling logic. The images that animated this logic in 17th century England, however, took shape against a background of contested social processes, such that calls for 'security' against 'thieves' lent themselves to being used by the wealthy in their efforts to eliminate people who stood in their way. For instance, as modern capitalism developed, English elite sought to privately enclose community land to pursue more lucrative sheepherding and private industries. This led to the dismantling of feudal and village agriculture, dismissal of farm labourers and retainers, disbanding of feudal armies, and displacement of the people who inhabited common lands (Allen, 1992, Marx, 1967, p. 448). Meanwhile, English law made burglary and minor shoplifting punishable by death. In this context, many of the 'thieves' punishable by execution were people pursuing acts of survival upon being left homeless and unemployed by land enclosures. In addition, 'witchcraft' laws – which led to the torture and execution of over 100,000 people across Western Europe – specifically targeted village women, thereby fragmenting the communities who lived on the common lands and disrupting their resistance to enclosure (Starhawk, 1982). In fact, many of Locke's contemporaries were aware (as a 17th-century folk poem put it) that the law locks up the poor but 'leaves the lords and ladies fine/Who take things that are yours and mine' (Anon, n.d.).

The contemporary 'tough-on-crime' imaginary

In today's world, 'criminal' may seem a fit label for someone who has broken a law; and punishment of criminals may seem a rational means to security. The ruses of colonialism and of Locke's England, however, caution us to consider how today's 'security' and 'criminal' may operate as part of a deceptive social imaginary: an imaginary that obfuscates state violence by inventing depraved subjects against whom violence is cast as 'good for everyone.' I argue below that today's criminal-justice images are, in fact, such cultural inventions.

Myths of 'security'

The 'security' that drives today's mass incarceration has a specific history. It has roots in early modern identifications of 'security' with punishment of lawbreakers. It also stems from more recent U.S. 'tough-on-crime' rhetoric, which calls for the punishment to be particularly severe. Some scholars trace this tough-on-crime rhetoric to the social unrest of the 1960s and 1970s, when conservatives found it useful to blame the turmoil on 'bad people' (Alexander 2011, pp. 40–43, Irwin, 2005, pp. 229–31). Academics contributed to this outlook by theorising '[w]icked people' who posed a threat to 'innocent people' (James Wilson cited Irwin, 2005, p. 229). In this account, although crime rates did rise in the 1960s, the emerging 'tough on crime' rhetoric was a political invention. It called for 'security' against 'wicked people' to promote an agenda of aggressive incarceration that would detract attention from social problems and bring disgruntled social groups under state control.

The call for 'tough-on-crime security' has materialised in specific legal practices. Under the banner of 'tough-on-crime,' states have implemented stiff criminal codes, laws that facilitate police search and seizure, hardline (or non-existent) parole boards, and laws that strip legal rights from people who are incarcerated (Alexander 2011, pp. 61–72, Oleson, 2002, Irwin, 2005, von Wilpert, 2011, Gopnik 2012, Mayeux, 2015, Ghandnoosh, 2017). These practices exhibit 'toughness,' but their security-value rings hollow for many Americans. In fact, studies do not show that aggressive incarceration practices have increased security (Ghandnoosh, 2017, Human Rights Watch., 2007, Wildeman, 2012). Neither do these practices respond to real security-needs, for they often have corresponded to declining crime rates (Alexander 2011, Peláez, 2016).

Moreover, tough-on-crime practices have made many Americans *insecure*. For people in low-income neighbourhoods, 'tough-on-crime' has meant greater vulnerability to apprehension by police and abuses after apprehension. For instance, laws that make it easier for police to arrest for 'gang activity' and 'loitering' have led people to be jailed for activities as benign as standing outside with friends or waiting for a bus (Casey & Watkins, 2014, p. 142, Van Cleve 2016, p. 170). Aggressive pursuit of criminals also has backlogged criminal courts, so that people without bail money can be kept in dangerous jails for extended periods, sometimes years, while they await trial (Gonnerman, 2014). In addition, the increased number of people being prosecuted, with the number of public defenders remaining constant, has meant that indigent people are receiving increasingly inadequate legal counsel. At the same time, recent laws restrict a person's ability to challenge a wrongful conviction, even in the case of clear attorney negligence (von Wilpert, 2011). Additionally, laws that criminalise immigration have exposed many people to racial profiling, detainment, and abuse by instruments of the law simply for 'being brown' (Casey & Watkins, 2014, pp. 140–144, Rodriguez, 2015, Van Cleve 2016, p. 82).

Within prisons, calls for 'tough-on-crime security' have bred cultures of punishment that expose incarcerated individuals to all kinds of violence. Unrestrained beating, macing, and rape of incarcerated individuals by guards as well as other egregious forms of abuse, including fatal suffocation and submersion in scalding water, have all passed unprosecuted (Oleson, 2002, pp. 854–58, Gonnerman, 2015, Dole, 2018, Grasha, 2017, Hawkins, 2017, Mills, 2017, Protect 2017). The same cultures of punishment have sanctioned regular 'disciplinary' practices so severe that they constitute torture. For instance, for 'infractions' as minor as 'insolence' or refusing sexual advances by guards, guards can send people to solitary units where they spend 23–24 hours per day in a cell of 'gray walls, a solid steel door, no window, no clock, and a light that [is] kept on twenty-four hours a day' (Solitary Watch, n.d, citing resident testimony). For years, or even decades, their only physical contact with another human being 'is the incidental brushing up against the guards who must first place them in handcuffs and chains' before removing them from cells (Solitary Watch, n.d., citing Craig Haney). Another state-sanctioned abuse is the regular use in some states of tactical teams that storm through prisons with clubs and pepper spray, whoop and bang their clubs on bars as they yell at inmates to 'get asshole naked,' keep inmates contained for hours without water or bathrooms while they ransack cells, and commit other unconscionable abuses, such as forcing inmates to march 'nuts-to-butts,' bent over and in close proximity, only partially clothed. Prison officials defend the raids as 'necessary [security] measures' (Dolinar, 2017, January 2).

Myths of 'the criminal'

Like 'security,' America's 'criminal' is also a cultural invention. The narrative that identifies 'security' with harsh punishment also transforms the target of punishment from a person who has broken a law to 'an undifferentiated mass of uncontrollable criminality' (Mayeux, 2015). Multiple cultural practices shore up this fantastical image of 'the criminal' as the embodiment of malignance.

The media, for instance, actively constructs people who are in police custody as despicable beings. A regular feature of television news is the 'perp walk,' in which a person who has been arrested is paraded before media cameras, often in handcuffs and prison attire, thus appearing as an objectified and debased 'criminal' – even before the person has been tried (Dole, 2014, pp. 8–14). The media also distributes mugshots of arrested persons, in which 'the unflattering bright light, the drab background, the name and prisoner ID at the bottom – tells us we are looking at a "criminal,"' an objectified bad guy (Davis 2015). The extent to which America's 'criminal' is a cultural invention is betrayed by the recent trend of Halloween haunted houses that advertise themselves as 'haunted prisons' and offer costumed 'monster-criminals' for Halloween entertainment (Bellware, 2016).

The cultural manufacturing of America's 'criminal' is revealed, also, by its class and race dimensions. As is now well known, African Americans do not use or sell drugs any more than whites; however, African Americans are targeted by police and incarcerated for drugs at much greater rates (Alexander 2011, p. 99). Moreover, as in Locke's time, when the poor were hung for taking a goose off the pasture but lords got away with appropriating entire pastures, 'criminal' applies uniquely to the underclass. As Alexander (2016) puts it, we tolerate the Wall Street executives who destroyed the savings of millions of American families in 2008 and the politicians who 'take millions of dollars from private prisons, prison guard unions, pharmaceutical companies, oil companies, tobacco companies, the NRA and Wall Street banks ... killing us softly ... But selling CDs or loose cigarettes? In America, that's treated as a serious crime, especially if you're black.'

Tellingly, when those who fit society's image of 'the criminal' are convicted of crimes, they regularly face decades-long prison-sentences and permanent demonisation (Alexander 2011, pp. 14–177, Davis, 2009, Dole, 2014, pp. 213–22). Yet if upper-class persons are apprehended, their crimes tend to be distinguished as 'white-collar crimes,' for which they receive limited sentences in federal prisons, upon completion of which they are dubbed *former* white-collar criminals.' Some have been invited to speak about business ethics at major universities, where they find understanding and empathy. Walter Pavlo (who served 2 years for a 6 million-dollar fraud scheme) was invited to Temple University because they wanted students 'to understand how easy it can be to make a mistake that results in prison time' (Farrell & O'Donnell, 2005). According to the teacher who invited Pavlo, 'The last thing we wanted was finger-wagging, or someone saying, "You better be good people" ... Most people are good, and then they enter an arena with incredibly high pressure' (Terry Halbert cited Farrell & O'Donnell, 2005). Such empathetic reception has earned Havlo hundreds of thousands of dollars in speaking fees while it has spared affluent people from having to imagine someone like themselves as a 'bad guy.' The attitude that 'most people are good' and environment pressures them to do bad things is not afforded, however, to the many under-privileged people whose brushes with the law have reduced them to 'outcast[s], undeserving of a second chance ... pariah[s] for life' (Dole, 2014, p. 213).

The 'tough-on-crime' imaginary and the institutionalization of state violence

If today's 'monster-criminal' and 'tough-on-crime-security' are cultural inventions analogous to colonialist myths, then the comparison to colonialism challenges us to consider how these myths have been instrumental in fostering state violence. First, the comparison challenges us to examine how our criminal-justice myths, like colonial myths, contribute to an ensemble of institutional practices that regularise the abuse of people defined as violable subjects. For instance, the myth of 'tough-on-crime-security' has focused legal institutions on punishment and encouraged those institutions to treat people convicted of crimes as mere objects of punishment. In this context, prison employees tend to be trained only in methods of restraint and empowered to punish with little oversight. If long-term solitary confinement and vicious tactical units have become routine, and if physical assaults on incarcerated individuals regularly go unprosecuted, then this is because myths of security through punishment of objectified 'criminals' have organised all facets of the criminal-legal system. Tellingly, when the state of California was charged with severe overcrowding and human-rights violations in state prisons, even the state's attorney acknowledged 'very significant violations of constitutional rights' but argued that the main cause of the violations was not overcrowding but 'the culture of disregard for the inmate' (cited in Mayeux 2015).

The comparison to colonialism also highlights how myths of 'the criminal' (not unlike myths of 'the Indian') encourage state officials to treat people who are so labelled as if they were inferior beings, which effectively turns those people into social inferiors. For instance, a study of Chicago's Cook County court system (Van Cleve 2016) describes how judges and lawyers tend to 'criminalise' underprivileged defendants – regardless of their actual relation to the crime in question. The disdain that court professionals held toward people in their custody was clear from the terms they used for them, which included '"scum," "pieces of shit," "bad guys" – even "banana suits" (which refers to the jail jumper that defendants in custody must wear in court)' (Van Cleve 2016, p. 57). The most common term for the defendants was 'mopes,' an epithet signifying lack of work-ethic, which translated in court culture to inherent culpability. 'Professionals find it difficult to regard a defendant as anything but a mope,' reports Van Cleve. 'By the professionals' logic, if someone was motivated, hardworking and competent, he or she would not be charged with a crime' (2016, p. 58). Armed with these biases, the courts reduce many of the people in their custody to the stereotypes they hold of them: riffraff to be swiftly processed or abominations to be prosecuted to the fullest extent possible (Van Cleve 2016, pp. 69–73).

When we compare the 'tough-on-crime' imaginary to the colonial imaginary, we likewise challenge ourselves to consider how many of us (like colonial Europeans) have become alienated from the human beings targeted by our myths. The comparison challenges us to consider how we may have detached from incarcerated people in ways that have impaired our own responsiveness to barbarism. For instance, Stateville Correctional Center in Illinois regularly warehouses men for 22–23 hours a day in barren, often sweltering, unventilated, walk-in-closet-sized cells, without even a desk or chair. Meals often consist of spoiled and cockroach-tainted food, are eaten in rooms infected with bird droppings, and are announced over loudspeakers twice a day as a directive to 'line up for feed-time.' And yet, when state inspectors visit, they speak only to the guards about their capacity to control the imprisoned men. They do not speak with the men who are incarcerated or ask them about their treatment as human beings. Similarly, when politicians or students tour prisons, they hear only from prison officials. 'It's like they're visiting a zoo; the prisoners are only there for display' (J. Dole, personal communication, 2 March 2017).

The criminal-justice imaginary and the silencing of incarcerated voices

The comparison to colonialism also prompts us to consider how, as in the crushing of indigenous voices under colonialism, our criminal-justice myths facilitate the forceful silencing of incarcerated people. For instance, under the guise of 'security,' many prisons deny journalists access to prisons and some states explicitly prohibit any interviewing of inmates (Gonnerman, 2015). Some states also prohibit incarcerated people from having social-media sites (managed by friends on the outside) where they can post their work (Kelkar, 2017).

In the context of multiple prison rules that obstruct communication across prison walls, incarcerated individuals can express their critical perspectives on prisons only via hunger strikes, work strikes, or buildings taking-overs. Even when incarcerated individuals risk severe punishment by taking such actions, the media tends either to ignore them or reduce their efforts to 'security threats.' For instance, a recent strike against prison labour by thousands of incarcerated individuals across the country received little news coverage (Kim, 2016). At Kinross prison in Michigan, before men went on strike, they attempted to peacefully express their concerns about abusive conditions. The prison responded by punishing those who relayed the grievances. Subsequent peaceful stands of unity by inmates were met with indiscriminate tear-gassing and physical abuse (Thompson, 2017). Another recent strike at Vaughn Correctional Center (known for its severe overcrowding and excessive punitive measures) received media attention when hostages were taken. A rare perspective from inside prison walls reached the public when an anonymous inmate used a stolen phone to explain the strikers' demands: 'education first and foremost,' rehabilitation programs, and accountability for the prison budget; they also were reacting against 'Donald Trump. Everything that he did' (Thompson, 2017, citing anonymous striker). Such perspectives were lost to television news, however, which focused solely on tactics used to crush the strike, the death of a guard, and statements by prison officials promising to punish those responsible. In typical manner, the prison responded with indiscriminate brutality against all men in the facility (Cherry, 2017, Thompson, 2017).

Such drastic responses to prison strikes betray another level of brutality associated with 'tough-on-crime' myths: incarcerated people who share their critical perspectives on incarceration are reduced to 'security threats' and severely punished. As I write, my friend Lacino Hamilton, in response to having shared his views on incarceration in a radio interview, sits in an isolated cell and faces charges that can keep him in lockdown/isolation for years (L. Hamilton, personal communication, 20 September 2017). In response to his political writings, Keven Rashid Johnson was gassed while handcuffed and then left in the gassed cell; he was assaulted with gas again after reporting the incident (Protect Kevin 'Rashid' Johnson from prison repression, 2017, Thompson, 2017). Other incarcerated individuals who have worked for prison reform have been physically assaulted and sent to isolation for years or even decades (Blau & Grinberg, 2016). Human-rights groups report that 'solitary confinement is widely employed against prisoners who are perceived as representing any kind of threat to the absolute power of prison authorities. This is true even if inmates are seeking to organize for positive change and even if they are completely nonviolent' (Ridgeway & Casella, 2011, citing Solitary Watch). Incarcerated individuals have little opportunity to challenge such charges, because the charges 'are levied, adjudicated, and enforced by prison officials with little or no outside oversight' (Solitary Watch, n.d.).

In circular fashion, the repression of incarcerated people's voices has helped maintain the myth that incarcerated people have nothing worthwhile to say. It has allowed systemic inattention to incarcerated individuals to pass unnoticed.

The silencing of incarcerated voices likewise has prevented many of us from seeing the human beings beneath the 'criminal' label. It has prevented us from seeing that the targets of aggressive incarceration have been largely people with mental illnesses, young adults whose only family have been gangs and in whom the state has had no interest until charging them with crimes, people of low socio-economic status who have been targeted by police and who lack adequate legal representation, and even people like the displaced of Locke's era who have been apprehended by the state in order to make way for economic ventures of the wealthy (Alexander 2011, pp. 97–139; Castro, 2015, Dole, 2014, pp. 19–93, Hamilton, 2015, 2017, Van Cleve 2016, von Wilpert, 2011). The repression of incarcerated voices also has denied recognition to the many individuals who have educated themselves while in prison, worked hard to improve their lives, and are "looking to get back some self-worth by somehow giving back" (Dole, 2004).

Conclusions: the need for resistant imagination

Finally, a comparison of today's criminal-justice imaginary to the colonial imaginary directs us to consider how the criminal-justice imaginary has thwarted the imaginative work necessary for those of us outside of prison to understand mass incarceration. Arendt has explained how imaginative 'visiting' of other people's standpoints is essential to understand political phenomena. Feminist standpoint theorists have underscored the need to 'visit,' in particular, the standpoint from marginalised lives, for such standpoints offer unique insight into social contradictions that ruling beliefs obscure (Stone-Mediatore, 2003, pp. 162, 179–184). In the case of contemporary mass incarceration, however, incarcerated people have been so thoroughly demonised that the missing perspective is hardly noticed. In addition, the brutal silencing of incarcerated people who attempt to express their political views has reinforced the myth that incarcerated people have no views beyond those projected onto them. 'Tough-on-crime' myths even encourage self-satisfaction in our indifference to the targets of our 'toughness.' 'Criminals,' says Alexander (2011, p. 141), 'are the one social group in America we have permission to hate.'

If edifying myths and brutal reinforcement of those myths have treated incarcerated people as voiceless and violable subjects, then the comparison to colonialism also challenges us to reexamine our most deeply ingrained notions of 'violable subject.' It challenges us to consider the perspective of the people we have presumed to have no perspective. For those of us outside of prison, imagining the perspective of people locked within prisons is no simple task. As feminist critics warn, imagining the perspective of people in situations radically different than our own demands arduous practical work as well as openness to the unsettling of familiar narratives. In this case, it means destabilising the divisions between 'good' and 'bad' people, and between law and violence, around which many of us have oriented our lives. It also demands endeavours such as close engagement with the work of incarcerated writers and artists, reaching out through letters to incarcerated individuals, or joining practical struggles with incarcerated people or their families.

Fortunately, various journals, websites, and prison-justice organisations facilitate such endeavors by sharing the work of incarcerated writers, artists and activists. The stories shared through these forums help make palpable the monstrosities of U.S. prisons as well as the resilient humanity of the individuals confined within them. For instance, in his story of the animals he encounters while serving a life-sentence, Joseph Dole highlights the irony of being labelled an 'animal' by a society that 'misunderstands both incarcerated people and animals' (2017, p. 143). His story invites us into a world where 'yard time' means being locked into a solitary concrete box; 'violent criminals' nurture a baby turtle; 'jailbirds' connect with 'the free world' by exchanging chirps with real birds; and 'one of society's alleged bogeymen' risks punishment to help a baby bird return to its mother (Dole, 2017, pp. 132–138). When Dole recounts the guards threatening him as he gently coaches a frail bird to safety; and when he describes 'clanking along in shackles, a waist chain, and handcuffs encased in a black, steel padlocked box,' while to his amazement 'a large rabbit jumped out of the hedges along the path, and passed right between [his] legs, brushing the shackles' (2017, p. 140), the images confound familiar narratives of 'human' and 'animal,' 'good guy' and 'criminal.' They guide us in imagining the unimaginable: the caging of human beings. When Dole proposes that his fellow Americans 'stop painting us all with a broad stigmatizing brush' and 'start acting more like the animals in here,' who judge the incarcerated men as individuals, he provokes a new look not only at incarcerated people but at ourselves as jailers, who keep 'hundreds of thousands of people incarcerated for life, long past the time they cease posing any threat to society' (2017, p. 143).

Although fraught with challenges, the task of engaging the voices and imagining the perspective of people who are incarcerated is vital to undermining the mechanisms of institutionalised violence. We can respond 'to people who say "prison shouldn't be a picnic,"' says Hamilton (2015), only when we 'shift conceptions of the humanity of the incarcerated' and begin to face incarcerated people as human beings. Documentation of the myriad abuses of human dignity and bodily integrity that are systemic to U.S. prisons is also crucial; however, if the abuses are not to be refashioned into ruses of 'just punishment' and 'necessary security measures,' then we need to begin viewing these phenomena from the standpoint of people who are incarcerated.

I cannot anticipate all the ways that the standpoint of the incarcerated would illuminate the U.S. criminal-legal system. Based on my analysis, however, I anticipate that such endeavours would raise troubling questions. For instance: How can we distinguish between law and violence when routine legal practices violate human integrity? How does the systematic disregard for the voices and humanity of incarcerated individuals degrade our own humanity? And how can we heal our communities and secure all members of our society from violence? Careful engagement with incarcerated voices and imagination of their perspective does not provide easy answers. Nor does it directly confront the extreme power imbalances that facilitate violence against incarcerated people. Still, by raising such questions and encouraging us to approach them with a sense of connection to the lives from which many of us have been alienated, the diligent 'visiting' of incarcerated standpoints could help us resist some of the mechanisms of institutionalised violence and reckon more honestly with that violence.

Note

1. In this paper, I use the first-person plural to refer to people who have not been incarcerated. I hope that my readers will include people on both sides of prison bars; however, my argument about the need to imagine the standpoint from incarcerated lives is directed to people who lack first-hand experience of incarceration.

Acknowledgments

I am grateful to the two anonymous reviewers, Mihaela Mihai, John Stone-Mediatore, Debbie Stone Bruell, and Joseph Dole for illuminating feedback on earlier versions of this paper.

Disclosure statement

No potential conflict of interest was reported by the author.

References

ACLU. (2011). Abuse of the human rights of prisoners in the United States. Submission to the United Nations Human Rights Commission 16th session on solitary confinement [online]. Retrieved March 10, 2017, from https://www.aclu.org/files/assets/ACLU_Submission_to_HRC_16th_Session_on_Solitary_Confinement.pdf

Alexander, M. (2011). *The new Jim Crow: Mass incarceration in the age of colorblindness*. New York: The New Press.

Alexander, M. (2016, July 9). Following horrific violence, something more is required of us. *Moyers & company* [online]. Retrieved March 10, 2017, from http://billmoyers.com/story/following-horrific-violence-something-required-us/

Allen, R. C. (1992). *Enclosure and the yeoman*. New York: Clarendon Press.

Anon., (n.d.). The goose and the common. Retrieved February 16, 2017, from http://unionsong.com/u765.html

Arendt, H. (1953a). A reply. *A Review of Politics, 15*, 76–85.

Arendt, H. (1953b). Understanding and politics. *Partisan Review, 20*, 377–382.

Arendt, H. (1958). *The human condition*. Chicago: University of Chicago.

Arendt, H. (1982). *Lectures on Kant's political philosophy*. Chicago: University of Illinois Press.

Bellware, K. (2016, October 31). Many people already see prisoners as monsters. Do 'haunted prisons' make it worse? *Huffington post* [online]. Retrieved March 10, 2017, from http://www.huffingtonpost.com/entry/haunted-prisons-halloween_us_58173d9de4b0990edc320e42

Blau, B., & Grinberg, E. (2016, October 31). Why U.S. prisons launched a nationwide strike. CNN U.S. edition, [online]. Retrieved March 9, 2017, from http://www.cnn.com/2016/10/30/us/us-prisoner-strike/

Casey, E., & Watkins, M. (2014). *Up against the wall: Re-imagining the U.S.-Mexico border*. Austin: University of Texas Press.

Castro, F. (2015, March 5). Gangs of the state. The Hampton Institute [online]. Retrieved August 14, 2017, from. http://www.hamptoninstitution.org/gangs-of-the-state.html#.WZMQPFWGOUk

Cesaire, A. (1972). Discourse on colonialism. In *Trans*. New York: Monthly Review Press.

https://www.thenation.com/article/prison-education-reduces-recidivism-by-over-40-percent-why-arent-we-funding-more-of-it/

Cherry, A. (2017, April 18). Behind the walls. WDEL [online]. Retrieved August 14, 2017, from http://www.wdel.com/news/video-behind-the-walls-letters-from-smyrna-s-vaughn-inmates/article_a4b63686-23b8-11e7-922b-57d75356615e.html

Davis, A. (2009). *Arbitrary justice*. Oxford: Oxford University Press.

Davis, C. (2015, February 4). Against mugshots Truthout [online]. Retrieved March 9, 2017, from http://www.truth-out.org/news/item/28903-against-mugshots-photos-of-the-state-s-latest-catch-don-t-belong-in-a-free-press

Dilts, A. (2014). *Punishment and inclusion: Race, membership, and the limits of American liberalism*. Fordham: Fordham University Press.

Dole, J. (2004). I'm sorry. In, *Katy ryan (ed* (pp. 1–2). Lockdown prison heart. New York: iUniverse.

Dole, J. (2014). *A costly American hatred*. Berryville, AR: Midnight Express Books.

Dole, J. (2017). Yard time with the animals. *Columbia Journal, 55*, 132–143.

Dole, J. (2018). Endless punishment: what happens after a staff assault. justice. *Power, and Resistance, 2*(1), 189-203.

Dolinar, B. (2017, January 2). Truthout [online]. Accessed March 10, 2017, from http://www.truth-out.org/news/item/38941-orange-crush-the-rise-of-tactical-teams-in-prison

Dussel, E. (1995). *The invention of the Americas*. (M. Barber, Trans). New York: Continuum.

Everest, L. (2013, July 7). Interview with Carol Strickman. Prisoners' struggle against 'cruel and unusual punishment amounting to torture. *Revolution newspaper* [online]. Retrieved March 7, 2017, from http://www.revcom.us/a/309/interview-with-Carol-Strickman-en.html

Fanon, F. (1967). *Toward the African revolution*. (H. Chevalier, Trans). New York: Grove Press.

Farrell, G. & O'Donnell, J., (2005, November 15). Ethics training as taught by ex-cons. *USA Today* [online]. Retrieved February 25, 2017, from http://usatoday30.usatoday.com/money/companies/management/2005-11-15-ethics-cov-usat_x.htm

Ghandnoosh, N. (2017, January 31). Delaying a second chance. *The sentencing project* [online]. Retrieved March 9, 2017, from http://www.sentencingproject.org/publications/delaying-second-chance-declining-prospects-parole-life-sentences/

Gonnerman, J. (2014, October 6). Before the law. *The New Yorker* [online]. Retrieved March 20, 2017, from http://www.newyorker.com/magazine/2014/10/06/before-the-law

Gonnerman, J. (2015, September 10). Prisoners' lives matter. *The New Yorker* [online]. Retrieved February 22, 2017, from http://www.newyorker.com/news/news-desk/prisoners-lives-matter

Gopnik, A. (2012, January 30). The caging of America. *The New Yorker* [online]. Retrieved March 9, 2017, from http://www.newyorker.com/magazine/2012/01/30/the-caging-of-america

Grasha, K. (2017, January 30). Woman alleges rape by Warren County jail officers. *Cinncinati* [online]. Retrieved March 9, 2017, from http://www.cincinnati.com/story/news/2017/01/30/woman-alleges-rape-warren-county-jail-officers-lawsuit/97259510/

Hamilton, L. (2015, June 23). Understanding the human cost of imprisonment. *Truthout* [online]. Retrieved August 14, 2017, from http://www.truth-out.org/news/item/31406-understanding-the-human-cost-of-imprisonment

Hamilton, L. (2017, April 30). The gentrification-to-prison pipeline. *Truthout* [online]. Retrieved August 14, 2017, from http://www.truth-out.org/news/item/40413-the-gentrification-to-prison-pipeline

Hawkins, D. (2017, March 20). An inmate died after being locked in a scalding shower for 2 hours. His guards won't be charged. *The Washington Post* [online]. Retrieved

August 14, 2017, from https://www.washingtonpost.com/news/morning-mix/wp/ 2017/03/20/an-inmate-died-after-being-locked-in-a-scalding-shower-for-two-hours-his-guards-wont-be-charged/?utm_term=.685518569028

Hegel, G. W. (1956). *The philosophy of history*. (J. Sibree, Trans). Mineola, NY: Dover.

Hobbes, T. (1968). *The leviathan*. New York: Penguin Books.

Human Rights Watch. (2007). No easy answers. *Human Rights Watch Report* [online]. Retrieved March 9, 2017, from https://www.hrw.org/report/2007/09/11/no-easy-answers/sex-offender-laws-us

Irwin, J. (2005). *The warehouse prison*. Oxford: Oxford University Press.

Kelkar, K. (2017, January 29). Resistance builds against social media bans in Texas prisons. PBS news hour [online]. Retrieved March 5, 2017, from http://www.pbs.org/newshour/updates/social-media-ban-texas-prisons/

Kilgore, J. (2017, February 28). Mass incarceration in the cornfields. *Truthout* [online]. Retrieved March 29, 2017, from http://www.truth-out.org/news/item/39651-mass-incarceration-in-the-cornfields-shattered-families-and-racial-profiling-in-small-town-america

Kim, T. (2016, October 3). A national strike against 'prison slavery'. *The New Yorker* [online]. Retrieved March 5, 2017, from http://www.newyorker.com/news/news-desk/a-national-strike-against-prison-slavery

Locke, J. (1980). *Second treatise of government*. Indianapolis: Hackett.

Marx, K. (1967). The German ideology. In L. Eason & K. Guddat (Eds.), *Writings of the young Marx*. Garden City: Doubleday, 403-473.

Mayeux, S. (2015, March 22). The unconstitutional horrors of prison overcrowding. *Newsweek* [online]. Retrieved March 10, 2017, from http://www.newsweek.com/unconstitutional-horrors-prison-overcrowding-315640

Mignolo, W. (2005). *The idea of Latin America*. Malden, MA: Blackwell.

Mills, S. (2017, July 17). How did Terrance Jenkins die? *The Chicago Tribune* [online]. Retrieved September 30, 2017, from http://www.chicagotribune.com/news/local/breaking/ct-pontiac-inmate-death-20170717-story.html

Oleson, J. C. (2002). The punitive coma. *California Law Review*, 90(3), 829–902.

Ortega, M. (2006). Being lovingly, knowingly ignorant. *Hypatia*, 21, 56–74.

Peláez, V. (2016, August 28). The prison industry in the United States: Big business or a new form of slavery? *Global Reach* [online]. Retrieved July 15, 2017, from http://www.globalresearch.ca/the-prison-industry-in-the-united-states-big-business-or-a-new-form-of-slavery/8289

Protect Kevin 'Rashid' Johnson from prison repression. (2017, January 19). Block report radio [online]. Retrieved March 10, 2017, from http://www.blockreportradio.com/index.php/news2/item/407-protect-kevin-rashid-johnson-from-prison-repression

Quijano, A. (2000). Coloniality of power, Eurocentrism and Latin America. *Nepantla: Views from the South*, 1(3), 533–580.

Ridgeway, J., & Casella, J. (2011, June 17). Confronting torture in U.S. Prisons. *Solitary Watch* [online]. Retrieved August 14, 2017, from http://solitarywatch.com/2011/06/17/confronting-torture-in-u-s-prisons-a-qa-with-solitary-watch/

Rodriguez, R. (2014). *Our sacred maíz is our mother: Indigeneity and belonging in the Americas*. Tucson: University of Arizona Press.

Rodriguez, R., 2015. 'Not Counting Mexicans or Indians': The many tentacles of state violence against Black-Brown-Indigenous communities [online]. Retrieved March 9, 2017, from http://www.truth-out.org/news/item/28921-not-counting-mexicans-or-indians-the-many-tentacles-of-state-violence-against-black-brown-indigenous-communities

Rovner, J. (2016, July 1). Juvenile life without parole: An overview. *The sentencing project* [online]. Retrieved March 9 2017, from http://www.sentencingproject.org/publications/juvenile-life-without-parole/

Smith, A. (2005). *Conquest: Sexual violence and American Indian genocide*. Cambridge: South End Press.

Solitary Watch. FAQ, (n.d.), [online]. Retrieved March 10, 2017, from http://solitarywatch.com/facts/faq/

Starhawk. (1982). *Dreaming the dark*. Boston: Beacon Press.

Stone-Mediatore, S. (2003). *Reading across borders: Storytelling and knowledges of resistance*. New York: Palgrave Macmillan.

Taylor, C. (1993). Positioning subjects and objects: Agency, narration, relationality. *Hypatia*, *8*(1), 55–80.

The Sentencing Project. (n.d.). Criminal justice facts [online]. Retrieved January 9, 2019, from: https://www.sentencingproject.org/criminal-justice-facts/

Thompson, H. (2017, February 17). What happened at Vaughn prison? *Jacobin* [online]. Retrieved February 27, 2017, from https://www.jacobinmag.com/2017/02/vaughn-prison-hostage-attica-uprising/

Todorov, T. (1984). *The conquest of America: The question of the other*. New York: Harper & Row.

Van Cleve, N. G. (2016). *Crook county: racism and injustice in america's largest criminal court*. Stanford: Stanford University Press.

von Wilpert, M. (2011). Holland v. Florida: A prisoner's last chance, attorney errors, and the antiterrorism and effective death penalty act's one-year statute of limitations period for federal habeas corpus review. *Fordham Law Review*, *79*, 1429–1476.

Wildeman, C. (2012, April 24). Mass incarceration. *Oxford bibliographies* [online]. Retrieved March 10, 2017, from http://www.oxfordbibliographies.com/view/document/obo-9780195396607/obo-9780195396607-0033.xml

The subversive potential of Leo Tolstoy's 'defamiliarisation': a case study in drawing on the imagination to denounce violence

Alexandre Christoyannopoulos

ABSTRACT
In his later years, Leo Tolstoy wrote numerous books, essays and pamphlets expounding his newly-articulated denunciations of all political violence, whether by dissidents or ostensibly legitimate states. If these writings have inspired many later pacifists and anarchists, it is partly thanks to his masterful deployment of the literary technique of 'defamiliarisation' – or looking at the familiar as if new – to shake readers into recognising the absurdity of common justifications of violence, admitting their implicit complicity in it, and noticing the process which numbed them into accepting such complicity. This paper discusses Tolstoy's use of the imagination to defamiliarise and denounce violence, first by citing several typical examples, then by reflecting on four of its subversive characteristics: its disruption of automated perception, its implicit concession of some recognition, its corrosion of conventional respect for traditional hierarchies, and its encouragement of empathy.

Introduction

Leo Tolstoy (1828–1910) is mainly remembered as the author of two of the world's most praised novels: *War and Peace* (1869) and *Anna Karenina* (1877). Less frequently recalled nowadays is that, when he passed away, a few years before the First World War and the Bolshevik Revolution, he was just as famous for what might be described as his controversial Christian anarcho-pacifist views. Both then and since, numerous writers, scholars, politicians, religious figures and public intellectuals have engaged and often disagreed with various aspects of his political thought. A mark of the peculiarity of Tolstoy's views is that, despite the clear Christian and anarchist themes, both his Christian and his anarchist credentials have been disputed (Greenwood, 1978; Kolstø, 2006; Matual, 1992; Maude, 1930; Préposiet, 2005; Schmidt & van der Walt, 2009; Spence, 1967; Wilson, 1988). The level-headedness of his pacifism has also often been questioned, though here the main focus of criticism has been not so much on his denunciations of violence as on his stubbornly puritanical stance (Kennan, 1887; Maude, 1930; Spence, 1963; Tolstoy, 2001b). Nevertheless, Tolstoy's pacifist writings have inspired many, including of course Gandhi, who also notoriously moved countless activists and thinkers (Lavrin, 1960; Tolstoy, 1937b). Tolstoy stirred many conscientious objectors, encouraging them to adopt a pacifist stance – even if the stance adopted was not always as absolute as Tolstoy's (Alston, 2014; Denner, 2010; Fueloep-Miller, 1960). Controversial though he certainly was, Tolstoy sits as a central figure at the origins of modern pacifism – an ardent ally to those looking to denounce violence (Atack, 2012; Brock, 1972).

One of the reasons Tolstoy proved controversial was his style: his allegedly simplistic arguments, his reductive syllogisms, his seemingly childish naivety (Abraham, 1929; Berdyaev, 1948; Greenwood, 1978; Lenin, 1908; Maude, 1930; Seeley, 1978; Wilson, 1988). Yet that style was always also in part what made him so appealing to his supporters: Tolstoy deliberately wanted his readers to cut through the deceitful fog of misleading complications and distractions: the simplistic purity of his arguments is partly what makes them sharp, accessible and potent. There is a candid and attractive innocence both in the substance of his claims and in the style with which he puts them across.

A particular rhetorical device which generates this impression of naivety, and which Tolstoy used frequently, is what Viktor Shklovsky (in a seminal text for Russian Formalism) called *ostranenie* (остранение) (Shklovsky, 2006). The term has been translated as 'making strange', 'estrangement', and 'defamiliarisation'. Tolstoy, Shklovsky shows, likes to get his readers to look at the familiar as if seen for the first time, in a childlike manner. He does so by pointedly not calling what he is describing by its accepted name, instead describing it by its component parts, and ignoring the wider context which to most observers gives it its normal meaning and coherence (paraphrasing Knapp, 2002, p. 163, Buchanan, 2010, s.v. 'ostranenie'). This allows Tolstoy to describe social, political, religious and other phenomena with the innocence of a child not familiar enough with all the conventions the implicit acceptance of which adults automatically bring to their observation of the phenomenon. It disrupts conventional understandings, and is thus potentially subversive. Knapp agrees: '*ostranenie* is an effective instrument of social critique' (2002, p. 163). Tolstoy's use of it when articulating his radical views contributed to making them controversial.

The aim of this article is to illustrate and reflect on Tolstoy's use of defamiliarisation in his Christian anarcho-pacifist writings, in particular as a tool to question the conventions that authorise violence and spark a pacifist critique. What the article will not provide is a critical discussion of these views – such discussions can be found elsewhere (Bartlett, 2010;

Christoyannopoulos, forthcoming; Guseinov, 1999; McKeogh, 2009; Wilson, 1988). After a brief first section introducing Tolstoy's anarcho-pacifism, the second section illustrates Tolstoy's use of defamiliarisation for subversive purposes, particularly to denounce violence. The third reflects on what makes defamiliarisation powerful and subversive. Ultimately, what this article intends to demonstrate is that Tolstoy provides a model for applying defamiliarisation to violence, which has not only unsurprisingly lit a pacifist spark in the past, but that still has power and relevance today. Thus it can still inspire us to creatively denounce violence and domination in our own evolving context in the unfolding future.

Tolstoy's Christian anarcho-pacifist turn

The direction of Tolstoy's life changed around 1879 when, after a decade-long and increasingly turbulent existential crisis, he 'converted' to Christianity, or rather to a peculiar and rationalistic understanding of Christianity, based on which he preached a form of anarcho-pacifism. It is conventional for biographers to reject the idea that there are two Tolstoys, one before and one after his conversion (Eikhenbaum, 1967; Gustafson, 1986; Medzhibovskaya, 2008; Orwin, 2002; Wilson, 1988). They rightly point out the numerous continuities between the two periods. It is also the case that the separation of Tolstoy into the writer of brilliant fiction (to be read assiduously) and the social critic (wacky, dangerous and best ignored) is one sponsored by the Bolsheviks, for clear political reasons. The Soviet authorities made sure this separation was enforced as the accepted one across the Soviet bloc (Avrich, 1968; Denner, 2010; Lenin, 1908; Struve, 1960). But Tolstoy (1987) himself insisted on the biographical break. Moreover, his writings after 1879 clearly have a different purpose – an engaged and primarily political and religious one. Despite the clear continuities, therefore, and without discounting their importance, one can nonetheless approach his 'fame' (Stepun, 1960, p. 157) and his corpus as twofold: what he wrote up to his 'conversion', and what he wrote in light of it thereafter (fiction and non-fiction included). When he died in 1910, he had certainly become notorious both in Russia and abroad for both his fiction *and* his political and religious views. The main focus of this article is on the latter.

Here is not the place to expand in great depth on Tolstoy's Christian anarcho-pacifism. What is important to note by way of summary is that Tolstoy did not start believing in the resurrection, the miracles, the sacraments or many of the church's dogmas. What he converted to wholesale is the *ethics* preached by Jesus and its implied analysis of violence, particularly the Sermon on the Mount and Jesus' counsels on turning the other cheek and, more generally, Jesus' teachings on (and prefiguration of) love and forgiveness. Based on this new moral outlook, Tolstoy spent the rest of his life bitterly denouncing the violence human beings inflict on each other. He denounced the state for exacting violence on an industrial scale without more legitimacy than a protection racket, contemporary violent revolutionaries for foolishly using fire to try to put out fire, and the church for burying Jesus' important and radically pacifist ethics under thick layers of superstitions and stupefaction in exchange for state-protected comfort (Christoyannopoulos, 2008, 2016). These themes will emerge in the examples of defamiliarisation given below.

Tolstoy's ideas survived him despite the Great War, the Bolshevik revolution, and the persecution of his followers in that tumultuous context. He was read across the world. His Christian anarcho-pacifist writings famously moved Gandhi (with whom Tolstoy had exchanged brief letters), but also influenced Romain Rolland, Ludwig Wittgenstein, and many others (Alston, 2014; Love, 2008; McKeogh, 2009; Rolland, 1978). Tolstoy's pacifist writings also enraged some readers. They certainly provoked thought and discussion, in no small part due to the brilliance of his defamiliarisation of violence.

Defamiliarising violence

Tolstoy is not the only writer to master the technique of making the familiar strange. Nonetheless, when Shklovsky coined the term to describe his preferred purpose for art, Tolstoy was the author he chose to rely on to illustrate it – indeed he cited him at length, and then only briefly mentioned a few other authors in what reads almost as an afterthought. This may not be surprising: when Shklovsky wrote and published his essay (in 1916–1917), Russia was unstable, at war, and pregnant with revolutionary spirit. This was also a time when Tolstoy's political corpus was widely read and discussed: as Denner puts it, 'For the radicalized intelligentsia of pre-Revolutionary Russia – a description that suits Shklovsky – Tolstoy was something of a patron saint.' (2008, p. 373) Shklovsky had also just been reading Tolstoy's extensive diaries when he was writing his essay. Either way, Tolstoy is the main author Shklovsky cites in his seminal text.

Shklovsky's concern is to portray art as a tool with which to break 'the automatism of perception' (2006, p. 779). He argues that we all naturally settle into 'unconsciously automatic' interpretations of what we observe, that 'perception becomes habitual'. Shklovsky cites holding a pen and speaking a foreign language as examples of automation, but then broadens his argument to suggest that this process of 'habitualization' applies to all aspects of life (2006, p. 778). For Shklovsky, then, as Denner puts it, 'art's purpose, its task, is to cure our diseased knowledge of the world' (2008, p. 376). In Shklovsky's words, its aim 'is to impart the sensation of things as they are perceived and not as they are known' (2006, p. 778). Art should make us approach the familiar without 'the automatism of perception'.

As Denner observes, such an understanding of art in fact resembles Tolstoy's in *What Is Art?* (1897) (Denner, 2008; Tolstoy, 1904) Besides, one of Tolstoy's recurring themes in his later writings is indeed that people have become hypnotised by habit and deceit into not seeing acts of violence and oppression for what they are. Tolstoy wanted, through his writings, to shake the public out of this hypnotised state, and he saw the purpose of art as to contribute to that.

It is not the intention of this article to comment on whether the whole purpose of art is to be defined so narrowly, i.e. as something that must always make the familiar strange. Instead, what this article argues is that defamiliarisation is a potent tool in disrupting the narratives of the violent political status quo, a technique therefore worth analysing and deploying in denouncing violence and oppression. Let us now therefore consider some examples.

The very first example Shklovsky gives of Tolstoy using this technique in his essay is a description of flogging – a punishment then recently reintroduced in Tsarist Russia. As quoted by Shklovsky, Tolstoy describes it as:

> 'to strip people who have broken the law, to hurl them to the floor, and to rap on their bottoms with switches', and, after a few lines, 'to lash about on the naked buttocks'. Then [Tolstoy] remarks: 'Just why precisely this stupid, savage means of causing pain and not any other – why not prick the shoulders or any part of the body with needles, squeeze the hands or the feet in a vise, or anything like that?' (Tolstoy, 1896; Shklovsky, 2006, p. 779)

Shklovsky comments that, here, 'The familiar act of flogging is made unfamiliar both by the description and by the proposal to change its form without changing its nature.' (2006, p. 779) Tolstoy invites us to look at the act through the eyes of a child, even, as Denner comments, 'using words drawn from the readers' memories of their punishment as children' (2008, p. 381). According to Shklovsky, this example 'is typical of Tolstoy's way of pricking the conscience' by 'not naming the familiar' and thus making it 'seem strange', by describing it 'as if he were seeing it for the first time' (2006, p. 779).

Shklovsky immediately follows this example with another much more extensive quote where Tolstoy defamiliarises this time the notion of private property by seeing it through the eyes of a horse (Tolstoy, 1886; Shklovsky, 2006, pp. 779–780). Shklovsky then gives several more examples, and notes that hundreds of further examples can be found in Tolstoy's work.

One of the more notorious passages of Tolstoy doing this is with his lengthy depiction of Sunday mass in prison in *Resurrection* (1899), which includes a classic defamiliarisation of the Eucharist (1966, p. 181). The two full chapters were compressed by the Russian censor to no more than three words: 'The service began.' (Edmonds, 1966, p. 13) The book also sealed

Tolstoy's excommunication. Church authorities thus certainly did perceive Tolstoy's defamiliarised accounts as subverting orthodox rituals and beliefs by representing them out of context, as if through the eyes of a seemingly inadvertently insolent child. According to Fernandez, it is indeed perhaps 'especially to criticise religion and priestly hypocrisy' that defamiliarisation has been 'most formidable' (Fernandez, 2010, p. 67 [my translation]). But Tolstoy also targeted other established institutions which he saw as complicit in violence.

Chapter 30 in *Resurrection* (1966, pp. 148–150) scans the prisoners of a cell, and describes the reason they found themselves imprisoned, in a way that clearly intends to implicitly question the justice of the criminal system. Similar presentations of convicts appear later in the book (1966, p. 235). Throughout the novel, defamiliarisations of various aspects of the judicial system contribute to a relentless ridiculing of it, whilst nonetheless laying bare the severe implications of institutional violence. McLean comments that

> One of the most searing representations of senseless cruelty in the penal system is the picture of the departure for Siberia of a large group of prisoners. On a day of intense summer heat the victims are lined up in the sun, counted, counted again, and finally marched through the streets of Moscow to the railway station. Several prisoners die of sunstroke or heat exhaustion; all suffer. It is one of those instances, as Nekhliudov analyzes the causes, where it is impossible to pin responsibility for the misery. Every official is just doing his job, following orders; but the result is suffering and death. Official, legal duties make people impervious to the human law written by God in their heart, just as pavement makes a road impervious to rain. (2002, p. 108)

Earlier in the novel, in an illustrative passage too long to cite in full here, Tolstoy introduces an 'aged general' who had received an 'extremely flattering Cross in the Caucasus because under his command close-cropped Russian peasants dressed in uniforms and armed with guns and bayonets had killed more than a thousand men who were defending their liberty, their homes and their families' (1966, pp. 344–345). Throughout *Resurrection*, Tolstoy thus paints defamiliarised pictures of prisoners and prison officers in a manner which clearly means to trigger reflection about both the absurdity and the violence of the justice system. Law courts are not spared, and also get what McLean calls 'a savagely critical representation' where 'the courtroom and its regalia [are presented] through the naive eyes of Nekhliudov, who is seeing these for the first time' (2002, p. 103). Tolstoy's 'picture of upper-class life' in it is also 'unrelentingly critical', as McLean goes on to explain (2002, p. 106).

There are many examples of the same technique applied in other late Tolstoyan writings, in particular to depict the horrifying absurdity of violence. In *The Kingdom of God Is within You* (1893), the text most frequently cited as the main and fullest exposition of his Christian anarchist thinking, Tolstoy describes the demands of the state like this:

> Take a man of our time – be he who he may – [...] living quietly when suddenly people come to him and say: 'First you must promise and swear to us that you will slavishly obey us in everything we prescribe to you, and obey and unquestioningly accept as absolute truth everything we devise, decide on, and call law. Secondly you must hand over to us part of the fruits of your labour (we shall use the money to keep you in slavery and to prevent you forcibly resisting our arrangements). Thirdly you must elect others, or be yourself elected, to take a pretended part in the government, knowing all the while that the administration will proceed quite independently of the foolish speeches you and others like you may utter, and that things will proceed according to our will – the will of those in whose hands is the army. Fourthly you must at the appointed time come to the law-courts and take part in the senseless cruelties we perpetrate on erring people whom we have perverted – in the shape of imprisonments, banishments, solitary confinements, and executions. And fifthly and finally, besides all this, although you may be on the friendliest terms with men of other nations, you must be ready, as soon as we order it, to consider as your enemies those whom we shall point out to you, and co-operate, personally or by hiring others, in the destruction, plunder, and murder of their men, women, children and aged alike – perhaps also of your own fellow countrymen or even your parents, should we require that.' (2001b, pp. 238–239)

Painted this way, these central functions of the state obviously look rather unattractive. This particular portrayal is in fact quoted in a classic compilation of Tolstoy's writings on anarchism and nonviolence as evidence of his anarchism (Stephens, 1990, p. 13). Yet this is but one example among many of similar defamiliarisation of state functions which Tolstoy uses to denounce state violence.

Tolstoy's denunciations of state violence are not limited to domestic affairs. In 'Christianity and Patriotism' (1894), Tolstoy looks ahead to the next war he expects Russia to inevitably find itself engaged in:

> And hundreds of thousands of simple kindly folk, torn from their wives, mothers, and children, and with murderous weapons in their hands, will trudge wherever they may be driven, stifling the despair in their souls by songs, debauchery, and vodka. They will march, freeze, suffer from hunger, and fall ill. Some will die of disease, and some will at last come to the place where men will kill them by the thousand. And they, too, without themselves knowing why, will murder thousands of others whom they had never before seen, and who had neither done nor could do them any wrong (2001a, p. 449).

Similarly ten years later, as the Russo-Japanese war was breaking out, Tolstoy depicts the collective endeavour to kill with classic defamiliarisation in 'Bethink Yourselves!' (1937a, pp. 212–213) in the hope it might jolt some compatriots out of their hypnotic contribution to the war effort – a hypnotic condition for which Tolstoy frequently laid particular blame on patriotism and on the church.

In *The Kingdom of God Is within You*, Tolstoy reflects on how state violence is made possible by the way it is organised: the act is subdivided into several separate tasks, each performed by different persons, all of whom feel the responsibility for the act rests somewhere else, not on them (2001b, pp. 342–368). Tolstoy here anticipates Arendt's famous arguments about the banality of evil (2006), whereby state atrocities are not necessarily caused by atrocious people but merely by human beings each playing their professional role and administering their local task with proud efficiency. That is, according to Tolstoy, hypnotised by conventional political and religious rationalisations and intoxicated by the self-importance of their routinised duties, human beings will collectively commit violence many of them deep down know they should be more questioning of.

There are many more examples of defamiliarisation in Tolstoy's writings. What the limited sample mentioned above hopes to demonstrate is that, whether or not we agree with Tolstoy's broader views on the state or on religion, and even whether or not we still think that some violence is unfortunately sometimes necessary for peace, for order or for some other important cause, the defamiliarisation of organised violence provides a potent device to trigger reflection on exactly what is implicitly authorised by members of the body politic when endorsing mainstream positions and arguments which routinise the infliction of violence.

Defamiliarisation's subversive potential

What makes Tolstoyan defamiliarisation potentially subversive? In what manner does defamiliarisation affect those exposed to it such that they might reconsider their assumptions? My heuristic suggestion is that defamiliarisation is effective due to at least four reasons: it disrupts routine thinking and briefly opens a moment for reflection; it helps establish some implicit agreement on what is being observed through the complicit bond that underlies the sharing of humour, irony or ridicule; it relativises constructed hierarchies and strips them of their self-importance; and it generates empathy by gazing at the familiar through the eyes of someone else.

Disrupting routine thinking

Firstly, reading a defamiliarised description of a familiar phenomenon disrupts our automated perception of it. It reminds us of how we may well have approached the phenomenon for the first time as a child, and how much we have become accustomed to the conventional perception, labelling and rationalising of it. The curious description, avoiding the accepted name and describing it with candid sharpness, strikes the reader as refreshingly unusual, and invites pause and reflection. Put back in the mind of a child gazing at it for the first time, one may well in turn be reminded of the questions a child would then ask about why this has to be how it is.

It might be worth remarking in passing that Tolstoy was fond of what he saw as the pure-hearted innocence with which children encounter the world (for instance: Tolstoy, 1910). This is just one of several Rousseauian themes in Tolstoy (Rousseau is probably the thinker that influenced Tolstoy the most: Hamburg, 2010; Knapp, 2002; Paperno, 2010), and this also influenced the way Tolstoy interpreted Jesus' sayings on children (Tolstoy, 1933, 1934). That is, Tolstoy took Jesus as sharing his view about children being as yet still untainted by the depraved morality of adults, and by the numbed conscience which will soon enough corrupt them too. Tolstoy wanted to reawaken that uncorrupted conscience in his readers.

Disrupting routine perception was of course precisely one of the purposes which Shklovsky saw in defamiliarisation. As explained above, he argued that 'perception becomes habitual' and 'automatic', and that defamiliarisation is precisely a technique which helps break that (2006, p. 778). It shakes us out of hypnotic, 'anaesthetising' habit, to quote Denner (2008, p. 380). Moreover, as de Goede explains (citing Michel Foucault), 'denaturalizing, or *making strange*, political practices that appear as natural or common sense' is where the 'practice of criticism' indeed 'begins' (de Goede, 2005, p. 381, my emphasis). If one therefore wishes to draw attention to an injustice caused by conventional approaches to a problem, such disruption is an effective first step, a way of provoking reflection. Tolstoy was actually explicitly hoping that his writings would jolt his readers into revisiting conventional perceptions of political violence, that they might 'bethink' themselves out of the hypnotised mindset upon which countless arguments that led to violence and injustice were blindly legitimised (Tolstoy, 1902, 1933, 1934, 1937a, 1937c, 1948, 2001b, 2001c, n.d.).

There is of course no guarantee that defamiliarisation *will* disrupt routine perception. There is therefore also no guarantee that jolting readers with anarcho-pacifist defamiliarisations of violence will lead them to anarcho-pacifism. Readers who are moved might eventually settle for liberal arguments for example, or for cold – but perhaps more conscious – *realpolitik*. Much like comedy (Brassett, 2016), although defamiliarisation destabilises, the political and ideological end-result is unpredictable. Tolstoy hoped, of course, that his writings might help generate some kind of pacifist momentum. Nonetheless, to the extent that it has the *potential* to jolt readers into asking why they have labelled and perhaps legitimised something which as a child they would have probably perceived differently, defamiliarisation is a subversive device.

Conceding implicit agreement

Secondly, what defamiliarisation also tends to do is implicitly concede some recognition of a particular reality. That is, at least if written well, a defamiliarised account will not be queried about the seemingly factual and frank validity of what it describes. What might be disputed is whether that description covers – or not – all that one needs to consider before passing final judgement (the description could be slated as too naïve because omitting some broader aspects which a more mature analysis needs to consider). However, the description itself will be accepted as true enough. In other words, critical readers may immediately think beyond what is described and consider explanations that ultimately legitimise what has been described rather innocently, but they will probably still implicitly agree with the description – acknowledging the often-ignored or relativised violence of the situation.

Moreover, the touch of humour, irony, or satire inherent in the presentation of a defamiliarised account contributes to this securing of some recognition. The already-converted will be entertained, but the as-yet-unconverted may be jolted by their laughter because, when one is at least a little amused by a particular, defamiliarised portrayal, that amusement typically rests on the validity of that perspective being implicitly recognised. Critchley writes: 'Humour both reveals the situation, and indicates how that situation might be changed' (2002, p. 16). Humour helps a perspective get recognised. Take for example any of the more politically subversive stand-up comedians and entertainers (such as Bill Hicks, Mark Steel, Frankie Boyle or John Oliver), the humorous interventions of some anti-establishment dissenters (such as the Discordians, the Yes Men or the Clown Army), or the political comments in popular American cartoons (such as *The Simpsons, South Park* or *Team America*): when you laugh at their depiction of a particular issue, are you not also implicitly recognising a particular 'truth' about it without which the portrayal would not be amusing? That is *not* to say that what is affirmed with a touch of humour necessarily induces critical reflection or sympathy with a progressive agenda – humour can after all be aggressive, absurd, discriminatory and so on. Humour facilitates a convergence of opinion, but there is no guarantee that this will be a convergence on a progressive or critical viewpoint.

Nevertheless, part of what makes defamiliarisation subversive is this potential to invite implicit recognition of an otherwise routinised and overlooked injustice through humour. The moment one chuckles, one has in effect expressed some agreement about the injustice of what has been described. For instance, if one is at least tickled by the satirical description of flogging relayed above, is one not also implicitly recognising that it is in hindsight quite random and farcical an invented yet also cruel punishment?

If one feels drawn to the sarcastic tone with which preparations for war are mentioned above, is one not also thereby by implication acknowledging the scale of the collective effort, the impressively widespread dedication to it by the full breadth of society, and the potency (yet also the questionability) of the ideological spell which legitimises the whole endeavour? By joining Tolstoy in the sarcasm, one is arguably also implicitly converging towards his perspective.

This again does not guarantee eventual agreement with the defamiliariser's ultimate conclusions. Even if one might implicitly concede some recognition for the perspective being portrayed sarcastically, one might still move to cite 'good reasons' to still tolerate what is being criticised. But when the recognition that has been implicitly secured concerns otherwise robotically tolerated acts of institutional violence, then even merely getting an acknowledgement of that raw violence can be subversive. Defamiliarisation thereby helps break the spell of the typical spin, double-speak or propaganda which usually downplays uncomfortable aspects by exposing and focusing one's gaze on what should be uncomfortable clearly and bluntly.

Deriding hierarchies

Thirdly, Tolstoy's defamiliarisations also erode the respect and the deference that, by convention, adults are expected to show for political and religious hierarchies. As discussed above, this applies as much to the church as to state institutions, like courts and the army. By describing the administrative performances which constitute them out of their context and through the eyes of a child, these hierarchies look like any other performance – playground games for adults except, of course, that the reader knows (and sometimes is pointedly made aware of) the serious and real consequences for human victims. Moreover, Tolstoy's reader gets the impression that anyone could be there, performing this or that solemn role high up a hierarchy. Tolstoy's accounts suggest the people up there are no better than us. The sense of special duty and high-brow professionalism conventionally associated with these roles no longer look as convincing. This was Tolstoy's intention: he *wanted* to query the reverence people are expected to show for institutions that administer violence, he wanted to encourage empathy for the victims, and he knew his depictions could have that effect.

To anyone ascribing significant value to such hierarchies, Tolstoy's defamiliarised depictions are indeed profane. Defamiliarisation is irreverent because it refuses to respect the depicted institution's pomp and ceremony (it even insolently refuses to call it by its accepted name and title), yet what makes it particularly powerful is that it does not simply preach at the reader, but instead presents the observation as seemingly innocent and naïve, as a perspective the reader can relate to and be amused by. Given the seriousness with which the public is expected to approach the mission of political and religious hierarchies, the cynical absence of deference in defamiliarisation is subversive.

The humorous undertones in Tolstoyan defamiliarisation further contribute to this irreverence. There are parallels here with the similarly subversive potential of other forms of humour. Brassett discusses the extent to which the British comedy of Russell Brand, Charlie Brooker and Stewart Lee acts as a form of resistance to the 'dominant forms of market subjectivity' produced by the global political economy (2016, p. 168). De Goede argues that carnival and laughter in dissent and resistance against the global financial industry can actually contribute to challenging its power (2005). Odysseos shows how Aristophanic comedy amounted to an acerbic critique of Athens' religious and political orthodoxies (2001). To these examples can now be added Tolstoyan defamiliarisation, even though it essentially consists of one particular kind of satire (the candid irony of an innocent child) and has here been discussed primarily for one particular kind of resistance (an anarcho-pacifist critique violence).

Facilitating empathy

Fourthly and finally, defamiliarisation is important for yet another reason: it facilitates empathy. For one, Brassett argues (following Rorty) that irony 'can foster a greater sensitivity to the suffering of others by recognising [...] the practical effects of seeing more and more people as fellow sufferers' (2009, p. 221). Moreover, Tolstoy thought one of the purposes of art was to transmit the feelings that one experienced, in other words to encourage empathy in the reader for the feelings one is expressing (Emerson, 2002; Tolstoy, 1904). To look at a phenomenon as if for the first time is to try to approach it unconstrained by the emotional attachments and allegiances that had come to automatically derive from one's actual position in the social canvas. It means both that familiar affections are suspended and that affections for people hitherto disregarded might be discovered. In other words, new patterns of empathy might emerge. Tolstoy's defamiliarised accounts of violence are quite deliberately crafted to incite the reader to feel the injustice, the absurdity, and the suffering caused. One is made to feel for the victims, and one is left pondering how one would react if confronted with the same treatment.

Tolstoy saw the core ethical teaching of all religious traditions as essentially a variation on the Golden Rule, the ethical guideline that calls us to do unto others as we would prefer be done to us (Christoyannopoulos, 2014). This Golden Rule is premised on a reciprocal treatment of each other as equals. By relativising constructed hierarchies and by framing our gaze as that of an innocent child, Tolstoy's defamiliarised accounts flatten our differences and, in effect, encourage ethical reflection (potentially) framed through the Golden Rule. To be clear: defamiliarisation on its own does not guarantee that individuals will embrace the kind of empathetic reciprocity embedded in the Golden Rule, but it acts as an invitation in that direction.

To encourage empathy is to possibly subvert legitimisations of violence because few are those who like to be at the receiving end of violence. Empathy challenges attempts to dehumanise those portrayed as enemies. Once their humanity is reinstated, the suffering inflicted on them cannot be ignored. If the arguments supposed to justify violence against enemies turn out to be comparable to those mustered by those on 'the other side' to be violent themselves, then the absurdity of both sides' violence is vividly exposed. Both dehumanisation and defamiliarisation modify perception, but in opposing directions: Tolstoyan defamiliarisation tends to 'rehumanise' by reawakening a purer gaze, untainted by conventional hierarchies and moulded identities, a gaze more open to empathy. It is more difficult to inflict violence when one feels empathy for the victim and, therefore, to the extent that defamiliarisation promotes empathy, it undermines the agenda of the advocates of such violence.

Concluding reflections

Defamiliarisation is not new, nor was Tolstoy the only one to use it. My contention, to sum up, is that Tolstoy, who is the main example repeatedly cited by Shklovsky in the text that coined the term for this artistic technique, is also a writer whose defamiliarised depictions of violence are still compelling and potentially subversive. They provide examples that might inspire others. One need not agree with Tolstoy on the radical anarchism or his proposed solutions to share his indignation about the violence he is disclosing, and feel moved to do something about it. Defamiliarised descriptions of the violence that humans inflict on each other are moving: they disrupt routine perceptions, concede some recognition of systemic violence, relativise hierarchies and encourage empathy.

Unlike Shklovsky, I am not claiming defamiliarisation is '*the* purpose of art' (2006, p. 778, emphasis added); nor do I wish to limit its use to those who define themselves as artists. What I am claiming is that it is a potent tool to raise public awareness – be it about injustices, the raw reality of violence, the role of institutions in administering it, or any other automated social practice. It is because of this subversive potential that twentieth-century artistic movements such as Dada and intellectual perspectives of poststructuralism have advocated and used similar techniques. More recent counter-cultural activities such as culture-jamming, subvertising, and satirical news production have been employing it too. The wider public also seems to enjoy taking part in defamiliarisation when posting and reposting memes and news commentaries that seek to provoke reflection through it.

Furthermore, defamiliarisation is only one of a broader range of aesthetic devices and practices that suspend or disrupt reality in different ways. From Bakhtin's 'carnival time' to Art Spiegman's *Maus*, from anti-capitalist street theatre to Banksy, there are many ways to try and turn the world upside down, to disrupt the unthinking and automatised reproduction of modes of behaviour and frames of thought that we all readily settle into as we busily navigate the social landscape. There is never any guarantee that any such attempts to disrupt routine will work, let alone that any successful unsettling will ultimately lead to the new perspectives and practices sought by those who seek change. Sometimes, they do. There is no guarantee that reading Tolstoy will disrupt one's tacit acceptance of the mechanised administration and legitimisation of violence and open space for potential critical reflection, but for some readers, it has done.

Admittedly, such causal influences can be difficult to establish unequivocally: they involve shifts in perception in the minds of audiences and readers, which are difficult to measure; there may also often be other contextual factors that are contributing to a shift in opinion; and sometimes the seeds of a new perception might have been growing in one's mind for a while already anyway. Nonetheless, evidence of shifts in perception includes the biographies, confessions and autobiographies of those who revised their views after what they describe as a disruptive jolt. Alston for instance cites many a Tolstoyan convert of this kind, ranging from lawyers and judges who abruptly walked away from their stable profession after having read Tolstoy, experienced soldiers who felt moved enough to wholly adopt and advocate Tolstoyan pacifism, and of course Gandhi, who credits Tolstoy for impressing upon him the importance of a firm moral commitment to non-violence (Alston 2010; Jahanbegloo, 1998). Tolstoy gained a sufficient-enough following to worry public authorities and move them to censor his writings and repress his disciples. Defamiliarisation is not the only ingredient that makes Tolstoyan pacifism a subversive concoction, but it does contribute to its particular flavour.

Today, the same aesthetic ingredient can help raise awareness of more contemporary types of political violence, including, for instance: the violence caused by borders and routinised discourses and procedures concerning international migration; the violent enforcement of economic inequalities; or the violence sold by a military-industrial complex and the trading of weapons for profit. Indeed, perhaps defamiliarised accounts of global production processes might help unmask some of the indirect culpabilities tied to the consumption of products stained by violence, from raw material extraction that funds civil wars, to brutal employment practices and habitat destruction. More generally, defamiliarisation can help disrupt the often rather quick and unquestioning endorsement of routinised violence and war as means to an end – whether domestically in dominant regimes of disciplining and punishment, or internationally, when evoking Just War arguments as facile excuses for war-making. Artistic disruptions of routinised violence thus add a dimension to the literature that seeks to think about credible and more peaceful alternatives to the violent human practices which enforce today's global geopolitical economy.

Tolstoy hoped to reach many different kinds of readers – the Russian intelligentsia, socialists, Christians, the aristocracy, the literary public, etc. – each playing different roles and differently complicit in the systemic violence he denounced. Today's global society is even more complex, and the type and degree of complicity of the different cogs of the current system considerably more complicated too. Globalised neoliberal capitalism, policed by the Westphalian order, is effective at hiding its production processes from consumers, hiding the effect of pension funds and private savings on the victims of their investments, hiding the front-line from the distant clerk, hiding the impact of economic austerity from the busy middle classes. If anything, this makes even more apposite and urgent the deployment of techniques of defamiliarisation to help expose the complex causalities underlying today's systemic violence.

Deep down, most citizens know there are deep injustices in the world, do not like it when they are victims of violence, and are aware that much violence is inflicted out there because of the various accepted realities of the twenty-first century world. Yet the acceptance of this reality rests on automated perceptions and arguments which, when queried through the eyes of an innocent child, can be harder to justify. That child-like naivety poses a challenge to those complicit in perpetrating or accepting the perpetration of violence. For those who have assimilated the conventional justifications of violence, a dose of defamiliarisation can disrupt and invite critical reflection. To a humanity still contaminated by violence and injustice, perhaps one could do worse than advise the reading of some of the later writings of the celebrated author of *War and Peace*.

Acknowledgments

I would like to thank the organisers of this special number and of the ECPR Joint Session workshop that preceded it, all those who participated at that workshop, those who commented at presentations of earlier drafts at Loughborough, and the anonymous reviewers.

Disclosure statement

No potential conflict of interest was reported by the author.

References

Abraham, J. H. (1929). The religious ideas and social philosophy of Tolstoy. *International Journal of Ethics*, *40*(1), 105–120.
Alston, C., (2010, June 10). Tolstoy's guiding light. *History Today* [online]. Retrieved from http://historytoday.com/charlotte-alston/tolstoys-guiding-light
Alston, C. (2014). *Tolstoy and his disciples: The history of a radical international movement*. London: I. B. Tauris.
Arendt, H. (2006). *Eichmann in Jerusalem*. London: Penguin.
Atack, I. (2012). *Nonviolence in political theory*. Edinburgh: Edinburgh University Press.
Avrich, P. (1968). Russian anarchists and the civil war. *Russian Review*, *27*(3), 296–306.
Bartlett, R. (2010). *Tolstoy: A Russian life*. London: Profile.
Berdyaev, N. (1948). The voice of conscience from another world: An introduction. In *Essays from tula* (pp. 9–18). London: Sheppard.
Brassett, J. (2009). British irony, global justice: A pragmatic reading of Chris Brown, Banksy and Ricky Gervais. *Review of International Studies*, *35*(1), 219–245.
Brassett, J. (2016). British comedy, global resistance: Russell Brand, Charlie Brooker and Stewart Lee. *European Journal of International Relations*, *22*(1), 168–191.
Brock, P. (1972). *Pacifism in Europe to 1914*. Princeton: Princeton University Press.
Buchanan, I. (2010). *A dictionary of critical theory* [online]. Oxford University Press. Retrieved May 10, 2016, from http://www.oxfordreference.com/view/10.1093/acref/9780199532919.001.0001/acref-9780199532919-e-501
Christoyannopoulos, A. (2008). Leo Tolstoy on the state: A detailed picture of Tolstoy's denunciation of state violence and deception. *Anarchist Studies*, *16*(1), 20–47.
Christoyannopoulos, A. (2014). The golden rule on the green stick: Leo Tolstoy's international thought for a 'postsecular' age. In L. Mavelli & F. Petito (Eds.), *Towards a postsecular international politics: New forms of community, identity, and power* (pp. 81–102). London: Palgrave Macmillan.
Christoyannopoulos, A. (2016). Leo tolstoy's anticlericalism in its context and beyond: a case against churches and clerics, religious and secular. *Religions*, *7*(5), 59. doi:10.3390/rel7050059
Christoyannopoulos, A. (forthcoming). *Tolstoy's Political Thought: Christian Anarcho-Pacifist Iconoclasm Then and Now*. Abingdon: Routledge.
Critchley, S. (2002). *On humour*. London: Routledge.
De Goede, M. (2005). Carnival of money: Politics of dissent in an era of globalizing finance. In L. Amoore (Ed.), *The global resistance reader* (pp. 379–391). London: Routledge.

Denner, M. A. (2008). Dusting off the couch (and discovering the Tolstoy connection in Shklovsky's "art as device"). *The Slavic and Eastern European Journal, 52*(3), 370–388.
Denner, M. A. (2010). The 'proletarian lord': Leo Tolstoy's image during the Russian revolutionary period. In D. T. Orwin (Ed.), *Anniversary essays on Tolstoy* (pp. 219–244). Cambridge: Cambridge University Press.
Edmonds, R. (1966). Introduction. In *Resurrection* (pp. 5–16). London: Penguin.
Eikhenbaum, B. M. (1967). On Tolstoy's crises. In R. E. Matlaw (Ed.), *Tolstoy: A collection of critical essays* (pp. 52–55). Englewood Cliffs: Prentice-Hall.
Emerson, C. (2002). Tolstoy's aesthetics. In D. T. Orwin (Ed.), *The Cambridge companion to Tolstoy* (pp. 237–251). Cambridge: Cambridge University Press.
Fernandez, D. (2010). Subrepticement subversif. *Le Magazine Littéraire*, November, 66–67.
Fueloep-Miller, R. (1960). Tolstoy the apostolic crusader. *Russian Review, 19*(2), 99–121.
Greenwood, E. B. (1978). Tolstoy and religion. In M. Jones (Ed.), *New essays on Tolstoy* (pp. 149–174). Cambridge: Cambridge University Press.
Guseinov, A. A. (1999). Faith, God, and nonviolence in the teachings of Lev Tolstoy. *Russian Studies in Philosophy, 38*(2), 89–103.
Gustafson, R. F. (1986). *Leo Tolstoy, resident and stranger: A study in fiction and theology*. Princeton: Princeton University Press.
Hamburg, G. M. (2010). Tolstoy's spirituality. In D. T. Orwin (Ed.), *Anniversary essays on Tolstoy* (pp. 138–158). Cambridge: Cambridge University Press.
Jahanbegloo, R. (1998). *Gandhi: Aux sources de la non-violence*. Paris: Félin.
Kennan, G. (1887). A visit to count Tolstoi. *The Century Magazine, 34*(2), 252–265.
Knapp, L. (2002). The development of style and theme in Tolstoy. In D. T. Orwin (Ed.), *The Cambridge companion to Tolstoy* (pp. 161–175). Cambridge: Cambridge University Press.
Kolstø, P. (2006). The demonized double: The image of Lev Tolstoi in Russian orthodox polemics. *Slavic Review, 65*(2), 304–324.
Lavrin, J. (1960). Tolstoy and Gandhi. *Russian Review, 19*(2), 132–139.
Lenin, V. I., (1908). Leo Tolstoy and the mirror of the Russian revolution. *Marxist internet archive* [online]. Retrieved September 20, 2011, from http://www.marxists.org/archive/lenin/works/1908/sep/11.htm
Love, J. (2008). *Tolstoy: A guide for the perplexed*. London: Continuum.
Matual, D. (1992). *Tolstoy's translation of the gospels: A critical study*. Lewiston: Edwin Mellen.
Maude, A. (1930). *The life of Tolstóy: Later years*. London: Oxford University Press.
McKeogh, C. (2009). *Tolstoy's pacifism*. Amherst: Cambria.
McLean, H. (2002). Resurrection. In D. T. Orwin (Ed.), *The Cambridge companion to Tolstoy* (pp. 96–110). Cambridge: Cambridge University Press.
Medzhibovskaya, I. (2008). *Tolstoy and the religious culture of his time: A biography of a long conversion*, (pp. 1845–1887). Lanham, MD: Lexington.
Odysseos, L. (2001). Laughing matters: Peace, democracy and the challenge of the comic narrative. *Millennium: Journal of International Studies, 30*(3), 709–732.
Orwin, D. T. (2002). Introduction: Tolstoy as artist and public figure. In D. T. Orwin (Ed.), *The Cambridge companion to Tolstoy* (pp. 49–62). Cambridge: Cambridge University Press.

Paperno, I. (2010). Leo Tolstoy's correspondence with Nikolai Strakhov: The dialogue on faith. In D. T. Orwin (Ed.), *Anniversary essays on Tolstoy* (pp. 96–119). Cambridge: Cambridge University Press.
Préposiet, J. (2005). *Histoire de l'anarchisme, reviewed and expanded edition*. Paris: Pluriel.
Rolland, R. (1978). *Vie de Tolstoï*. Paris: Albin Michel.
Schmidt, M., & van der Walt, L. (2009). *Black flame: The revolutionary class politics of anarchism and syndicalism*. Oakland: AK.
Seeley, F. F. (1978). Tolstoy's philosophy of history. In M. Jones (Ed.), *New essays on Tolstoy* (pp. 175–193). Cambridge: Cambridge University Press.
Shklovsky, V. (2006). Art as technique. In D. H. Richter (Ed.), *The critical tradition: Classic texts and contemporary trends* (3rd ed., pp. 774–784). Boston: Bedford/St. Martin's.
Spence, G. W. (1963). Suicide and sacrifice in Tolstoy's ethics. *Russian Review, 22*(2), 157–167.
Spence, G. W. (1967). *Tolstoy the ascetic*. Edinburgh: Oliver and Boyd.
Stephens, D. (1990). The non-violent anarchism of Leo Tolstoy. In D. Stephens (Ed.), *Government is violence: Essays on anarchism and pacifism* (pp. 7–19). London: Phoenix.
Stepun, F. (1960). The religious tragedy of Tolstoy. *Russian Review, 19*(2), 157–170.
Struve, G. (1960). Tolstoy in Soviet criticism. *Russian Review, 19*(2), 171–186.
Tolstoï, L. N. (n.d.). *What to do?* London: Walter Scott.
Tolstoy, L., (1886). Kholstomeer: The story of a horse. The long riders guild academic foundation [online]. Retrieved May 10 2016, from http://www.lrgaf.org/training/kholstomer.htm
Tolstoy, L., (1896). Shame! [online]. Retrieved May 10, 2016, from http://www.non resistance.org/docs_htm/Tolstoy/Shame.html
Tolstoy, L. (1902). *What I believe <my religion>*. London: C. W. Daniel.
Tolstoy, L. (1904). *What is art?* New York: Funk & Wagnalls Company.
Tolstoy, L., (1910). The wisdom of children [online]. Retrieved May 10, 2016, from http://www.nonresistance.org/docs_htm/Tolstoy/Wisdom_of_Children.html
Tolstoy, L. (1933). The gospel in brief. In *A confession and the gospel in brief* (pp. 113–302). London: Oxford University Press.
Tolstoy, L. (1934). The teaching of Jesus. In *On life and essays on religion* (pp. 346–409). London: Oxford University Press.
Tolstoy, L. (1937a). Bethink yourselves!. In *Recollections and essays* (pp. 204–271). London: Oxford University Press.
Tolstoy, L. (1937b). Gandhi letters. In *Recollections and essays* (pp. 433–439). London: Oxford University Press.
Tolstoy, L. (1937c). Thou shalt not kill. In *Recollections and essays* (pp. 195–203). London: Oxford University Press.
Tolstoy, L. (1948). The slavery of our times. In *Essays from Tula* (pp. 65–136). London: Sheppard.
Tolstoy, L. (1966). *Resurrection*. London: Penguin.
Tolstoy, L. (1987). A confession. In *A confession and other religious writings* (pp. 17–80). London: Penguin.
Tolstoy, L. (2001a). Christianity and patriotism. In *The kingdom of God and peace essays* (pp. 422–500). New Delhi: Rupa.

Tolstoy, L. (2001b). The kingdom of God is within you: Christianity not as a mystical doctrine but as new understanding of life. In *The kingdom of God and peace essays* (pp. 1–421). New Delhi: Rupa.

Tolstoy, L. (2001c). Patriotism and government. In *The kingdom of God and peace essays* (pp. 501–529). New Delhi: Rupa.

Wilson, A. N. (1988). *Tolstoy: A biography*. New York: Norton.

Our wildest imagination: violence, narrative, and sympathetic identification

Jade Schiff

> **ABSTRACT**
> At this polarizing moment in American politics identifying with the experiences of others feels especially difficult, but it is vital for sharing a world in common. Scholars in a variety of disciplines have argued that narratives, and especially literary ones, can help us cultivate this capacity by soliciting sympathetic identification with particular characters. In doing so, narratives can help us to be more ethically and political responsive to other human beings. This is a limited view of the potential for narratives to solicit sympathetic identification, and it prevents us from identifying and grappling with our resistances to identifying with others. In this article I propose a more expansive view – inspired by Elizabeth Costello, a character in JM Coetzee's novel of the same name – that there are no bounds to our capacities for sympathetic identification. Through critical readings of *Waiting for the Barbarians* and *Animal Farm* I explore the possibility that we might identify with people who cause others to suffer, and perhaps even with animals too. Both sorts of identification engender fierce resistance. Identifying with those who cause suffering demands that we grapple with our own capacities for cruelty and violence. Identifying with animals demands that we confront what is animal in ourselves – the perilous instincts that, unmoderated, incline us to aggression. Acknowledging and working through – without rejecting or disavowing – our capacities for cruelty and our animal instincts is necessary for the practices of sympathetic identification upon which sharing a world depends.

'Bitzer is just weird: We cannot identify with him or wonder about him, for we sense that all within is empty.' Nussbaum (1995, p. 30)

'There are no bounds to the sympathetic imagination.' Elizabeth Costello (Coetzee, 2004, p. 80)

American politics is polarised as never before. In a stunning blow to the political establishment, Donald Trump defeated Hillary Clinton to capture the presidency with a campaign that deployed racist, misogynist and populist rhetoric to harness the anxieties and resentments of Americans who feel disenfranchised by and alienated from politics. The election exposed a seemingly unbridgeable gulf between an old order accustomed to setting the terms of political life, and a new order eager to redefine those terms. The old regards the new with fear and disdain; the new regards the old with resentment and a desire for vengeance. Such polarization partly reflects a failure of identification, an inability or unwillingness to see ourselves in others, and to see others in ourselves. Human capacities for identification are linked to our faculty of imagination, which enables us to project ourselves into others' lives and worlds and to see themselves as part of ours. Identification is no guarantee of peace or justice or self-determination. But it is a necessary condition of any effort to share a common world.

Are the chasms of perspective and experience generated by differences of class, race, sexual orientation, gender identity, and the relations of power and privilege that these differences engender insurmountable? Or are we just reluctant to cross them for fear of what we might find in others and ourselves? The epigraphs above – one from the philosopher Martha Nussbaum, the other from Elizabeth Costello, a character in J.M Coetzee's eponymous novel – help to clarify and develop these and related questions: Are there limits to our capacity to identify with others, and to the imagination that makes identification possible? Why might we sometimes insist that there are such limits? How might engagement with literary narratives help us approach these questions? In this article I do not provide settled answer these questions so much as I open them further, to explore how literary narratives might expand our capacity to understand ourselves and others.

Identifying with others can generate positive affective attachments like empathy and negative ones like anxiety, frustration and hostility. Many scholars have suggested that identification with those who suffer can make us more ethically and politically responsive (see e.g. Cohen, 2012; Nussbaum, 1995; Rorty, 1989; Schiff, 2014). But can we also identify with those who contribute to suffering? I think that we can but often prefer not to, and that reflecting on this resistance might help us confront in ourselves dispositions we prefer to leave unexamined. Identification and reflection are never neutral. They necessarily take place from our particular social and political perspectives that shape our understandings of ourselves and others. I will not catalogue a possible range of responses to identification, nor assign particular responses to particular kinds of people or groups. I seek only to suggest that identification is more complex, and potentially more expansive, than other scholars have suggested.

Finally, if our sympathetic imaginations are unlimited, can we identify with non-human beings? I think that an *a priori* insistence on limits to identification bespeaks discomfort with our capacities for violence and cruelty and with our animal instincts whose taming is vital for co-existence. Identification with those who contribute to suffering might help us work through these tendencies and the anxieties and resentments to which they give rise, rather than to unleash them on others. We risk being swept away by them, but if we flee this risk we miss opportunities to understand ourselves. Furthermore, if we can identify with non-human animals we might come to treat them – and our fellow human animals – more humanely.

In the first section, I defend Costello's suggestion that there are no limits to our sympathetic imagination against Nussbaum's insistence on such limits. In the second, I explore Costello's claim by reckoning with Colonel Joll, a magistrate in JM Coetzee's *Waiting for the Barbarians*. In the third, inspired by posthumanist displacement of human beings as privileged subjects and masters of nature, I suggest that George Orwell's *Animal Farm* invites us to identify with animal suffering and confront the animal in ourselves.

Identification without limits?

The capacity to imagine 'oneself as another' (Ricoeur, 1995) is critical for sharing a common world. Imagination is what allows us to project ourselves into the worlds of others. If we project ourselves into others' worlds we can perhaps begin to see that world from their point of view. This seeing is what I am calling 'identification.' Identifying with others involves knowing something about their circumstances and the ways in which they respond to them. It also involves *acknowledgment*, both that we share a world with them and that we may respond to our shared world in similar and different ways (Cavell, 2002; Markell, 2003). *Sympathetic* identification gives this activity emotional valence and emphasizes its relational character. Cohen (2012) called this capacity a 'talent for metaphor.' Hannah Arendt linked the capacity for identification with the faculties of thinking and judgment, and diagnosed in Adolph Eichmann an inability 'to think from the standpoint of somebody else' (Arendt, 2006). Iris Young (2000) suggested that identification with others could improve political deliberations. Coles (2016) suggests that it might facilitate democratic responses to environmental degradation. On the other hand, some scholars have emphasized the dark side of sympathetic identification and its relatives. Nietzsche (1989) criticized compassion because it made people weak. Arendt criticized the sentiment of pity in politics (Arendt, 1972). Paul Bloom suggests that cultivating empathy toward some can make us crueler toward others (e.g. Bloom,2016), while McGregor and McGregor (2013) that it can 'trap' us in unhealthy relationships. Similarly, I suspect that sympathetic identification might enable us to identify with those who contribute to suffering. But identification itself is only a first step. How we *respond* to this identification shapes our capacity to share a common world.

Concrete narratives about people's circumstances can nurture our capacities for identification, because they supplement abstract normative theories with descriptions of lived experience. Nussbaum (1995) has argued that identification with literary characters can generate more ethical legal and political judgments because literature can help us hone our 'ability to imagine the concrete ways in which people different from oneself grapple with disadvantage' (Nussbaum, 1995, p. xvi). Richard Rorty has argued that literary narratives can help us see others as fellow sufferers and cultivate solidarity with them because they offer 'detailed description of what unfamiliar people are like and...redescriptions of what we ourselves are like' (Rorty, 1989, p. xvi). These acts of imagination and identification, grounded in what we know about other people's lives, help us acknowledge their place in a world we share with them. In psychology, Mar, Oatley, and Peterson (2009) have demonstrated that certain kinds of literary narratives may increase our capacity for empathy (see also Mar, Oatley, Hirsh, Dela Paz, & Peterson, 2006). Although she is not concerned with literary narratives in particular, Young argues that 'without the thick description of needs, and problems and consequences that concrete stories can provide, political judgments may rest on social understandings that are too abstract' (Young, 2000, p. 20).

These scholars suggest that narratives have positive effects: they make their readers (or listeners) better. As Booth, 1989, p. 485) puts it, literature offers 'trial runs' at different ways of living that can make us more ethically responsive. But Booth also notes the seductive character of rogues (1983, p. 379), and some authors have noted that narratives can as easily constrict our ethical and political sensibilities as they can expand them (Schiff, 2014). Here I pursue the why and how of our identification with those who perpetrate violence and cruelty, and what its consequences are. I reject the position that Martha Nussbaum articulates in the epigraph above and want to understand the impulses from which it might arise. Her position emerges from observations about Bitzer, a character in Dickens' *Hard Times* who, she asserts, exceeds our capacities for sympathetic identification:

> Bitzer is chillingly weird and not quite human: From our first glimpse of his 'cold eyes' and his skin, 'so unwholesomely deficient in the natural tinge', we know that we are dealing with a monster. The monstrosity in Bitzer is his incapacity for any sympathy or commitment that extends beyond a use of others to serve his own ends...[T]his figure repels our sympathy and our identification; even asking what it is like to be him is difficult, so alien is he made to seem... Bitzer is just weird: We cannot identify with him or wonder about him' (Nussbaum, 1995, p. 30).

This assertion is startling in a work about the power of literature to solicit identification. Nussbaum implies that the inability to identify with Bitzer is universal, but nothing about him makes this necessary. To start with, his skin does not mark him as alien, but suggests albinism (McMaster, 1987, p. 177;

Sklenicka & Spilka, 1994, p. 166). In another Dickens novel, *David Copperfield* (2004), Uriah Heep is depicted as an 'ugly' albino. Bitzer is never described as ugly. Even if he were, he might elicit sympathetic identification because he is marked as irreducibly different, and the experience of being different in ways that disturb others is a common one. Nussbaum says that he instrumentalises relationships, using people for their own ends. People do this all the time. This suggests that some might be able to identify with Bitzer after all.

But as Nussbaum's response to Bitzer illustrates, his difference *might* lead us to resist identifying with him. While literature may solicit identification, we are not passive in the face of its solicitations, which Wayne Booth calls 'friendship offerings' (Booth, 1989, pp. 174–179). Whether we accept or refuse them is up to us. We might refuse identification because we are anxious about or resentful of the prospect of confronting what is different in us. We might be reminded of the burden of our own difference and our sense of responsibility for it and be moved to displace those burdens onto characters like Bitzer through projection and disavowal, just as Sartre's anti-Semite displaces responsibility for his condition onto the Jew (Sartre, 1995). We might inflate Bitzer's difference to reassure ourselves of our own 'normalcy' (Connolly, 2001; Foucault, 2004). People have many reasons, and many strategies, for resisting threatening identifications.

The imperatives of sympathetic identification and our strategies for resisting it feature prominently in *Elizabeth Costello*. Turning from a philosophical work to a literary one re-orients us from abstract reflection to the existentially much riskier terrain of concrete engagements that may help us examine our own resistances to identification. Unlike Mulhall (2009, p. 3), for whom we can only approach the questions Costello raises 'if we understand that our primary relation to her is as a literary creation', I think we can only explore these questions in existentially meaningful ways if we recall that literature allows us to see ourselves in her, which also means seeing her in us. Sympathetic identification enables crossings between literature and life that let us approach Costello as a human being, and not just a literary creation, whose world we can share, and who can share ours (Ricoeur, 1984; Schiff, 2014).

Costello is an Australian writer lecturing in the United States, where she is being honoured for her work. In 'The Philosopher and the Animals,' she addresses the (non-fictional) philosopher Nagel's (1974) question, 'what is it like to be a bat?' This encounter between a literary character and a 'real' person exemplifies the potential crossings between literature and life. Our Nagel becomes hers, and she invites us to meet him. For Nagel we cannot know what it is like to be a bat because 'our minds are not bats' minds.' A 'bat is a fundamentally alien creature...more alien than another fellow human being.' This raises the possibility that we might identify with *any* human being, even one as 'alien' as Bitzer. But Costello finds Nagel's view 'tragically...restrictive and restricted' (pp. 75–76) because 'being fully a bat is like being fully human, which is also to be full of being...to be alive is to be a living soul. An animal – and we are all animals – is an embodied soul' (pp. 77–78). Costello concludes that '"[t]here are no bounds to the sympathetic imagination"' (Coetzee, 2004, p. 80). To put it in the terms of imagination and acknowledgment that I used earlier, Costello is saying that our capacity to imagine – to project ourselves into the worlds of others – is unlimited, and that it depends upon acknowledging that, as animals, we share *being* with other animals.

For Costello, as for me, identification engages affect. She says it involves our heart, 'the seat of a faculty, *sympathy* that allows us to share at times the being of another' (p. 79). Here she surreptitiously introduces one limit to identification: We can share the being of another 'at times,' but perhaps not all the time. 'There are people who have [this capacity], there are people who have no such capacity...and there are people who have the capacity but choose not to exercise it' (p. 79). Our means of and capacities for resisting identification may be as limitless as the possibilities for identification themselves.

The perils of such limits become clear when Costello connects animal slaughter to the Holocaust and encounters fierce resistance. She notes the metaphors we use to talk about the treatment of the Nazis' victims: "They went like sheep to slaughter." "They died like animals..." The crime of the Third Reich, says the voice of accusation, was to treat people like animals' (pp. 64–65). This dehumanization affected the perpetrators, too: 'By treating fellow human beings...like beasts, they had themselves become beasts' (p. 65). She notes that the Poles near Treblinka denied knowing what happened there. They 'said that, while in a general way they might have guessed what was going on, they did not know for sure; said that, while in a sense they might not have known, in another sense they did not know, could not afford to know, for their own sake' (p. 64). Because of similar 'willed ignorance,' Germans 'of a particular generation are still regarded as standing a little outside humanity' (p. 64). She compares this willed ignorance to ignorance about the meat industry. In Waltham she 'saw no horrors, no drug-testing laboratories, no factory farms, no abattoirs.' But she is 'sure they are there... only we do not, in a certain sense, know about them' (p. 65).

Costello will not have this: 'Let me say it openly: we are surrounded by an enterprise of degradation, cruelty and killing which rivals anything that the Third Reich was capable of because 'ours is an enterprise without end' (p. 65). To 'claim that there is no comparison, that Treblinka' was devoted to death 'while the meat industry is ultimately devoted to life...is as little consolation to those victims as it would have been...to ask the dead of Treblinka to excuse their killers because their body fat was needed to make soap and their hair to stuff mattresses with' (p. 66). Like those whose willed ignorance made them complicit in Treblinka's horrors, meat eaters who feign ignorance of its origins are complicit in animal cruelty. Just as the former became beasts, the latter become less than human. Costello turns identification from a possibility into an imperative. Her comparison solicits sympathetic identification with the Nazis' victims to generate moral and political urgency about animal cruelty. Costello also wants us to see that our complicity in animal cruelty makes us like the Nazis. She wants us to identify with humans treated like beasts and with those who become like beasts. Crucially, it is the concreteness of her engagement, as distinct from more abstract, 'decontextualising' philosophical concerns about ethics (Mulhall, 2009, p. 22; see also Leist & Singer, 2010; Schiff, 2014), that makes this identification possible and heightens its urgency. But Costello does not abandon philosophy for poetics in an all-out 'war with reason' (Head, 2009, p. 83). She reasons with and against Nagel to expose the limits of philosophy.

Costello's invitation to identification meets resistance from the poet Abraham Stern. He skips a dinner in her honour, and leaves her an accusatory note:

> You took over for your own purposes the familiar comparison between the murdered Jews of Europe and the slaughtered cattle. The Jews died like cattle, therefore cattle die like Jews, you say… You misunderstand the nature of likenesses; I would even say you misunderstand wilfully, to the point of blasphemy. Man is made in the likeness of God but God does not have the likeness of man. If Jews were treated like cattle, it does not follow that cattle are treated like Jews. The inversion insults the memory of the dead. It also trades on the horrors of the camps in a cheap way (p. 94).

Stern's accusation betrays a misunderstanding, perhaps as wilful as the one of which he accuses Costello. While he says that she misunderstands likenesses, it is more accurate (and more useful) to say that they understand likenesses differently: Costello is not saying that Jews died like cattle and that *therefore* the Holocaust was like animal slaughter (and vice versa), but that the treatment of Jews dehumanized them *to the point of seeing them* as beasts, which turned the perpetrators into beasts themselves; and that the inhumane treatment of cattle similarly diminishes their being in a way that diminishes ours. What Jews and cattle share is a particular relationship to those who slaughter them: They are both 'wounded animals' (Mulhall, 2009).

Why Stern cannot (will not?) see this becomes apparent in his accusation of blasphemy, that Costello disturbs the hierarchy of animals, humans, and God. But for Costello there *is* no morally relevant hierarchy. Humans and animals share being, and that is what matters. Stern's interpretation of Costello's claim reflects theological anxieties and concerns about profaning the Holocaust. But Costello reveres the dead by insisting that *all* life ought to be revered. Stern's anxieties about identification make me wonder how our own anxieties might forestall possibilities for identifying others, human and not. In the next two sections, I pursue her suggestion that identification is boundless by exploring two apparently *un*sympathetic characters: Colonel Joll in *Waiting for the Barbarians*, and the pigs in *Animal Farm*.

The lesson of Colonel Joll

JM Coetzee tells the story of the Magistrate at an outpost of an empire facing a 'barbarian' threat. Initially a faithful functionary he eventually acknowledges his implication in the empire's cruelty partly through his relationship with Colonel Joll, a ruthless representative of imperial rule. Ultimately, the Magistrate turns against the system he administers. The story is told from the Magistrate's perspective, so we are invited to share in his experiences. His first encounter with Joll establishes the Colonel's strangeness: 'I had never seen anything like it' (Coetzee, 1980, p. 1). From his description – 'two little discs of glass suspended in front of his eyes in loops of wire' that 'protect one's eyes against the glare of the sun' – they are obviously sunglasses, but this description conveys otherness. 'Is he blind?', the Magistrate asks himself. 'I could understand it if he wanted to hide blind eyes' (Ibid.). This musing illuminates metaphorically a crucial insight about sympathetic identification: it depends upon making ourselves vulnerable to others. In shielding ourselves from others we make it difficult for them to identify with us – except insofar as they might identify with our desire for self-concealment. And in shielding ourselves, we obstruct our view of them. The Colonel can see through his sunglasses, but more dimly than without them. Similarly, the vulnerability identification requires is uncomfortable and so we may resist it.

Colonel Joll arrives at the outpost 'under emergency powers' (Ibid.) a phrase that evokes post-9/11 security practices and their justifications. Reading the novel today might bring us back to that time, without demanding that we read it in strictly allegorical terms that can limit the ethical and political significance we might draw from it by fixing it in a specific time or place (Attridge, 2004; Dooley, 2010; Schiff, 2014). 9/11 is not merely an analogy: it provides an historical context in which we might encounter Joll, and seek or refuse identification with him. Like the barbarian threat, the 9/11 attacks exposed anxieties about American empire, and Joll seeks to eliminate the threat to imperial rule just as the US government seeks to eradicate terrorism. Both the empire and the US government sanctioned torture to do so. The Magistrate engages Joll in an eerily familiar conversation about these methods: 'What if your prisoner is telling the truth,' asks the Magistrate, 'but finds that he is not believed?' 'Imagine: to be prepared to yield...to have nothing more to yield, to be broken, yet to be pressed to yield more! And what a responsibility for the interrogator! How do you ever know when a man has told you the truth' (p. 5)? The Magistrate invites Joll to imagine himself a tortured prisoner in order to question his own role in it. The final question is put so generally that it might be an invitation to us as well: How do we know when we are told the truth, and what responsibilities do we bear when we ask? Recall the 'enhanced interrogation' techniques employed at Guantanamo and CIA 'black sites.' We did not see them at first, but – remember Costello – perhaps we knew and couldn't afford to know because we feared what was being done in our name and the responsibility to protest it that attends such knowledge (Arendt, 2003). The infamous 'human pyramid' photo from Abu Ghraib shed a light on torture so that we could not look away. How do we know that we tell *ourselves* the truth about our own complicity in this torture – that we do not disavow, deflect, deny, or otherwise deceive ourselves? The deceptively simple question that the Magistrate poses opens possibilities for sympathetic identification with Joll – if we are receptive to his invitation. Some scholars have worried about the morally corrosive effects of identification with 'bad' characters like the Colonel (e.g. Booth, 1983; Valdés, 1991). That risk may be real. But if we flee from it we lose an opportunity to ask ourselves these vital questions.

From the Colonel's answer it is clear that he refuses the invitation altogether. 'A certain tone enters the voice of a man who is telling the truth. Training and experience teach us to recognize that tone.' He refuses the very general terms of the Magistrate's question, insisting that he is 'speaking only of a special situation...in which [he has] to exert pressure to find' the truth. 'First I get lies...then pressure, then more lies, then more pressure, then the break, then more pressure, then the truth' (p. 5). Torture is a technical question, not a moral or political one, and he never addresses the question of responsibility. Perhaps he is so immersed in his role that it never occurs to him, or perhaps he sees truth-seeking as his sole responsibility. Perhaps he has thought about and dismissed it. Perhaps it haunts him and he must refuse it repeatedly. Perhaps he can avoid it now because he works invisibly in the outpost's granary. He hides himself and so answers to nobody, including himself.

Joll's reasoning recalls arguments supporting torture after 9/11: It was an efficient way to extract reliable information (it wasn't) to capture terrorists and foil their plans. Indeed, according to one poll from 2014 a majority of Americans believed that CIA interrogation techniques had worked, even while nearly half acknowledged that they constituted torture (Goldman & Craighill, 2014). They believed, along with Colonel Joll, that the pursuit of security justifies treatment that is otherwise morally reprehensible and that, today, is illegal. To the extent that Joll legitimizes their anxieties and reflects back to them their view of the necessary trade-off between humanity and security, they might identify with him easily. He might exemplify Booth's 'seductive rogue,' enticing us into justifying torture. Indeed, anyone who recalls the terror, confusion and anxiety on 9/11 might identify with a man who seeks to root out evil for the sake of peaceful living. There were, are, days when I might. I would like to say I could never identify with him. But I cannot say that. Can any of us honestly say it with absolute confidence?

If the answer is no – as I think it must be – Colonel Joll's later actions might make us want to disavow the part of ourselves that we see in him. When twelve prisoners are brought to the outpost, at his direction '[four] of the prisoners kneel on the ground...The kneeling prisoners bend side by side over a long heavy pole. A cord runs from the loop of wire through the first man's mouth, under the pole, up to the second man's loop,' and so on.

> [A] soldier slowly pulls the cord tighter and the prisoners bend further till finally they are kneeling with the faces touching the pole. One of them writhes his shoulders in pain and moans. The others are silent...concentrated on moving smoothly with the cord, not giving the wire a chance to tear their flesh (p. 105).

This is the only scene in which torture is public. We cannot shield ourselves from it any longer. I have read that passage many times, and every time I do it becomes more powerful. I can imagine, can almost *feel*, the bending, the twisting, the sting of the wire. But to imagine that, to *feel* that, I must face something else: Joll is no longer simply the dispassionate seeker of truth, but a man who oversees a public spectacle of torture and humiliation; and if Joll is that, than perhaps I am, or could be. The Magistrate recounts:

> The Colonel steps forward: Stooping over each prisoner in the turn he rubs a handful of dust into his naked back and writes a word with a stick of charcoal. I read the words upside down: ENEMY...ENEMY...ENEMY...ENEMY. He steps back and folds his hands. At a distance of no more than twenty paces he and I contemplate each other. Then the beating begins (p. 105).

In this public spectacle the veil is dropped: Joll reveals the anxiety and cruelty that boil beneath the surface of his other, coolly efficient efforts to secure the empire. The prisoners are thoroughly dehumanized, reduced to mere bodies. The image of them bent over a pole recalls animals roasting on a spit, although without the fire – perhaps imperial rage burns hot enough. Like animals, they are branded – not with hot pokers, but with sand. The word branded on their backs – 'ENEMY' – marks their difference, and the threat they pose not just to the security of empire, but to its *identity*, its self-understanding as representative of civilisation: right, good, pure, just and clean (Connolly, 2001; Freud, 1989).

The revelation of the empire's spectacular cruelty may make us recoil – it makes *me* recoil – but too late. If we could see ourselves in the dispassionate Joll, and see what lies beneath that dispassion, those same impulses and dispositions may lie in us as well. In recoiling from Joll we recoil from that possibility, but it stalks us like prey. How do we respond to this haunting intimation of our capacities for spectacular cruelty? We might examine those capacities closely, to see what anxieties and resentments lie beneath – anxieties about the loss of power and privilege, for example, or about the exquisite vulnerability that the 9/11 attacks exposed (Butler, 2006); to work with them, to work through them, so that they might not overtake us. Or we might unleash them upon other people by designating them less than human, as the Nazis did to their victims; and as the US did by declaring suspected terrorists 'enemy combatants' (note the resonance with Joll's 'ENEMY'), depriving them of basic rights, and subjecting them to brutal torture (the use of 'stress positions' in particular recalls the contorted bodies of Joll's prisoners). This possibility resonates with Costello's observations about animal cruelty and genocide: by dehumanizing others, we dehumanize ourselves.

The lesson of Colonel Joll, in short, is this: We can identify with a person who acts cruelly, if we are open to it. If we do, we have two choices: We can attend to the anxieties, resentments and fears that fuel our own capacities for cruelty and desires for vengeance, and hope to attenuate them; or we can unleash them upon others from whom we steadfastly distance ourselves through the same kinds of practices of dehumanization that Joll undertook. That choice is ours, and ours alone.

The lesson of the pigs

Pursuing Costello's claim that there are no limits to our sympathetic imagination, I have suggested that we might identify with people who cause others to suffer and explored how and why we might resist doing so. But Costello goes further by suggesting that we can identify with animals, and she presses her audience to do this by connecting animal suffering at the hands of human beings to the suffering of the Nazis' human victims. In her response to Nagel, Costello says that we can know what it is like to be a bat because we know what it is like to *be*, and since bats also *are*, we can identify with them. Therefore, we can identify with their suffering. We can do so because 'an animal – and we are all animals – is an embodied soul.' Moreover, animals, like humans, have survival instincts like aggression, they form attachments, they feel pain, and so on. But Costello overlooks something important. We *know* what we share with animals, but coming to terms with it can be difficult because it may mean partly relinquishing our sense of being a higher form of life – a sense that justifies the domination of nature for our own ends, as in the case of animal slaughter. Coming to terms with our own animality calls for a posthumanist perspective that 'decenters' the human as a privileged subject (Braidotti, 2013; Wolfe, 2009). One strand of posthumanism, animal studies (Weil, 2012), urges us to incorporate our relationships with animals more fully into our sense of the world. This perspective is implicit in Costello's view that we ought to identify with animal suffering.

Posthumanism suggests an unconventional reading of George Orwell's *Animal Farm*, a satirical, allegorical warning about the dangers of communism. I can only begin that reading here. In a classic study of allegory, Angus Fletcher wrote that '[i]n the simplest terms, allegory says one thing and means another' (2012, p. 2). In this case, the story of the animals of Animal Farm signifies Orwell's assessment of communist visions of society. De Man (1972, p. 72) approaches the allegorical mode as a more dynamic one and suggests that it is structured by a perpetual tension between the allegory itself and the thing of which it is an allegory. This view is better suited to thinking about sympathetic identification, since the tension between allegory and what it represents catches the reader between two worlds and invites them to examine their own from a different point of view. While in one sense the animals in Orwell's novel are anthropomorphized humans – they speak, they experience human emotions, they engage self-consciously in political resistance – Orwell widens the gap between our world and theirs by emphasizing the animal *being* of the farm's denizens. The pigeons 'fluttered up to the rafters;' the horses, Boxer and Clover, walked on 'vast, hairy hoofs,' and so on (p. 4). He pays careful attention to what distinguishes us from them in a way that maintains their specific differences while inviting us to identify with beings that remind us of our selves. In Costello's terms, Orwell reminds us that *being* is something that we share with animals.

The animals rebel against their human oppressors and take over Manor Farm. They rename it Animal Farm, destroy most vestiges of human habitation (they retain some connections to the world of human beings – for instance, they leave parts of the main house intact) and develop an antihuman system of thought called Animalism, whose seven principles can be reduced to one: 'Four legs good, two legs bad' (p. 34). Led by a pig named Napoleon, the pigs of Animal Farm establish a regime ostensibly based on radical equality but that enriches them at the expense of the other animals. This regime ultimately devolves into violence, and in the end the animals adopt the ways of their former oppressors, the pigs marching on their hind legs while the sheep chant an altered version of the Animalist slogan: 'Four legs good, two legs better' (p. 133). The novel concludes with a sinister rapprochement between the animals and their former oppressors.

Orwell solicits our identification in three ways: First, he invites us to see ourselves in and as human beings complicit in the immiseration of animals. He also solicits our identification with animals in ways that support Costello's expansive view of the sympathetic imagination. He invites us to identify with them in two ways – as victims of violence and oppression, and as perpetrators of it, driven by instincts that we share with them as animals ourselves. Major, the old pig, gives voice to the experience of oppression in a diatribe against human beings, and later to the dream of freedom. He asks:

> Now, comrades, what is the nature of this life of ours? Let us face it: Our lives are miserable, laborious and short...those of us who are capable of it are forced to work to the last atom of our strength; and the very instant that our usefulness has come to an end we are slaughtered with hideous cruelty. (pp. 6–7)

Because we hear this description from one who lives such suffering, the animals' plight has even more urgency and an even stronger claim upon our moral and ethical attention than it had for Costello's audiences. And we hear, too, Major's diagnosis of the animals' oppression: 'But is this simply part of the order of nature?...No, comrades, a thousand times no!'

> Why then,' he asks, 'do we continue in this miserable condition? Because nearly the whole of the produce of our labour is stolen from us by human beings. There, comrades, is the answer to all our problems. It is summed up in a single word: Man. Man is the only real enemy we have. (p. 7)

With this stirring speech and a song of liberation that came to him in a dream, Major inspires dreams of freedom in the other animals and sows the seeds of revolt. Orwell's solicitation of our identification here is twofold: He invites us to see our own implication in their suffering *because* we are human, and he also invites us to identify with their suffering. Major accuses not just the owners of Manor Farm, but 'human beings,' or 'Man.' Read alongside Costello's indictment of the meat industry and humans' complicity in it, we might feel the weight of Major's accusation. And we might be tempted to deny or disavow our implication in animal suffering, just as seeing ourselves in Colonel Joll might repel us. One way to do so might be to deny the being that Costello insists we share with them – to insist, with Stern, that we are beings of a higher order and that animals exist for our use and consumption, nothing more.

But we might also identify with Major, and with the suffering of the animals for which he speaks. From this perspective, *Animal Farm* is an allegory of revolution that evokes human desires to determine the conditions of our own existence. Such desires animated the Russian, French and American revolutions against absolutism and, more recently, the 'Battle of Seattle,' a protest of the 1999 WTO meeting that erupted into violence against the 'rule' of global capitalism. The Occupy movement was similarly animated. Even the campaign and election of Donald Trump reflected a desire for liberation from an elitist politics by which his voters felt alienated and disenfranchised. Those who struggle for self-determination might see themselves in the struggle for self-determination at Manor Farm.

However, *Animal Farm* also reminds us that such violence can turn against revolutionary ideals – witness the Terror of the French Revolution,

Stalin's gulags, and even the rhetoric of freedom that animated the 'war on terror.' Witness, too, the creeping authoritarianism that marks the beginning of Trump's presidency. Just as struggles for freedom can turn in on themselves, the revolution in the name of freedom at Manor Farm devolved into a violent tyranny, rife with accusations of treachery and demands for ideological purity. For example, Molly the mare's fondness for human things like ribbons and beds made her especially suspect. Similarly, after 9/11 suspicions that anyone – especially Muslims – sympathized with the attackers engendered mistrust and rage in many citizens and in the state. Like 9/11 in relation to *Barbarians*, these are not mere historical and contemporary analogies – they are contexts of reception and narrative engagement. Perhaps we can also identify with this desire for purity in a time as polarized as ours, in which others are 'with' us or 'against' us and compromise is easily seen as betrayal. If we can identify with revolutionary impulses against suffering, we might equally identify with their perversion – another uncomfortable possibility that might repel us. After all, we might say, our ideals are pure. Our circumstances force us to betray those ideals – we do not choose to. That is one way, for instance, to justify torture in the wake of 9/11.

Thus far, my reading of *Animal Farm* suggests that it is as plausible to identify with the suffering of animals and the cruelty to which revolutions in the name of freedom may lead, as it is with the cruelty enacted by Colonel Joll in the name of security. But identifying with the animals and their struggle is harder because it requires us to loosen our grip on what makes us distinct as human beings, recognize what is animal in ourselves and relinquish the hierarchy of human and animal that Costello rejected, and upon which Abraham Stern insisted. Like Stern, we might cling to that hierarchy on theological grounds, or on grounds of a secular humanism which we may feel we cannot cede without ceding our humanity. Loosening our grip on humanism means letting go of something else, too: Enlightenment's conceit that human beings are masters of non-human nature (Connolly, 1991), a conceit that today underlies everything from factory farming to the production of genetically modified foods and the recent creation of embryos containing pig and human cells (Anonymous, 2017). In inviting us to identify with animals, Orwell presses us to recognize that we are driven by the same animal instincts that our 'civilization' represses (Freud, 1989). Reading *Animal Farm* reminds us of our evolutionary history, and that we are distinguished from animals not by the lack of these instincts, but by our capacity to reflect upon, modulate, channel and repress them through reason and the institutions of civilization.

Identifying with the pigs of animal farm reminds us, too, of the fragility of that repression. If we do not work through this fragility, work to acknowledge what is instinctual and animal in us, we may be more likely to unleash those same instincts on our fellow human beings. We might be seeing something like that today in American politics, where those alienated from politics and those who fear the rise of authoritarianism lash out at each other in the name not only of American values that each defines differently, but of survival itself. The conclusion of *Animal Farm* highlights the stakes of grappling with our animal instincts, and with humanity's fragility. The pigs and humans are playing cards. The game pauses and Napoleon makes a toast. Some of the other animals watch through a window, and observe the pigs' faces are changing: 'Some had five chins, some had four, some had three' (p. 60). The card game resumes and an argument erupts. Through the window, the other animals watch as the pigs' transformation is completed: The animals 'looked from pig to man, and from man to pig, and from pig to man again; but already it was impossible to say which was which' (Ibid.). The identification with animals that Orwell solicits is finally explicit: The pigs have become humans – suggesting that perhaps they were not simply anthropomorphized humans at the outset. Perhaps in them we can now see ourselves for the animals that we have always been – not only as fragile beings, but as dangerous ones too. Acknowledging both our fragility and our more dangerous instincts might enable us to work through them, concede our vulnerability and respond to its exposure with greater receptivity and generosity, and less cruelty and violence.

Conclusion

Our capacities for sympathetic identification might be more expansive than some imagine. We can identify not only with those who suffer – whether humans or perhaps even animals – but also with those whose actions contribute to suffering. The lesson Colonel Joll and Orwell's pigs teach us is that through sympathetic identification we may learn of our own capacities for cruelty and be reminded of our animal natures. We may respond with fierce resistance, denial and disavowal. We may even lash out at those who provide these reminders. But if we can accept and work through our capacities for cruelty we may cultivate receptivity and generosity toward others. This possibility has profound political implications: even in polarizing times we might be able to identify sympathetically with those whose experiences and worldviews seem so distant from and anathema to our own, and traverse the bridge across which we currently glare with derision, fear and anger. And we might, too, be more generous and receptive to the non-human world rather than simply dominating it for our own ends. There is no reason, in principle, why we cannot do these things. The choice to do so, or not, is ours.

Acknowledgments

The author wishes to think Bernard Schiff and two anonymous reviewers for helpful comments on earlier drafts of this essay.

Disclosure statement

No potential conflict of interest was reported by the author.

References

Anonymous. (2017). Human-pig embryo made. *Nature: International Weekly Journal of Science* [online], *542* (9). Retrieved November 9, 2017 from http://www.nature.com/nature/journal/v542/n7639/full/542009b.html
Arendt, H. (1972). *On revolution*. New York, NY: Penguin Classics.
Arendt, H. (2003). Collective responsibility. In J. Kohn (Ed.), *Responsibility and judgment* (pp. 147–158). New York, NY: Schocken.
Arendt, H. (2006). *Eichmann in Jerusalem*. New York, NY: Penguin Classics.
Attridge, D. (2004). *J.M. Coetzee and the ethics of reading*. Chicago: University of Chicago Press.
Bloom, P. (2016). *Against empathy: The case for rational compassion*. New York, NY: Ecco.
Booth, W. C. (1983). *The rhetoric of fiction*. Chicago: University of Chicago Press.
Booth, W. C. (1989). *The company we keep: An ethics of fiction*. Chicago: University of Chicago Press.
Braidotti, R. (2013). *The posthuman*. Cambridge: Polity Press.
Butler, J. (2006). *Precarious life: The powers of mourning and violence*. London: Verso.
Cavell, S. (2002). The avoidance of love. In (ed), (pp. 267–354).Cambridge: Cambridge University Press.
Coetzee, J. M. (1980). *Waiting for the barbarians*. New York, NY: Penguin Books.
Coetzee, J. M. (2004). *Elizabeth Costello*. New York, NY: Penguin Books.
Cohen, T. (2012). *Thinking of others: On the talent for metaphor*. Princeton: Princeton University Press.
Coles, R. (2016). *Visionary pragmatism: Radical and ecological democracy in neoliberal times*. Durham: Duke University Press.
Connolly, W. E. (1991). *Political theory and modernity*. London: Wiley-Blackwell.
Connolly, W. E. (2001). *Identity|Difference: Democratic negotiations of a political paradox*. Minneapolis: University of Minnesota Press.
De Man, P. (1972). *Allegories of reading: Figural language in Rousseau, Nietzsche, Rilke and Proust*. New Haven: Yale University Press.
Dickens, C. (2004). *David Copperfield*. New York, NY: Penguin Classics.
Dooley, G. (2010). *J.M. Coetzee and the power of narrative*. Amherst: Cambria Press.
Fletcher, A. (2012). *Allegory: The theory of a symbolic mode*. Princeton: Princeton University Press.
Foucault, M. (2004). *Abnormal: Lectures at the Collège de France, 1974–1975*. (G. Burchell, Trans.). New York, NY: Picador.
Freud, S. (1989). *Civilization and its discontents*. (J. Strachey, Trans.). New York, NY: WW Norton.

Goldman, A., & Craighill, P. (2014). New poll finds majority of Americans think torture was justified after 9/11 attacks. *Washington Post* [online]. Retrieved November 9, 2017 from https://www.washingtonpost.com/world/national-security/new-poll-finds-majority-of-americans-believe-torture-justified-after-911-attacks/2014/12/16/f6ee1208-847c-11e4-9534-f79a23c40e6c_story.html?utm_term=.85d4be5e3cc4

Head, D. (2009). *The Cambridge introduction to J.M. Coetzee*. Cambridge: Cambridge University Press.

Leist, A., & Singer, P. (2010). *J.M. Coetzee and ethics*. New York, NY: Columbia University Press.

Mar, R. A., Oatley, K., Hirsh, J., Dela Paz, J., & Peterson, J. B. (2006). Bookworms versus nerds: Exposure to fiction versus non-fiction, divergent associations with social ability, and the simulation of fictional social worlds. *Journal of Research in Personality, 40*(5), 694–712.

Mar, R. A., Oatley, K., & Peterson, J. B. (2009). Exploring the link between reading fiction and empathy: Ruling out individual differences and examining outcomes. *Communications, 34*(4), 407–428.

Markell, P. (2003). *Bound by recognition*. Princeton: Princeton University Press.

McGregor, J, & McGregor, T. (2013). *The empathy trap: understanding antisocial personalities*. UK: Sheldon Press.

McMaster, J. (1987). *Dickens the designer*. Houndsmill: The Macmillan Press.

Mulhall, S. (2009). *The wounded animal: J.M. Coetzee & the difficulty of reality in literature and philosophy*. Princeton: Princeton University Press.

Nagel, T. (1974). What is it like to be a bat? *The Philosophical Review, 83*(4), 435–450.

Nietzsche, F. (1989). *On the genealogy of morals and ecce homo*. (W. Kaufmann, Trans.). New York, NY: Vintage.

Nussbaum, M. (1995). *Poetic justice: The literary imagination and public life*. Boston: Beacon Press.

Orwell, G. (2012). *Animal farm*. New York, NY: Signet Classics.

Ricoeur, P. (1984). *Time and narrative, volume one*. (K. McLaughlin and D. Pellauer, Trans.). Chicago: University Chicago Press.

Ricoeur, P. (1995). *Oneself as another*. (K. Blamey, Trans.). Chicago: University of Chicago Press.

Rorty, R. (1989). *Contingency, irony and solidarity*. Oxford: Oxford University Press.

Sartre, J. (1995). *Anti-Semite and Jew: An exploration of the etiology of hate*. (G. Becker, Trans.). New York, NY: Schocken Books.

Schiff, J. L. (2014). *Burdens of responsibility: Narrative and the cultivation of responsiveness*. Cambridge: Cambridge University Press.

Sklenicka, C., & Spilka, M. (1994). A womb of his own: Lawrence's passional/parental view of childhood. In E. Goodenough, M. A. Heberle, & N. Sokoloff (Eds.), *Infant tongues: The voice of the child in literature* (pp. 164–183). Detroit: Wayne State University Press.

Valdés, M. J. (1991). *A Ricoeur reader: Reflection and imagination*. Toronto and Buffalo: University of Toronto Press.

Weil, K. (2012). *Thinking animals: Why animal studies now?* New York, NY: Columbia University Press.

Wolfe, C. (2009). *What is posthumanism?* Minneapolis: University of Minnesota Press.

Young, I. M. (2000). *Inclusion and democracy*. Oxford: Oxford University Press.

On representation(s): art, violence and the political imaginary of South Africa

Eliza Garnsey

ABSTRACT
The purpose of this article is to explore the multiple layers of representation which occur in the South Africa Pavilion at the Art Biennale in Venice in order to understand how they constitute and affect the state's political imaginary. By analysing three artworks (David Koloane's *The Journey*, Sue Williamson's *For thirty years next to his heart*, and Zanele Muholi's *Faces and Phases*) which were exhibited in the 2013 Pavilion, two key arguments emerge: 1) in this context artistic representation can be understood as a form of political representation; and, 2) these artists are simultaneously state and citizenry representatives. A tension emerges between the political imaginary desired by the South African state and the political imaginary enacted by its representatives. The article draws on seven months of participant observation fieldwork at the Biennale, which involved 76 interviews with people associated with the South Africa Pavilion, including government representatives, exhibition organisers, artists, and visitors. Part I explores the concept of representation in order to establish the two philosophical trajectories (political and artistic) with which this article engages – with particular reference to Michael Saward's framework of the representative claim. Part II explores the multiple representative claims which the three artists and their artworks enact.

Abbreviations: Biennale: Venice Art Biennale; DAC: Department of Arts and Culture; For thirty years: For thirty years next to his heart, by Sue Williamson; TRC: Truth and Reconciliation Commission; US: United States of America

Every two years around 85 states stage national pavilions at the Art Biennale in Venice (the Biennale). Membership of the Biennale is highly political, dependent on recognition by the Italian Government and other member states. Permanent member states – under half of the participants – are for the main part the geopolitical axes of the mid-twentieth century, a grouping that predominantly emerges from post-war Europe. The US, Great Britain, Germany, France, Russia, Israel, Japan and Egypt (to name a few) reside side by side in architecturally distinct art embassies at the geographical centre of the Biennale, the *Giardini* (gardens). Semi-permanent member states – those enjoying time-limited participation rights – are largely emerging out of periods of authoritarian rule or conflict to assert their position in the international community. South Africa, Argentina, Kosovo, Turkey, Indonesia, Lebanon and Chile are examples. These states exhibit inside converted warehouses in the *Arsenale* (arsenal), arms-length from the permanent members, under the watchful eye of an active naval base next door. Temporary member states – those which have to apply each year to participate – are often post-colonial states, or states whose political activities make the permanent members uneasy. Zimbabwe is a case in point. The exhibitions of these states are dotted around the city alongside those of nations which the Biennale does not officially recognise as states, such as Taiwan and Palestine.

Amid these geo-political cradles of influence in Venice, and the symbolic struggles over state power and legitimacy captured by the Biennale, the issue of representation – both political and artistic – is paramount. How states represent themselves through art affects how they are perceived and received by the international community, itself constituted through the exposition. This representation also reflects how states understand themselves at the national level. Artists become political representatives, selected (rather than elected) to represent the state, while art becomes the medium through which representation occurs.

The purpose of this article is to explore the multiple layers of representation which occur at the Biennale in order to understand how they constitute and affect the state's political imaginary, specifically in relation to South Africa. During the cultural boycott of apartheid (1968–1993), South Africa was banned from participating in the Biennale. It was not until the prospect of political change and democratic elections emerged that the state was invited to return. South Africa's contemporary participation in the Biennale is marked by this historically tense relationship. Its first national pavilion as a semi-permanent member in 2013 made efforts to show the breadth of the state's artistic output since the end of apartheid – to reinsert its art history back into the Biennale.[1] Three artworks in this exhibition stand out for how they draw attention to remembering, recording, and restoring violence as key acts of representation in post-apartheid South Africa. These artworks are David Koloane's *The Journey*, Sue Williamson's *For thirty years next to his heart*, and Zanele Muholi's *Faces and Phases*. Each artwork captures how the pervasive practices of discrimination and violence live on in South Africa, questioning what it means to represent a nation-state and citizenry that is in flux.

By undertaking a close analysis of these artworks, two key arguments emerge, specifically in relation to South Africa. First, in the context of the Biennale, artistic representation can be understood as a form of political representation.[2] The normative position contained in this argument posits that conceptions of representation should be expanded in order to more fully grapple with the politics that occurs through artistic processes outside of the bounds of the state. Second, artists at the Biennale are simultaneously state and citizenry representatives. They represent the state as well as the claims of citizen groups – the latter most often occurs through their artworks. In the 2013 South Africa Pavilion, the artists interrogated the state of the nation through the lens of the past. A tension arose between the political imaginary desired by the state and the political imaginary enacted by its representatives.[3]

The article adopts an interpretive standpoint, drawing on seven months of participant observation fieldwork at the Biennale, which included 76 interviews with people associated with the South Africa Pavilion, including government representatives, exhibition organisers, artists, Biennale staff members, and visitors, as well as archival research.[4] As such, the claims made throughout are particular, rather than universal, referring specifically to the South African case study. The article deliberately engages two research approaches – the analytical methodology of political theory and the narrative prose of art theory – in order to arrive at the discursive meditation and 'self-reflectiveness required to understand the complexities of visual global politics' (Bleiker, 2015, p. 872).

Part I briefly explores the concept of representation in order to establish the two philosophical trajectories with which this article engages. Part II analyses artworks by Koloane, Williamson and Muholi, exploring the multiple forms of representation which these artists and artworks enact.

The clash of representations

The concept of representation encompasses a wide range of meanings, approaches, and emphases for different areas of study. Broadly speaking, political representation remains most commonly conceived as a 'substantive acting for others' (Pitkin, 1967). That is, the process through which governments and their officials are responsive to constituents, which in turn establishes the legitimacy of democratic institutions. How this process occurs and what it achieves is the subject of continued debate (Brito Vieira, 2017; Brito Vieira & Runciman, 2008; Shapiro, Stokes, Wood, & Kirshner, 2010). Struggles over the meaning of political representation continue to captivate numerous political theorists. Efforts to define political representation highlight its contested semantic domain (Sintomer, 2013) as well as the concept's impurity (Disch, 2012).

The same can be said of artistic representation, although art theory appears somewhat more comfortable with the ambiguity of the concept . Artistic representation most often relates to the manner in which meaning is communicated through signs and symbols (Fernie, 1995, pp. 358–360, Hall, 1997). How this representation functions aesthetically rather than mimetically, and what the value of this communication is – power, knowledge, or myth production – remains the subject of discussion within art theoretical discourse (see Nochlin, 1999; Pollock, 1988). Representation in relation to art also often bears the implication that artworks resemble 'real life' objects. Such representation (or naturalism) in art is sometimes denigrated as being aesthetically unsophisticated or as limiting interpretation. Representation in these terms can be pejorative.

The multifarious understandings of representation across both political and artistic domains mean that the concept remains open to a variety of interpretations. While this may cause confusion within the literature, this article is less interested in pinpointing a correct theory of representation. Rather, it seeks to understand what political and artistic representation are *doing*, and what claims are being made about representation, through close interpretive engagement with an empirical case study.

Despite its conceptual pluralism, the word representation contains an inherent paradox which remains foundational to most discussions of the concept regardless of disciplinary boundaries. That is, the paradox of simultaneous presence and absence: 'the presence that comes from being re-*presented*, and the absence that comes from needing to be *re*-presented' (Brito Vieira & Runciman, 2008). Representatives stand in place of absent constituents, in order to present the concerns of constituents to government. Signs and symbols signify absent objects and ideas in order to impart knowledge about their value. The act, or event, of representing involves the implicit presence of the person, group, object, or idea being represented, at the same time as it necessitates their absence. The dynamic potential of representation simultaneously emerges from its multiple modes of operation (political, artistic) which are connected by this underlying presence-absence paradox.

Until recently aesthetics has been largely sidelined in discussions of political representation, having been perceived at best as an analogy of political representation and at worst as a distraction from politics. This is despite the aesthetic turn in international political theory being relatively long established. Recent scholarship on political representation has begun to recognise the value of aesthetics and the close relationship between aesthetic and political representation (Ankersmit, 2002; Saward, 2010), as well as to revive the performative and imaginative aspects of political representation which are largely overlooked in foundational accounts (Brito Vieira, 2017; Disch, 2012). This scholarship shares key ideas about political representation being a dynamic and creative act constituted through a process of exchange. Political representation contains an aesthetic moment because the represented has to be evoked by the representive and judged by the represented (Saward, 2010). In this moment emerges a gap between the represented and the representative (Ankersmit, 2002): this gap is the very location of politics (Bleiker, 2001, p. 510).

The aesthetic moment and performative act are key to understanding artistic representation as a form of political representation. Michael Saward (2010, p. 44) argues that political representation is an ongoing process of claim-making and claim-receiving rather than 'a fact established by institutional election or selection'. He proposes that representative claims consist of five interconnected dimensions: maker, subject, object, referent, and audience. For example, '[a]ntiglobalization demonstrators (makers) set up themselves and their movements (subjects) as representatives of the oppressed and marginalized (object) to Western governments (audience)' (Saward, 2010, p. 37). The referent in this example is the actual people who comprise the oppressed and marginalized. This framework places particular emphasis on the making of symbols of the represented, as well as the role of the audience in not simply receiving claims but making counter-claims. By doing so, Saward shows how political representation is deeply connected to aesthetic representation and the circular (performative) relationship between represented and representative.

This article goes one step further to explore how artistic representation can be understood as a form of political representation. The distinction between aesthetic and artistic locates the article specifically in relation to art, rather than aesthetic philosophy broadly understood. Taking Saward's framework as a starting point, the next section explores how Biennale viewers (audience) play a central role in receiving the claims of artists and artworks (both makers) about violence (subject) as representatives of South Africa (object) and particular citizen groups (referent) within the state and make counter-claims about the artworks on display.[5] The institutional structure of the Biennale in the form of national pavilions imposes state-centered political representation onto artworks which in another context may be interpreted very differently. Herein lies the gap between representative and represented which both designates particular artworks as highly political and locates the political imaginary being enacted through artistic representation.

Although political theory has begun to recognise the close relationship between political and aesthetic representation, and although art theory regularly grapples with politics in discussions of representation, neither side has gone as far to suggest that artistic representation can be understood as a form of political representation. This article seeks to fill this gap. Only then is it possible to more fully comprehend political representation as it increasingly occurs in transnational spaces (outside of state confines) and through 'non-traditional' actors. The article also responds to five gaps in discussions of political representation noted by Saward (2010), the need to: 1) focus on what representation is doing (not fix upon what it is); 2) understand the constitutive role of representation; 3) employ interpretive depth (not normative theorising); 4) highlight the dynamics of what is going on in representation (not focus on an ideal typology); and, 5) take non-electoral modes of representation seriously. Addressing these gaps enables greater understanding of the role of representation(s) in seeing how politics functions (for and through whom) and how it might function differently. In the context of South Africa, these imperatives are critical.

State of representation

In his speech opening the South Africa Pavilion, Arts and Culture Minister Paul Mashatile (2013) said that the exhibition was 'about using the arts to question and challenge our reading of the past, to reach a new understanding of it and to craft a new and inclusive narrative for our country'; calling the 17 artists in the exhibition ambassadors, their 'voices... as rich and varied as those of the citizens of our beautiful land'. Artists are interpellated by the Government as being agents of the state; they have diplomatic roles as ambassadors and representatives of the state. The artists also have political roles as representatives of different groups of citizens within the state. This creates a tension between the artists representing the interests of the state, and the artists (and their artworks) representing the interests of citizens which do not necessarily align with those of the state.

Contrary to the Government's desired reinterpretation of the past to create a new inclusive narrative, the exhibition, entitled *Imaginary Fact: Contemporary South African Art and the Archive*, used the lens of the past to draw attention to the ongoing conflicts which persist within the state. The disruption of the state's political imaginary was made possible by the structure of the Pavilion. After a public tender process, the Department of Arts and Culture (DAC) selected the National Arts Festival – a non-profit arts organisation – to stage the exhibition based on the theme of *Imaginary Fact*. However, many of the exhibiting artists were only selected and announced after the tender was already awarded. This meant that the state had limited prior knowledge or control over the content of the exhibition; effectively being kept at arms-length to the artistic decisions made by the curatorial committee. Although this process was deliberately enacted by DAC in order to distance itself from the opaque selection process and ensuing accusations of nepotism which plagued the 2011 Pavilion (see Blackman, 2012), it resulted in an exhibition which created the conditions for a tension to arise between the state's desired representation and the artists' representation of the state.

Imaginary Fact drew on two invitations proffered by the overarching theme of the Biennale, *The Encyclopedic Palace* (Gioni, 2013) – to journey and to assemble. The theme encouraged an encyclopedic journey through history; to see how knowledge is produced through the organisation of artworks and how artworks organise certain kinds of knowledge. The theme also implied monumentality and the assemblage of artworks on an encyclopedic scale. The 17 artists in *Imaginary Fact* presented a journey over 20 years through diverse methods and mediums (Maart, 2013). The exhibition's title alluded to the creation of knowledge and the knowledge of creativity; playing on the idea that facts evolve from imaginative processes over time as well as from the gathering of these processes through archives. *Imaginary Fact* suggested it would impart facts and simultaneously invited reflection on these facts and their construction, the veracity of which were always in question through reference to imagination.

Violence was a dominant subject within *Imaginary Fact*: the unresolved violence of apartheid-era crimes; the structural violence of pervasive practices of discrimination; and, the physical violence which people continue to be subjected. Three artworks stood out for the ways in which they emphasised that remembering violence, recording violence, and restoring violence are crucial responsibilities of political representation within South Africa. These artworks were David Koloane's *The Journey*, Sue Williamson's *For 30 Years next to his heart*, and Zanele Muholi's *Faces and Phases*.

Koloane (b. 1938), Williamson (b. 1941) and Muholi (b. 1972) are highly influential figures within South African contemporary art. In their roles as practicing artists, curators, writers, and educators, they are all involved in forms of arts activism and have founded key arts organisations. All three artists regularly exhibit internationally, all are represented by major commercial galleries in South Africa and abroad, all have artworks in the permanent collections of major arts institutions around the globe, and between them they have won every major art award in South Africa (see Perryer, 2004; Williamson, 2009). Their artworks which were exhibited in the South Africa Pavilion are regularly shown in major exhibitions overseas. The reputation of these artists and the exhibition history of their artworks is important in establishing these artists as representatives, especially in the context of the Biennale where they serve as representatives of the state, but their artworks create a critical view of the state's political imaginary.

Remembering violence

David Koloane's *The Journey* 1998 (Figure 1) is a series of 19 oil pastel works on paper which reconstructs the sequence of events that lead to Steve Biko's death: from his arrest, interrogation, detention, and autopsy. Biko was leader of the Black Consciousness Movement and an anti-apartheid activist, whose murder in 1977 at the hands of members of the Security Branch became a discursive event in the fight against apartheid and remains a discursive event in the nation's transition – one that often arose in interviews and conversations with South African decision makers and artists.

Figure 1. David Koloane *The Journey* (1998) series of 19 acrylic and oil pastels on paper, each 29 × 42 cm (details). Courtesy of the artist and Goodman Gallery.

The Journey engages multiple layers of representation. Firstly, by imagining the events of Biko's death Koloane is making a claim to represent a pivotal figure and moment in South Africa's struggle for humanity. Koloane created *The Journey* in response to observing the perpetrators of Biko's death seeking amnesty at the Truth and Reconciliation Commission (TRC). Having worked with Biko at Black Community Programmes – an organisation running development projects – in the 1970s, the process of making the artwork was a way for Koloane to remember Biko's murder and reflect on the subsequent process of amnesty: 'It left a deep impression in my mind... to see how dangerous the apartheid government was, that people could just disappear and be killed like that' (Interview Koloane). *The Journey* is deeply personal and at the same time highly political. The artwork depicts the intimate scenes of Biko's torturous journey; restoring 'the simplicity of the horror of torture and murder to a collective consciousness' (Maart, 2013, p. 18). It is a product of Koloane's reaction to Biko's death: 'It was one of the most brutal things I've ever experienced emotionally' (Interview Koloane). By drawing on his personal response to the murder in order to imagine the event, the artist memorialises Biko, representing his prominent legacy in the anti-apartheid struggles and continued legacy in the post-apartheid transition.

Secondly, the artwork bears witness to the contested truths which emerged during the perpetrators' testimonies at the TRC; questioning what it means to enact truth and reconciliation. In 1999 – the year after Koloane created *The Journey* and in the same year the artwork was first exhibited abroad – the five surviving policemen (Harold Snyman, Daniel Petrus Siebert, Jacobus Johannes Oosthuysen Beneke, Rubin Marx, and Gideon Johannes Nieuwoudt) responsible for Biko's death were denied amnesty on the grounds that they failed to disclose the full truth and that their version of how Biko died was 'so improbable and contradictory that it had to be rejected as false' (Truth and Reconciliation Commission, 1999).

Despite admitting to taking part in Biko's murder and being denied amnesty for it, the five men were never prosecuted. In 2003, the South African Justice Ministry announced it had insufficient evidence to prosecute for murder and that it would be unable to lay any other charges because the timeframe for prosecution had expired. While the amnesty hearings afforded an important opportunity for public confession, the TRC has been criticised for not asking more detailed questions during these hearings which would facilitate criminal prosecution if amnesty was denied. The result of the TRC and the inability of the Justice Ministry to prosecute, means that Biko's killers have in effect received de facto amnesty (Nagy, 2004, p. 25). The lack of resolution around Biko's death remains an open wound in post-apartheid South Africa, particularly for Biko's family who challenged the constitutionality of the amnesty process at its initial stages (see Mihai, 2016). Given Koloane created *The Journey* one year before Biko's killers were denied amnesty and six years before the Justice Ministry's decision not to prosecute, the commemoration of Biko's murder in the artwork takes on heightened political significance; it becomes an unintended symbol of the limitations of South Africa's transition, representing the unresolved issues which Biko's case has come to exemplify. *The Journey* complicates the progressive narrative of the TRC by drawing attention to its limitations; reflecting the ongoing claims for truth and justice which exist in South Africa.

Thirdly, the artwork is received by viewers as a warning against the repetition of such crimes: 'It's a constant reminder to say look this is where we were and we can't go back there' (Interview Exhibition Management). This claim aligns with Koloane's intention: 'to remind people that even if we have a black government it doesn't mean things are going to be rosy. This [Biko's death] could still happen with a black government' (Interview Koloane). By remembering the events surrounding Biko's death, the artwork contemplates how those events came to be, but also how these circumstances are potentially not unique to apartheid.

It is not necessary to be familiar with Biko's story in order to access the politics of, and racial conflict within, *The Journey*. In the context of the South Africa Pavilion, *The Journey* is circumscribed by the nation's political tensions and oppressive past. The sequential images portray the torture of a black body at the hands of white bodies. The repeated figure of Biko is Christ-like, each frame becoming a station of the cross, progressing through the final days of life. This sense of martyrdom was increased by the artwork being hung in a low-lit area of the Pavilion. The imagery in *The Journey* is abstracted by the densely coloured layers of oil pastel. This style increases the tension; the artwork becomes more disturbing the more it is looked at: 'there is a quality in those works, an impressionistic quality that, for me, keeps it trembling and living now' (Interview Curatorial Team Member). The blurred lines between abstraction and realism in *The Journey* avoid sensationalising torture and death. The symbolism and style of the artwork, coupled with its deliberate installation, implicates Biko in a redemptive narrative. His sacrifice comes to symbolize South Africa's sins. Rather than representing the reconciled political imaginary of the state Koloane comes to represent the ongoing struggles of a nation and the people within its borders.

Through his art Koloane is also making a broader claim to be reclaiming the space which was restricted under apartheid: 'Apartheid was a politics of space more than anything... and much of the apartheid legislation was denying people the right to move... Claiming art is also reclaiming space' (Koloane, 1999). Not only is the South African state reclaiming their space in the international community by participating in the Biennale (from which they were previously banned), but through the exhibition Koloane is reclaiming the space which under apartheid he was denied. This reclaiming of space is about physically inhabiting space through art, as well as believing in the right to that space. There is a sense then that the issues of representation at stake in Koloane's *The Journey* are about enacting claim-making and claim-receiving, as well as *re*-claiming political representation through art.

Recording violence

Sue Williamson's *For thirty years next to his heart* 1990 (Figure 2) portrays evidence of the apartheid Pass Laws. The artwork depicts 49 colour laser prints of Ncithakalo John Ngesi's *dompas* (passbook) – a document required under the apartheid government to be carried by every black South African over the age of 16 at all times. Dompas contained personal information – photographs, fingerprints, and addresses – employment history, employer's signatures and reports, travel and residential permissions, and other identification information. A person's rights to live, work in, and visit, certain areas – as well as their family's rights – were jeopardised if an employer did not endorse their dompas, regardless of the reason. Around 18 million arrests for failure to produce a dompas on demand occurred between its introduction in 1952 and repeal in 1986 (Savage, 1986). As a document of oppression and control, the dompas was a hated symbol of apartheid.

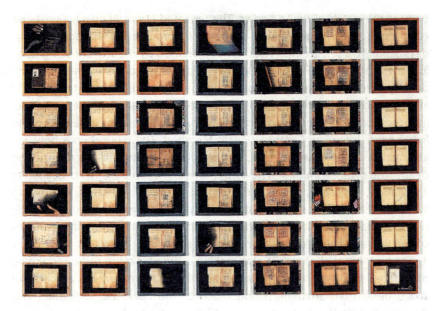

Figure 2. Sue Williamson, *For thirty years next to his heart* (1990) series of 49 photocopies in unique hand-crafted frames, 182.9 × 261 cm. Courtesy of the artist and Goodman gallery.

Unlike *The Journey*, which re-claims space through the imaginative remembering of pivotal events, *For thirty years* draws attention to the restriction of space through the recording of a document designed to deny people the right to move. The artwork becomes evidence of several claims about representation. This is not to say it only serves a mimetic function, rather it captures the invasion of private life by public authorities. In doing so, the artwork subverts the apartheid claims on private life by making these claims public; enabling claims about the representation of structural violence to be made and received.

Firstly, *For thirty years* represents a highly personal item carried by Ngesi, recording aspects of his life; his movement, his employment, his earnings, his encounters with other people. As the title suggests, the dompas was held close to his heart. Yet it is not an object of love, but an object forced upon Ngesi's body by the apartheid government; tellingly, Ngesi gave his dompas to Williamson, he did not want it back (cited in Maart, 2013, p. 163). The dompas was highly personal, but at the same time it was also highly depersonalised, being an instrument of discrimination against the majority of the population, perpetrated by the state. The inhumanity of the apartheid system is exposed by its invasion into, and regulation of, Ngesi's personal life.

The tension between private and public, personal and political, is evident not only in the subject matter of *For thirty years* but in the way the artist depicts the dompas. Glimpses of Ngesi's hands remind viewers that this document belongs to someone, it is about someone's life. By contrast, the highly gridded display of the artwork is symbolic of bureaucratic control. Each frame is made from material relating to the page pictured. For instance, bank notes cover the frame of the taxes section and tin is used to make the frame of the employment section, referring to Ngesi's work in a mine. Using a colour photocopier to create the prints reinforces the sense of officialdom in the artwork.

Secondly, *For thirty years* is simultaneously evidence of Ngesi's life and evidence of apartheid's mechanisms of control; an indictment of the system and a warning against it. Williamson draws on this evidence to expose the gross injustices which the Pass Laws proliferated: the artwork testifies to this effect. The artist documented a dompas so people who never had to carry one did not 'forget about quite how horrific they were' (Interview Williamson). Williamson is making dual representative claims about the people subjected to the dompas system and those who were not, preserving the dompas in order to prevent its return.

The artwork records the dompas system and it also becomes evidence of participation in that system. Names of companies and signatures of people are found on every page: 'One is implicated in the whole system of passbooks whether you want to be or not, because it's your signature, you as an employer have this power over the people that you wish to employ' (Interview Williamson). The artwork draws attention to the involvement of people beyond official levels, where so many ordinary people were complicit in proliferating an unjust system. It is not only evidence of Ngesi's life being circumscribed by state control, but it is also evidence of people observing and participating in that state control. The artwork implicates certain groups in the maintenance of apartheid, while revealing the structural violence of that system against other groups, divided along racial lines. This has the effect of creating a tension between the representative claims being made and the representative claims being received by multiple groups of people.

Thirdly, *For thirty years* presents a familiar visual vocabulary for viewers unfamiliar with the dompas. The dompas looks like a passport, which similarly allows and restricts freedom but on an international scale – an increasingly critical issue in current debates about statehood and migration. This familiar imagery also makes the artwork tangible. A viewer from Australia, almost in tears in front of *For thirty years*, said they were upset because they had been previously unaware of the severity of the injustices under apartheid. Through the representation of the evidence of structural violence, the artwork emphasises the continuing claims of people subjected to the dompas system, the complicity of others in enacting this system, and is an indictment of the system.

There is also an inherent paradox of freedom in *For thirty years*: it captures a false 'freedom' imposed by a repressive regime: 'it's a symbol of restriction and a symbol of freedom because if you had this passport you could go everywhere' (Interview Biennale Staff Member). The original unfreedom of the dompas is freely transported as an archive. The artwork is well travelled, being regularly exhibited outside of South Africa. Its transformation into an artwork turns a hated symbol of apartheid into a public denunciation of that regime.

Restoring violence

Zanele Muholi's series of portraits of LGBTI people in South Africa, entitled *Faces and Phases 2006-2013* (Figure 3), restores black queer visibility. The black and white photographs portray a marginalised segment of South African society – marginalized in terms of being erased from historical canons, and subjected to severe discrimination and physical violence resulting from ingrained heteronormativity and apartheid's major legacy of intolerance. Through the photographic series Muholi is restoring representation,

Figure 3. Zanele Muholi, *Faces and Phases* (2006–2013) series of 200 photographic prints, unframed black and white digital photographic prints, each 30.5 × 44 cm. Installation view of *Imaginary Fact*, 2013 Venice Art Biennale. Photography by Giovanna Zen, courtesy of the National Arts Festival.

creating 'images of people like me for reference point for posterity' (Interview Muholi), rebuilding a legacy of queer identity in the 'new' South Africa.

Ten gaps in the grid of 200 photographs signify the missing portraits of people who have been the victims of hate crimes. Homophobic violence is an ongoing problem in South Africa. Violence often takes the form of 'corrective rape' – where men rape women in order to 'cure' their lesbianism (Jody Kollapen cited in Martin, Kelly, Turquet, & Ross, 2009). These crimes are not only underreported due to associated stigma, but they are also under-recorded by the police and seldom prosecuted as hate crimes on the basis of sexual orientation, which contributes to the silence around such violence (see Mwambene & Wheal, 2015). The simultaneous presence and absence of the portraits draws attention to this violence.

Muholi defines herself as a visual activist rather than a visual artist (Williamson, 2009, p. 130). Her artistic practice arises from activism, but it is also a lived imperative. She documents ongoing cases of rape, assault, and murder: 'I [go] from one place to the next place documenting, listening to people, their needs. If there is a case that needs to be referred to an organisation, I refer that case' (Interview Muholi). By refusing to call herself an artist, Muholi is making a claim about the form of representation she is practicing. Her visual activism is explicitly political representation, yet it is also artistic representation as it is created and mediated through her photographic works which are exhibited in major art exhibitions.

While *Faces and Phases* restores black queer visibility, it is simultaneously an indictment of current discrimination in South Africa: a call to action. Muholi is advocating for equal rights and treatment, drawing attention to the violence and discrimination faced by the LGBTI community: 'The whole point is to educate the next person who is not a member of the LGBTI community' (Interview Muholi). There is a deliberate element of didacticism in Muholi's work. However, for audiences unfamiliar with these issues, it is difficult to grasp them from the photographs alone, without accompanying text or information which explains who is being represented and why. In the context of the Biennale viewers 'needed to be guided into that process' (Interview Exhibition Management). *Faces and Phases* successfully de-essentializes the gender of the people represented in and by the photographs, yet it does so to such a degree that the claims being made about representation require further elaboration. The claim-making of the artist does not easily, or necessarily, align with the claim-receiving of the audience.

There is a tension between celebration and bereavement in *Faces and Phases*. Five percent of the people represented in the artwork – whose portraits are absent – are the victims of fatal violence, while the remaining 95% embody an enduring community. The missing photographs mourn absent people, while the existing photographs celebrate the people present. The direct gaze of each person looking out from each photograph, creates a personal connection with viewers: 'Muholi's work really puts you in the moment of these women staring at you, being almost canonised in a way that makes you consider where they come from, who they are, and what they were subject to after all these years of democracy' (Interview Curatorial Team Member). This gaze also counter-exerts power, the photographs are of people not of art objects to be looked at (Maart, 2013, p. 23). The series is about more than looking. *Faces and Phases* is about restoring and celebrating representation, it is also about challenging why the absence of representation exists in the first place – both regarding individual representation of victims of hate crimes and the collective representation of the LGBTI community.

For the artist, *Faces* expresses the people in the photographs and her face-to-face encounters with them. While *Phases* signifies 'the transition from one stage of sexuality or gender expression and experience to another' (Muholi, 2010, p. 6). However, there is also a more disturbing association to the word 'phase' which is sometimes used pejoratively to refer to sexuality as something that can be overcome. In the context of South Africa phase also evokes a political association with the nation's transition.

Including *Faces and Phases* in the South Africa Pavilion draws attention to the politics within South Africa which surrounds Muholi's visual activism. In 2009, the then Arts and Culture Minister, Lulama Xingwana, refused to open an exhibition featuring Muholi's work on the basis that it was 'immoral' because it depicted images of lesbians: '[o]ur mandate is to promote social cohesion and nation building. I left the exhibition because it expressed the very opposite of this' (Xingwana in Munro, 2012, p. 219). This event sparked controversy in South Africa both within and outside of art circles; becoming a discursive event noted by many interview participants when speaking about Muholi's work.

The Minister's statement presupposes a vision of the nation circumscribed by heteronormativity. This gendered form of political identity in the 'new' South Africa betrays its disintegrating rainbow nationalism, but it also echoes apartheid-era strategies of silencing alterity. For Xingwana, social cohesion appears to be less about representing all citizens and in the process of doing so addressing the struggles of marginalised communities, and more about constructing an image of the nation built on a narrow conception of citizen-hood. The Minister's actions are indicative of the discrimination experienced by the LGBTI community at some of the highest levels, emphasising the vast gap between the conceptual liberalness of South Africa's constitution and its political practice: 'On the face of it we have this very liberal constitution which forbids discrimination of any kind and in fact it's just not adhered to, even by the government itself' (Interview Artist).

The inclusion of Muholi's work in the 2013 South Africa Pavilion challenges the views of the former Arts and Culture Minister. In opening the South African Pavilion, Arts and Culture Minister, Mashatile (2013) described all the artists in the exhibition as 'immensely talented and, as a nation, we are proud of them and of the opportunity to showcase them to the world'. The sentiment of this statement is significant because it stands in opposition to the views expressed by the previous minister and it also stands in opposition to the longer running history of discrimination against LGBTI people in South Africa. Despite Mashatile and Xingwana belonging to the same political party – the African National Congress – Mashatile's statement is a concerted effort to distinguish his leadership of arts and culture from his predecessor's.

While DAC ostensibly had little control over the inclusion of *Faces and Phases* in the South African Pavilion – the artist was selected and announced by the curatorial team at a late stage – it is significant that they did not distance themselves from the exhibition in light of the previous Minister's actions. Rather the Government embraced Muholi and her work as an example of South Africa's liberal development: 'to destroy the myth that Africa as a whole persecute people because of their sexual orientation' (Interview Molobi, Commissioner of the Pavilion and Consul-General of South Africa to Milan). The inclusion of *Faces and Phases* in this international context is intended to differentiate the state from other nations on the African continent who criminalise homosexuality. However, although homosexuality is not criminalised in South Africa, it is far from accepted. Muholi's artwork complicates the Government's political imaginary by exposing the ongoing struggle for representation in a society plagued by prejudice.

The inclusion of *Faces and Phases* stems from two competing attempts to restore representation: the Government's claim to restore South Africa's representation in the international community, seeking to cultivate an image of the state's inclusivity and to distinguish it from other states and, the artist's and the curatorial team's claim to expose continuing discrimination in the 'new' South Africa – and to restore representation of the black queer community. There is also a third dimension of restoring representation at stake. By exhibiting in *Imaginary Fact* Muholi is representing South Africa. This is important because it signals support for her artwork as one of the representatives of the state at the Biennale – which would not have been possible under the apartheid regime (or arguably under the former minister). This inclusion is significant because it is actively redressing the imbalances of representation directly resulting from apartheid.

Beyond its specific relationship to South Africa, *Faces and Phases* opens up a wider discussion about LGBTI representation in the member states of the

Biennale: 'People don't think about the past, as in all the other works [in *Imaginary Fact*], because it's something they immediately recognized as current and contemporary, a universal theme that is a social issue also in Italy' (Interview Biennale Staff Member). Although *Faces and Phases* is focused on practices of discrimination in South Africa, it also responds to broader practices of discrimination not unique to South Africa. In the context of the Biennale, Muholi's visual activism provokes reflection on the practices of other nation-states. This fourth representative claim is especially significant given that *Faces and Phases* is widely exhibited internationally.

Violence reverberates throughout the artworks by Koloane, Williamson and Muholi. Remembering, recording, and restoring violence become key responsibilities for these artists in their dual role as state representatives and citizenry representatives at the Biennale. Each artist questions what it means to represent a state that is in flux. They capture three ways in which the pervasive practices of discrimination live on in South Africa, leaving a sense that the process of political transition is not only unfinished, but must be remembered, recorded, and restored so as not to be repeated.

Conclusion

In the case of South Africa at the 2013 Biennale, the representations of violence enacted by particular artists and artworks can be understood as a form of political representation, constituted through creative acts and a process of exchange between representatives and represented. Returning to Saward's framework, the artists and artworks (makers), as representatives of South Africa (object) and particular citizen groups (referent), evoke images and symbols of violence (subject) which are judged by viewers (audience) in an ongoing process of claim-making and claim-receiving. Koloane makes claims about *The Journey* being a remembered archive of Biko's death, a way for him to personally process the emotion of the event. Through the artwork Biko is memorialised as a pivotal figure in South Africa's struggle for humanity. The artwork bears witness to the ongoing debates about truth versus justice which pervade contemporary South Africa, becoming an unintended symbol of the limitations of the state's transition. *The Journey* is received as a warning against the repetition of such crimes, while its presence also re-claims the space which was denied under apartheid.

Through the representation of the evidence of structural violence, Williamson's *For thirty years* emphasises the continuing claims of people subjected to the dompas system, the complicity of others in enacting this system, and is received by viewers as an indictment of the system. Like *The Journey*, it is a warning against the system. The artwork subverts the claims on private life made under apartheid by making them publicly visible. Muholi's visual activism makes a claim to restore black queer visibility and is simultaneously a call to action against ongoing discrimination. While the Government seeks to cultivate an image of the state's inclusivity through *Faces and Phases*, the artist and artwork expose the continuing practices of discrimination in the 'new' South Africa.

By understanding artistic representation as a form of political representation, it is possible to more fully engage with politics as it becomes dispersed to transnational spaces beyond state confines and is no longer the sole purview of elected representatives (if indeed it ever was). South Africa gains legitimacy through its membership of the Biennale, itself an international organisation. This legitimation occurs through artistic representation. Koloane, Williamson and Muholi are responsible not only for representing the state through the national pavilion to an international audience, but also for representing the differing claims of citizens through their artworks. Gaps emerge amid the representative claims which are made and received, creating a tension between the state's desired political imaginary of inclusivity and reconciliation, and the artists' political imaginary capturing the ongoing problems and divides within the state. Thinking about artistic representation as a form of political representation enables a better understanding of what can be seen and said, who has the ability to see it and say it, and how it is possible to *know* and *do* politics in different ways.

Notes

1. During the preceding decade (1993–2013) South Africa was a sporadic temporary member of the Biennale. In 2013 the Government secured a ten-year lease on an exhibition space, making South Africa a semi-permanent member.
2. This argument extends the idea that art is a radical form of political participation in times of political transition (Garnsey, 2016).
3. The concept of the political imaginary being engaged broadly relates to how political identities, groups, communities, and states are constructed and imagined by the people who perceive themselves to be part of them (Anderson, 2006).
4. Interviews were conducted May – December 2013 in Italy and May – November 2014 in South Africa. Statements made in interviews are non-attributable to individual people, only their titles will appear. Where a name appears, the quote is attributed with their permission.
5. The idea that artworks are makers may cause unease in the context of political representation, especially since Hannah Pitkin (1967) claimed that inanimate objects could not be held responsible to constituencies. However, in relation to artistic representation W.J.T Mitchell (1995) argues that artworks are animated beings with desires which have the power to affect political lives.

Acknowledgments

I would like to thank Mihaela Mihai, Mathias Thaler and the three anonymous reviewers for their invaluable comments and guidance. Thank you also to my doctoral supervisor Duncan Bell and to participants in the 'Imagining Violence' workshop at ECPR Joint Sessions 2016 for their insightful engagement with an earlier version of this article. Many thanks to all those interviewed, anonymous and named. Thank you to the artists, Goodman Gallery, and the National Arts Festival for their invaluable insight and support, and the use of images. This work is supported by the British Academy, grant number PF170086. The research was also supported by Ca'Foscari University; the Cambridge Political Economy Society Trust; the Centre of Governance and Human Rights at the University of Cambridge and the Centre for Human Rights and the Institute for International and Comparative Law in Africa at the University of Pretoria, through a grant from the David and Elaine Potter Foundation; Queens' College Cambridge; the Smuts Memorial Fund, managed by the University of Cambridge in memory of Jan Christiaan Smuts; the University of Cambridge Fieldwork Fund; and, the University of Witwatersrand.

Disclosure statement

No potential conflict of interest was reported by the author.

References

Anderson, B. (2006). *Imagined communities: Reflections on the origin and spread of nationalism*. London: Verso.
Ankersmit, F. R. (2002). *Political representation*. Stanford: Stanford University Press.
Blackman, M. (2012). *Taxpayers dish out R10m for 'private' exhibition [online]*. Retrieved June 6, 2016, from http://mg.co.za/article/2012-04-02-taxpayers-dish-up-for-private-initiative-exhibition
Bleiker, R. (2001). The aesthetic turn in international political theory. *Millennium, 30*, 509–533.
Bleiker, R. (2015). Pluralist methods for visual global politics. *Millennium, 43*(3), 872–890.
Brito Vieira, M. (2017). Performative imaginaries: Pitkin versus Hobbes on political representation. In M. Brito Vieira (Ed.), *Reclaiming representation: Contemporary advances in the theory of political representation* (pp. 25–49). New York: Routledge.
Brito Vieira, M., & Runciman, D. (2008). *Representation*. Cambridge: Polity. Unpaginated electronic book.

Disch, L. (2012). The impurity of representation and the vitality of democracy. *Cultural Studies*, *26*(2–3), 207–222.
Fernie, E. (Ed.). (1995). *Art history and its methods: A critical anthology*. London: Phaidon.
Garnsey, E. (2016). Rewinding and unwinding: Art and justice in times of political transition. *International Journal of Transitional Justice*, *10*, 471–491.
Gioni, M. (2013). *Il palazzo enciclopedico*. Venice: Fondazione La Bienale di Venezia.
Hall, S. (Ed.). (1997). *Representation: Cultural representations and signifying practices*. Milton Keynes: Open University.
Koloane, D. (1999). In D. Hardin & M. Grove (Eds.), *Claiming art reclaiming space: Post-apartheid art from South Africa*. Washington: National Museum of African Art.
Maart, B. (2013). *Imaginary fact: Exhibition catalogue*. Grahamstown: National Arts Festival.
Martin, A., Kelly, A., Turquet, L., & Ross, S. (2009). *Hate crimes: The rise of 'corrective' rape in South Africa*. London: Action Aid.
Mashatile, P. (2013). *Speech on occasion of the opening of South African pavilion at the 55th venice biennale* [online]. Retrieved September 20, 2015, from http://www.dac.gov.za/content/speech-paul-mashatile-occasion-opening-south-african-pavilion-55th-venice-biennale
Mihai, M. (2016). *Negative emotions and transitional justice*. New York: Columbia University Press.
Mitchell, W.J. T. (1995). *Picture theory: Essays on verbal and visual representation*. Chicago: University of Chicago Press.
Muholi, Z. (2010). *Faces and Phases*. Munich: Prestel Verlag.
Munro, B. M. (2012). *South Africa and the dream of love to come: Queer sexuality and the struggle for freedom*. Minneapolis: University of Minnesota Press.
Mwambene, L., & Wheal, M. (2015). Realisation or oversight of a constitutional mandate? Corrective rape of black african lesbians in South Africa. *African Human Rights Law Journal*, *15*(1), 58–88.
Nagy, R. (2004). Violence, amnesty and transitional law: 'private' acts and 'public' truth in South Africa. *African Journal of Legal Studies*, *1*(1), 1–28.
Nochlin, L. (1999). *Representing women*. London: Thames and Hudson.
Perryer, S. (2004). *10 years 100 artists: Art in a democratic South Africa*. Cape Town: Bell-Roberts.
Pitkin, H. F. (1967). *The concept of representation*. Berkeley: University of California Press.
Pollock, G. (1988). *Vision and difference: Feminism, femininity and the histories of art*. Abingdon: Routledge.
Savage, M. (1986). The imposition of pass laws on the African population in South Africa 1916–1984. *African Affairs*, *85*(339), 181–205.
Saward, M. (2010). *The representative claim*. Oxford: Oxford University Press. Unpaginated electronic book.
Shapiro, I., Stokes, S. C., Wood, E. J., & Kirshner, A. S. (2010). *Political representation*. Cambridge: Cambridge University Press.
Sintomer, Y. (2013). The meanings of political representation: Uses and misuses of a notion. *Raisons politiques*, *2*(50), 13–34.
Truth and Reconciliation Commission. (1999). *Amnesty decision on death of Steve Biko* [online]. Retrieved June 1, 2016, from http://www.justice.gov.za/trc/media/pr/1999/p990216a.htm
Williamson, S. (2009). *South African art now*. New York: Harper Collins.

The art and politics of imagination: remembering mass violence against women

Maria Alina Asavei

ABSTRACT
This paper addresses the role of artistic memory in processes of redressing political violence and historical injustices. Combining philosophical reflection, insights from memory studies and examples of artistic practices, it focuses on how memory and imagination coalesce in problematising mass violence against women and resisting its 'official' oblivion. The argument is that artistic memory work can foster collective memories of the painful past in ways that overcome both individual and national representations. To this end, this paper aims to explore various contemporary art productions as new models of memorialization, which deal with the representation of violence against women in armed conflicts and under political repression. The academic literature on the role of art in processes of dealing with the past tends to examine literature, film, theatre, painting and other more traditional artistic media of commemorating the victims of mass violence. In contrast, this paper explores the political potentialities of new artistic models of memorialization, namely participatory and collaborative artistic practices. Unlike the traditional media, they can commemorate victims performatively and collaboratively, simultaneously catalysing transnational solidarity and new forms of politics 'from below.'

Introduction

Generally, the academic literature on art and processes of dealing with the past focuses on literature, film, theatre, painting and other more traditional artistic media and genres of commemorating the victims of mass violence. These forms of artistic expression have been considered *symbolic* reparations (Simić & Volcic, 2014).[1] Here, I explore the political potentialities of new artistic models of memorialization – namely participatory and collaborative forms of artistic practice – employed in enacting the collective memory of mass violence against women. Dave Beech (2008) distinguishes between participatory and collaborative formats in contemporary public art practice.

While the collaborative formats encourage the co-authoring of the art pieces – allowing the participants (the public) to contribute to the artwork's final structure and foundational ideas – the participatory formats are built around an artist' idea. The degree of audience involvement is restricted by the conceptual and formal parameters established by the artist in advance (Beech, 2008).

The choice of addressing the issue of violence against women during political repression and armed conflicts through the mediation of artistic memory work is far from accidental. I use gender as an analytic lens as women and their struggles are often left out of national memory and history of the past in general.[2] Usually, in the 'era of commemoration' and 'memory boom' (Winter, 2006), women's voices and the memory of their ordeals are subsumed under the grand narrative of the 'whole nation'. Monuments, museums, print media, textbooks, and even legal battles over the 'right to memory' are typically framed by 'the nation'. In other words, mnemonic practices and their cultural materialisations are meant to recall how 'the nation' suffered from foreign invasions. Much less emphasis is put on the memory of certain victims, such as women, ethnic and sexual minorities, children, the elderly. Not all pasts receive equal attention: while some remain invisible, others are re-enacted in national museums, art galleries and other official institutions of remembrance. But what happens when the community of remembrance is not reducible to the nation? And what if it stretches beyond national borders?

This is, I argue, the case with women's experiences of violence. Women and girls are much more exposed to sexual violence as they are regarded as depositories of ethnic and cultural identity. And yet, their experiences of violence are often obscured from the official story for reasons I can only briefly review here. First, many suffer from depression and post-traumatic stress disorder (Simić & Volcic, 2014, p. 382), which means they will not easily make claims for redress. Second, victims often feel embarrassed to recall past sexual abuses. Their unwillingness to speak and to recall those experiences renders the pursuit of justice difficult. The fact that memories of sexual violence cannot be tackled openly is not surprising, and, as the artist Judy Chicago asks rhetorically, 'how open can you be when it is shrouded in shame?'[3] Third and importantly for this paper, transitional justice processes have mostly been legal processes. Law's insistence on replying on individual testimony to re-establish the truth about the past offers less space for *collective* memories by groups – in this case women – women who share experiences of violence.[4]

Shifting the focus away from law, this paper aims to illuminate the great potential of contemporary artistic practice to enable an active and *collective* remembrance of the painful past. As a matter of fact, judicial proceedings might be more beneficial for victims if their collective memories of violence were simultaneously vindicated and accounted for publicly outside the courtroom: this is where artistic practices can play a vital role. Participatory artworks can make possible survivors', witnesses' but also post-witnesses' collective engagement with past violence. In talking of 'post-witnesses' I build on Hirsh's concept of 'post-memory' (2008), which refers to how distant inheritors of trauma can remember 'other people's memory'.[5] In other words, 'post-memory' is that memory held by those who have not experienced first-hand the violence, whose memory is not direct: it is not the memory of the survivors, but a mediated memory. This paper argues that participatory, collective artworks can do this mediation work for those who are only indirect inheritors of the trauma. Moreover, through artistic encounters, the shared memory of traumatic events is instantiated imaginatively so that the survivor is not isolated and facing the risk of re-traumatization.

However, not all cultural responses to mass violence against women work in this personally and politically productive manner. In this paper, I contend that representations of mass violence against women should move beyond the sexualisation of violence and atrocity to avoid the trivialisation or the 'softening' of the memory of suffering, as well as the risk of exploiting the victims again. Thus, artistic representations of mass rape and other forms of violence against women that rely on exposing the body or its parts cannot count as forms of symbolic reparation. Nor do they establish relations across difference or across generations, as they do nothing to highlight women's agency in political, economic and social transformation within post-conflict societies.

Certain art pieces are politically effective in the way I suggested above because they have the power to capture painful experiences and trigger dialogical memories. Valorising the intimacy between art and imagination, artists provide *symbolic reparations* that can foster *new forms of politics and mobilization from below*. Certain artistic approaches to the violent past rely on imaginative strategies that amount to claim-making practices, thus emerging as new forms of grassroots politics. To be concrete, the lack of national and international mechanisms of addressing women's suffering sometimes gives rise to a 'creative vigour rising "from below" – from victims and survivors groups, community, civil society organizations, and artists' (Simić & Volcic, 2014, p. 384). Through art's mediation, groups and communities remember, imagine and construct their past and future creating new identities and initiating collective action.

This paper attempts to demonstrate that, unlike individual artistic production, the collective format catalyses a 'social turn' in art (Bishop, 2006). Individual art production and reception are grounded in the traditional metaphysical distinction between object and subject (art object – beholder). In collectively made art, the relationship between beholder-beheld (subject-object) is turned into a relationship of reciprocity/mutuality among participants. In other words, the focus is not on the relationship art object-art spectator but on a communal experience of co-authoring which prepares the ground for a dialogue. Unlike the individual artistic production, the collective formats appeal to the spectator's *sensus communis* (Kant, 1987, pp. 159–163). I here follow Kester's work (2004, p. 108), who, departing from Kant's theory, puts forth a particular understanding of the *sensus communis* as 'a sense of the commonness of cognition itself', which allows empathic identification with other subjects, as well as mutual understanding and respect. In this approach, *sensus communis* 'does not entail the conditions of possibility for the communicability of feelings in the absence of any conceptual grounds (as in Kant's aesthetic theory) but it rather refers to ethical (placing oneself in other's shoes) and conceptual grounds.' (Asavei, 2014, p. 74).

Let us now turn to the interplay between memory and imagination in participatory artistic encounters and explain how they enable the emergence of this type of *sensus communis* between spect-actors. In the following section, I will also develop what I understand by spect-actor, following Augusto Boal.

Post-memory through imagination

While there is no need 'to convince anybody that there is such a thing as an individual memory', the term 'collective memory' is not without detractors (Assmann, 2006, p. 222). For instance, Susan Sontag posits that 'all memory is individual and irreproducible', passing away at the same time with the person who experienced the event first-hand (Sontag, 2003, p. 115). Sontag concludes her book *Regarding the Pain of Others* by claiming that 'collective memory is a spurious notion' used by the official institutions of remembrance to convince people that this is the 'true narrative' about how it happened (Sontag, 2003). Along similar lines, the historian Reinhart Koselleck claims that 'there is no collective memory' (Koselleck quoted in Assman, 2004, p. 21), while the philosopher Rudolf Burger posits that 'memories die with individuals. In spite of what is claimed by mystagogues today, there is no collective memory' (Burger cited in Assmann, 2004, p. 21) I cannot do justice to the debate over whether there is such a thing as 'collective memory' here.[6] Instead, I begin with a useful distinction between the concept of 'collected memories' as the common recollections of those people who experienced the same event in the same place and time and the concept of 'collective memory' (Rigney, 2016). As Rigney convincingly points out, 'for memory to be "collective" it must involve not only recollections that are held in common, but reflections that are also self-reflectively shared ... and memory can only become collective in this specific sense when different acts of communication and representation, using whatever tools are available, have come into play' (2016, p. 65). Since this paper deals with the concatenation of memory and imagination in artistic memory work focusing on mass violence against women, 'the collective' and 'the cultural' are tackled as the two sides of the same coin. By scrutinizing the cultural foundations of collective memory, I argue that certain narratives, representations and aesthetic experiences become shared, linked to a transbiographical identity and socially interconnected. Therefore, a 'community of remembrance' – not necessarily connected to the national level – is actually a form of 'we', constituted and co-constituted through shared values, norms and politics.

But how does memory and the imagination work together in participatory artworks dealing with gender violence? The relationship between imagination and ethics or imagination and politics has been largely discussed in philosophy.[7] Theoretical accounts of imagination have been (at least up to the nineteenth century) of two types: those that associated imagination with a low (obscure, inaccurate) form of cognition (closer to what Hobbes called 'nothing but decaying sense'[8]), and those that thought imagination to be a faculty of the human mind *(facultas imaginandi)*, which binds perception with reason and memory.[9] Temporally speaking, the faculty of memory was associated with the past and imagination with the future. Consequently, memory was thought to be the faculty that 'worked through the past', while imagination was derogatorily associated with 'fabulation'.

These views persist today to a certain extent, in certain fields of inquiry. However, recent work by Keightley and Pickering has developed 'a sociological aesthetics of memory' (2012, p. 78), where imagination plays a crucial role in understanding the past. According to such unifying theories, memory and imagination are two separate mental faculties that complement each other (Garcia, 2005; Keightley & Pickering, 2012; Popescu, 2015). The concept of 'mnemonic imagination', formulated by Keightley and Pickering, refers to 'an active synthesis of remembering and imagining' through which 'we refine and resynthesize past experience, our own and that of others, into qualitatively new understandings, of ourselves and other people, including those to whom we stand in immediate or proximate relation' (Keightley & Pickering, 2012, p. 121).

In this paper, I rely on this more recent work and explore community imagining and remembering *via* artistic production. I embrace Kind and Kung's understanding of imagination as a way of knowing about the world (2016), that also mediates our knowledge about the past (our memories). By memory I mean here the public (cultural and social) dimensions of representing the past and not the biological/psychological aspects of remembering the past. Thus, memory in its social and cultural dimension is a process which allows us to know about the past *via* representations. These 'images' about the past are also fuelled by imagination as a major mobilising force in envisioning the future. Yet, memory and imagination are not one and the same thing, although they can and do become linked faculties of knowledge, sometimes overlapping for a limited period of time, without thereby collapsing into each other. As I shall show in what follows, both are experiential cognitive faculties.

The imagination 'is put to two different and seemingly incompatible kinds of uses', namely the *transcendent* use and the *instructive* use (Kind & Kung, 2016, p. 1). The transcendent use of imagination is that which enables us to supersede this world through pretending and daydreaming, while the instructive use refers to imagination's ability 'to enable us to learn about the world as it is.' Thus, contrary to those who conclude that the imagination is unnecessary and extraneous to knowledge acquisition, we can treat it as a reliable and valuable source of knowledge. Instructively, imagination can help us perceive how others might feel in a difficult situation we never experienced first-hand. It can also enable us to see the distant others and their concerns. Transcendently, by providing visions of hope, imagination keeps the knowledge of the past interconnected with the future.

Returning to this paper's focus, trauma is remembered and represented artistically even beyond the reference groups to which the traumatic experience is attributed. This 'de-territorialisation' of artistic memory work fosters the creation of *new communities of remembrance* (not necessarily formed by those who experienced violence first-hand) and *new forms of politics of resistance*. The concrete, 'tangible' individual memories are turned into relational, dialogical post-memories of painful experiences, materialised in imaginative artworks that seek to stimulate social responsibility. In this light, imagination is not the opposite of memory but a critical tool that opposes further injustices and oblivion. Through the imaginative discourse of art, the traumatic memories of women who suffered violence during or after armed conflict are instructively shared with others, who connect with the traumatic past even when they are not themselves survivors or second generation witnesses to those traumatic events. While for Knightley and Pickering the 'mnemonic imagination' can help us make sense of second or third generation witnesses' engagement with a traumatic past, my main concern in this paper is to shed light on new artistic memory practices involving distant witnesses of these memories, i.e. post-witnesses, with no biographical ties with the victim. In particular, my examination of contemporary artistic memory works aims to demonstrate that these new, collective mnemonic practices do not disclose or restate historical and political facts: they aim to engage the audiences in processes of shaping new accounts of that very past, by creating opportunities for solidarity with victims across biography, time and space. Instructive imagination can help certain spect-actors remember 'other people's memory' of violence and oppression by provoking reflections which are 'self-reflectively shared' (Rigney, 2016, p. 65). These reflections materialise in cultural responses – called by Levy and Sznaider 'unbounded cultural memories' (Levy & Sznaider, 2002, pp. 87–105). Thus, the interplay between memory and imagination occasioned by artworks that can transcendentally establish a political relationship to a history that the *spect-actor* has not personally experienced first-hand.

The founder of the 'Theater of the Oppressed', Augusto Boal, defines 'spect-actorship' as the double role of those involved in 'Forum Theatre' (1985). A spect-actor is for Boal simultaneously 'spectator' and 'actor'. The focus is not on the relationship art object – art spectator, but on a communal experience of co-authoring and co-performing a piece which takes place dialogically. Thus, the spect-actor is not a passive perceiver of the artwork but she engages with it directly. In other words, the spect-actor does not merely look at or listen to the artwork but she creates action by 'doing something' with the art piece and interacting with the other spect-actors. Imaginatively occupying both roles gives distant witnesses of traumatic memory the chance to acquire a certain type of experiential knowledge. Participating in these collaborative works, *spect-actors* 'imagine for themselves'. As Paterson points out, 'through this participation, the audience members became empowered not only to imagine change, but to actually practice that change, reflect collectively on the suggestion, and thereby become empowered to generate social action'. (Paterson, 2017) Therefore, the artistic memory work explored in this paper does not merely *transmit information* (e.g. that 'this happened there and there' and 'mass violence against women is morally questionable') but allows the viewer (the spect-actor) to *experience imaginatively* what it must have been like to be a woman in this or that situation. In other words, the participant to this artistic memory work is provoked to have a first and personal experience of the idea (the concept) central to the art piece: she does not merely think about that idea but she grasps, deals and involves herself with that idea.

Memory and imagination at work in artistic production dealing with mass violence against women

The active mingling of memory and imagination in artistic memory works dealing with violent pasts can dislocate hegemonic and skewed visions of history, giving rise to moral anxieties about the wrongdoings of the past and the present in the light of the future. Yet, social scientists seeking to explore political redress in the wake of political repression and historical injustices focus almost exclusively on memory with 'little if any attention paid to imagination' (Keightley & Pickering, 2012, p. 1). Moreover, since imagination is sometimes associated with 'fantasy' and the failure of the veracity tests, some theorists and mass violence survivors envision it as being at odds with memory. For example, in the aftermath of the Holocaust, there was a specific view, which still exists today to a certain extent, that the memory of this disconcerting event is possessed exclusively by its victims. According to this view, all contemporary representations of this heinous event (artistic or otherwise) are contaminated by imagination, and, therefore, they violate the real experience of the Holocaust and other traumatic events (Wiesel, 1989).[10]

Thus, memory and imagination are rendered incompatible because imagination is unable to fully embrace 'the horrors of the concentration camps'(Arendt, 1973, p. 444). By the same token, Theodor Adorno's dictum 'to write lyrical poetry after Auschwitz is barbaric' (1983, p. 34) has been interpreted as a vow of silence and as an injunction against the artistic representation of the Holocaust (Gubar, 2003; Ibsch, 2004; Whitfield, 2007). However, as some scholars have shown, although Adorno did not address much Holocaust memory *per se* in his work, he tackled the problem of *how* to remember the traumatic past or 'the *how* of education and remembrance'. (Martin, 2006) Far from calling for silence after Auschwitz, Adorno's dictum ought to be understood as a call for the post-Holocaust artist to bear witness to this horrendous violence. In other words, Adorno's dictum does not address the question of *whether* the Holocaust should be represented, but *how* it should be remembered. Not any work of art can represent the 'unrepresentable': art pieces relying on aesthetic stylization where the horrifying violence is rendered aesthetically pleasing are not ethically appropriate. At the same time, Adorno's dictum does not refer to a requirement for artistic witnessing limited to 'the real experience of the Holocaust' or to 'facts alone.' The *how* of remembrance does not command realism: artistic imagination and faithfulness to history are not mutually exclusive.

It is because of the work of the imagination that contemporary artistic productions about the Holocaust are as much about the past as they are about the present. It expands the boundaries of the Holocaust's meaning to encompass new sets of concerns, such as capitalist greed, desensitisation and alienation of the human being in contemporary societies, and much more. At the same time, these artistic productions work both instructively and transcendentally to re-visit and re-tell the past, while re-envisioning the future by mobilizing new forms of politics and new forms of opposing economic and cultural hegemony.

For example, feminist artist Judy Chicago (assisted by photographer Donald Woodman) addresses in her art installation *Double Jeopardy* (1993) the neglected issue of gender in the Nazi camps. The piece consists of six panels combining photographs, needlework and painting. One panel consists of a juxtaposition of two plans: an infamous black and white photograph of men (prisoners) experiencing Buchenwald's liberation and a pastel coloured image of women inmates being raped by British, Americans and Russians 'liberators'. The rape scene is graphically composed as a re-enactment of the notorious *Rape of the Sabine Women* painted by Rubens in 1635–1637. The abduction scene displays both the victims and the perpetrators, who are not exclusively Germans. As the artist recalls, the allusion was deliberate: 'I positioned my models in those same poses in part to suggest that rape has often been part of war' (Chicago 1993). Ethically informed, her work does not display photographs of the women victims' naked bodies to avoid their further exploitation.

Sexual violence against women during the Holocaust has rarely been represented through artistic engagements. Moreover, early research on Holocaust's survivors' testimonies revealed very little gender awareness, especially when it came to sexual violence.[11] Judy Chicago aimed to fill this gap in the official history of the Holocaust by going outside the conventional narrative to uncover evidence of women's traumatic experiences. She consulted survivors about the accuracy of the images displayed in her art installation. According to Rochelle Saidel and Sonja Medgepeth, the artist initially 'portrayed only Russian soldiers as rapists, because she had found references to this in the literature. She also accepted that the liberating American and British troops never raped women. But, a Holocaust scholar and survivor of Bergen-Belsen who was an adviser to the Holocaust Project told her, "No, Judy, everybody raped." So she changed the uniforms' (2010). Thus, this installation is not meant to function exclusively as a reminder of Buchenwald's liberation. This representation not only instructed viewers about the atrocities of one particular Nazi camp; it also recalled the horrors of the Holocaust in contemporary settings. At the same time, *Double Jeopardy* tackles the fear of rape in general, a fear shared by all women across the globe, not only by victims in conflict zones and wartimes. As Waxman points out, for Judy Chicago 'patriarchy itself is indicted as part of what made the Holocaust possible – she cites as evidence the fact that the architects of the Third Rich were exclusively male' (Waxman, 2007, p. 665). Although Chicago consulted several survivors to complete her art piece, she was not afraid to include in her work imagined scenes whose impetus was partly her own fear of rape, but also the need to disclose the story of other women's experiences. Through this *imaginative* dimension of her work Chicago goes beyond merely documenting violence against women.

While Chicago's memory work reveals an individual – non-participatory, non-collective – act of artistic resistance against oblivion and injustice, other pieces of contemporary art are conceived as 'collective work' that aim to foster transnational, communal resistance against the gendered dimension of political violence. One recent example in this respect is the project *Women Mobilizing Memory: Collaborative Archives, Connective Histories* (Santiago/Istanbul/New York, 2015). It brought together artists, human rights activists and academics from Turkey, Argentina, Chile and the US who co-authored 'collaborative archives of resistance' against political violence and atrocity. As the curators posit, various memories, both recent and distant, of political violence against women (but not only) 'became the occasion for solidarity across space and time' (Önol & Kohn, 2015, p. 7).

Avoiding the traumatic re-enactment of violent pasts, the artists dealt imaginatively with both personal and communal memories of trauma and displacement using a variety of media. These artistic projects provide the ground for constructing an active, collective memory, where women and other disenfranchised people – who have no national archives – can affirm their identity and common history of exclusion from the officially sanctioned institutions of remembrance. Thus, recent online and offline artistic memory projects engage the audience in what Adorno has called 'working through the past' (2012, pp. 292–309), which gets transfigured through art. Such transfigurations in turn provide new horizons for carrying out the work of memory.

Thinking of you and *the blue bra*

This section analyses two exemplary contemporary art pieces dealing with mass violence against women. Both pieces reveal collective formats of artistic memory production. The exquisite, gigantic art installation *Thinking of You* by the Kosovo born and British bred conceptual artist Alketa Xhafa-Mripa took place on the biggest football stadium in Kosovo in June 2015. The giant installation consists of more than 5000 skirts and dresses hung on washing lines in the central soccer stadium. The location juxtaposes memories of defeat and victory, as well as stereotypical representations of masculinity and femininity. While Judy Chicago re-enacted Rubens's painting *Rape of the Sabine Women* to suggest that 'rape has often been part of war' and its painful memory was neglected, Alketa Xhafa-Mripa chose the stadium as a place of crime, not only for women from the former Yugoslavia. In 2009, Human Rights Watch reported the mass rapes and massacres of mostly women on Conakry's Stadium in Guinea. Thus, *Thinking of You* employs the stadium as a *lieu de mémoire*, unbound by nationally restricted memories of mass violence against women. The clothes were mostly donated by Albanian and Bosniak women.[12] The public nature of this installation fostered an unprecedented engagement with this work commemorating victims of wartime rape.[13] Kosovar newspapers and international reported that Cherie Blair, the first female president of Kosovo Atifete Jahjaga, international pop stars, fathers, husbands, brothers, sisters, mothers and children of the victims of sexual violence supported the art project, donated skirts, and helped the artist install the exhibition (Bytyci, 2015; Tran, 2015).

Crucial for this paper, *Thinking of You* gathered also dresses and skirts from women and men from all over the world, who had no biographical ties with the victims of sexual mass violence. This collaborative piece of artistic memory sought both to commemorate and to empower victims of sexual mass violence, especially in a country where the background culture is rather conservative and where remembering and commemorating the victims of wartime rape could not be pursued without recognising the potential stigma and harms to 'family honour.' In the former Yugoslavia (especially in Bosnia and Herzegovina and Kosovo) 'family honour and ethnic group identity are enmeshed with female chastity' (Sharlach, 2000, p. 96).

According to the Kosovo Women Network, very few survivors of wartime rape have spoken publicly about their horrendous experience, and 'to date, there has been only one conviction at the International Criminal Tribunal for Former Yugoslavia based partly on sexual assaults...in Kosovo itself, there have been only two rape case prosecutions' (Tran, 2015). However, while the officially sanctioned institutions of remembrance in Kosovo remain silent about wartime sexual violence, the vernacular memories of these traumatic experiences resurface in collaborative artistic practices involving survivors, the direct inheritors and the post-witnesses of this horrendous experience.

Indeed, the participants in this collective and collaborative memory event are no longer spectators, but *spect-actors*. The new relations between spect-actors and politics are more socially responsible than those enabled by traditional, aesthetically disinterested or psychologically distanced spectatorship. The individuals who contributed dresses and skirts to the *Thinking of You* project co-authored this piece of artistic memory work while spectating it. Alketa Xhafa-Mripa envisioned the public's participation as part and parcel of the collective artwork's final form and meaning. The aesthetic experience was *dialogical* and intersubjective rather than a subject-object encounter: traditional aesthetics' distinction between *art object* and *beholder* was overcome. The aesthetic experience took place dialogically, and a sense of togetherness against oblivion and mass violence was encouraged. Relying for its creation and reception on the interplay between the faculties of imagination and memory (including here distant or mediated memory), this collaborative art piece reveals how both faculties are simultaneously private (individual) and collective (social).

Intersubjectivity, then, is a necessary concept for understanding how a process like imagination begins *internally* in the individual and shifts to a *communal process*. The art installation can also be understood as a *collaborative archive of resistance* mobilizing imagination and cultural memory's 'invocation as a catalyst for present-day agendas' (Zelizer, 1999, p. 114), affirming women's agency in political, economic and social transformation within a post-conflict, conservative society.

Thinking of You manages to represent the 'unimaginable' dimension of sexual violence by relying on the power of imagination as a weapon against oblivion and stigmatization. There is an inevitable tension between the social responsibility to remember the victims of sexual violence and the limited cultural means an artist has at her disposal. However, *Thinking of You* finds a collectively creative solution for dealing with painful events that 'defy sayability in the usual modes of public recollection' (Rigney, 2016, p. 66). At the same time, this work reflects on *who* is doing the remembering and *to what ends*: what is the impact of this memory work on the social relations and common futures of all women and men? I argue its public display functions as a 'working through the past' – to paraphrase Adorno – where the artistic rendering provides a form of 'symbolic reparation' (Simić & Volcic, 2014).

Importantly, this piece refuses any attempt at an aesthetic stylization of sufferance. The horror of the event of sexual violence is artistically rendered without futile aestheticization, without representing pain and distress in ways that occasion in viewers the feeling of cognitively unaffected aesthetic pleasure. *Thinking of You* eschews the trap of transfiguring the bareness of pain and despair, and thus restores truth and justice by declining to aesthetically alleviate the horrors of the rape camps. Unlike other pieces of art and exhibitions that deal with mass violence against women, *Thinking of You* circumvents the problematic representation of women's nakedness and body parts, avoiding the reproduction of exploitation. The artwork lets the donated skirts speak instead. For the *spect-actors* of this installation, the aesthetic experience is marked by the Kantian *play of imagination and understanding* minus the feeling of disinterested pleasure (Kant, 1987).

In the same activist register, another piece of public art displaying women clothes as a means of empowerment, this time a blue bra, emerged in Cairo during the Egyptian revolution in January 2011. The blue bra stencil commemorates a young, unknown Egyptian woman who was beaten and humiliated by the military police during the revolution. The violent treatment was recorded by cameras showing her blue bra exposed after her *abaya* (Islamic robe) had been stripped off (Salem, 2015). This violent image was widely shared online and became an icon of the Egyptian revolution. According to the international media 'the regime's thugs molest women as a form of political bullying – and harassment of women in the streets rises to epidemic levels' (Soueif, 2011). In the same register of endemic violence against women and young girls, the military police used the weapon of shame, subjecting the women protesters to virginity tests and gang rape. Only after the video of the beaten woman became viral online, the artistic works addressing this event started to be produced as cultural responses to the actual act of violence. These art pieces are the result of the spectators' collective engagement (memory) with a violent past they post-witnessed. This might be seen as a form of co-production of artistic memory work whose 'community of remembrance' transcends the national borders. Thus, the artistic responses to the actual act of violence might be regarded as yet another 'collaborative archive of resistance' against political violence. Those artists, activists and other cultural produces that further disseminated the

Blue Bra's artistic and political message became empowered to imagine change for women in conflict zones.

While the video of the unknown woman beaten in the Tahrir Square became the symbol of the Egyptian revolution, the blue bra stencils have become the epitome of women's resistance (Bardhan & Foss, 2016). The blue bra stencils have been reproduced and posted on the walls of the main squares of Cairo first, and then on online platforms. Just to mention one relevant example, the Facebook group *Blue Bra* has 318 members from all over the world, whose declared focus is 'on women's rights in Arab countries and on the discrimination, misunderstanding, and other human rights battles they face in the West.'[14] Thus, the memory of this violent event has been distributed and re-distributed by many internet users all over the world and re-interpreted artistically to connote women's empowerment.[15] The fact that the stencil displays a bra has considerable symbolic weight since the bra is viewed in the Egyptian culture as an element of shame and frivolity.[16] The artistic work resignifies the bra purging it of shame and embarrassment. As Bardhan and Foss posit 'in ancient Egyptian color symbolism, blue depicts prestige (Baines 1985); the woman has prestige – esteem, honor and reputation – because she is standing up to those beating her' (Bardhan & Foss, 2016, pp.12–13). At the same time, this memory work is not only a form of collective commemoration but also a form of political participation. Through multiplication and appropriation, the story of the blue bra – of the unknown beaten woman – becomes a group story, the story of all women who suffered at the hands of the military police. Therefore, the violent event of the beating experienced by the unknown Egyptian woman-protestor is shared with many other women and men all over the world. In this way, a transnational community is engaged in memory work through collective identification with the victim.

Both *Blue Bra* stencil and *Thinking of You* reveal the relationship between *personal* (individual) and *collective memories* of mass violence against women, as well as the interaction between *situated* and *mediated experiences*. As the experience of the violent past is mostly *mediated* – since most of the participants to this memory works have not experienced first-hand the painful events – the memory-imagination nexus is crucial to an ethical-political aesthetics. Both the *Blue Bra* stencil and the *Thinking of You* project rely for their production not only on *collective memory*, but also on the *imagination* and *collective forms of experiencing*. Therefore, the art projects do not depend for their realization only on recollections held in common by those who participate in these memory events, but also on 'reflections that are also self-reflectively shared' (Rigney, 2016, p. 65) as part and parcel of a critical collective memory driven by political imperatives.

At the same time, these public, participatory artworks capture and reveal women's experiences in conflicted societies, increasing awareness and attempting to restore women's dignity. Symbolic reparations through art have the great potential of fostering the creation of moral and political communities that condemn the wrongdoings of the past. By collectively engaging with the harm of sexual violence and reflecting on how painful the memories of abuse are, these artistic and political communities recall the painful past imaginatively.

Yet, to begin to grapple with *the pain of others*, we need to make special efforts. Acknowledging that what happened is morally bad is not enough, unless we also begin to grasp – however imperfectly – how it feels to be subjected to violence and injustice. Certain artworks have the power to foster in certain people the experiential knowledge of being subjected to mass violence and injustice: through art our imagination allows us to have a mediated experience of these painful pasts.

By occasioning collective experiential knowledge, the artistic memory of mass violence against women explored in this paper re-kindles our emotions and helps us rethink the idea of reparation. Reparation is re-conceptualised to exceed its pecuniary or formal apology dimension, encapsulating the redefinition of 'relations across difference, recognition of structural, gendered and intergenerational violence and a move away from its normalization' (Figueroa, 2015, p. 46).

Conclusions

Although artistic memory work is a source of experiential knowledge and grassroots mobilization for a 'never again', it would be mistaken to assume that any artistic memory work on its own would reveal the appalling, dehumanizing nature of violence against women. Not every piece of artistic memory dealing with violence against women fosters collective forms of experience that are 'self-reflectively' shared; not all artistic representations are equally able to trigger a critical collective memory, driven by emancipatory political imperatives.

Although the examples of artistic memory work addressed in this paper are far from exhaustive, they illustrate, in my view, effective ways of 'working through the past' in relation to the present and the future. Participatory artistic memory work has the merit of enabling witnesses and post-witnesses to mediatedly and collectively experience the painful past. Thus, they can facilitate the commemoration of all victims of mass violence, avoiding situations where memory artworks focus exclusively on the violent past of a certain category of women (e.g. Bosnian Muslim and Croatian women victims), while downplaying the hurtful experiences of other women (e.g. Serbian women).

The pieces of contemporary visual art explored in this paper aspire to imaginatively solve the tension between the social responsibility to remember the women victims of mass violence and the limited cultural means an artist has at her disposal. By breaking the borders between artist and public, the collective memory work investigated here employs those 'limited' cultural means to give voice to victims. At the same time, the collective representations of painful memories, experienced by both witnesses and post-witnesses, can trigger a critical collective memory whose cultural materializations avoid the further sexualisation and objectification of women and girls. Correspondingly, the archives (or the lack of archives) of women's painful memories are performed, co-performed and co-produced by mobilizing imagination to foster a trans-national, trans-biographical identity and social interconnectedness.

Notes

1. Symbolic reparations refer to cultural measures meant to restore victims' dignity. Memorialization is a form of symbolic reparation (Naidu, 2004).
2. Altinay and Petö write that 'women's memories and experiences have been left out of the historical scope and omitted from the official processes of justice and reconciliation, such as the Japanese women who were held in American concentration camps during the Second World War' (2016, p. 240). Schöllhammer also argues that 'women had been left out of official historiography' (2011, p. 1). For more studies see Bell and O'Rourke (2007, pp. 23–44).
3. Chicago quoted in Saidel and Medgepeth (2010).
4. There are some exceptions. Some legal scholars (Lopez, 2015; Osiel, 1997) have argued that the judicial system should also consider *collective* memory in the context of transitional justice procedures.
5. For more on the concept of 'post-memory' see Hirsh (2008, pp. 103–128).
6. Halbwachs is considered the first theorist of 'collective memory' by which he understands those recollections of the past held in common with others. See Halbwachs (1992).
7. For a theoretical discussion of the relationship between imagination and ethics see Tierney (1994) and Arendt (2003). For a detail account on the relationship between imagination and politics see Bottici and Challand (2001).
8. Hobbes (1909, reprinted from the edition of 1651, p.13).
9. The first type of understanding of imagination can be called Platonic, while 'the second type can be called Aristotelian' (Garrett, 2011).
10. See also Lanzmann (1994) quoted in Zelizer (2001, p. 150).
11. Later studies remedy this gap, tackling women's roles as caregivers, friends, mothers, sisters and resisters. See for example Gurewitsch (1998).
12. During the 1990s wars in former Yugoslavia, an estimated 20,000 Albanian women and men were abducted and raped by Serbian paramilitaries (see Radio Free Europe's Report online at https://www.rferl.org/a/kosovo-wartime-rape-victims-kept-secret/25403115.html).
13. A documentary about the production of the installation *Thinking of You* (see *The Making of Thinking of You* by Anna di Lellio and Fitim Shala 2015) reveals the impressive participation by post-witnesses of mass rape. This documentary (a fragment can be seen at https://www.youtube.com/watch?v=cvHk8iv6W_Q) follows the campaign to collect skirts and dresses all over Kosovo and includes

numerous interviews with participants. Some reflections by those who offered skirts and dresses for the installation can be read online at: http://irwgs.columbia.edu/blog/thinking-you. (Accessed 20 June 2017).
14. One of *Blue Bra* online communities can be found at: https://www.facebook.com/groups/204508666303145/ and https://www.facebook.com/groups/204508666303145/553001941453814/ (Accessed 10 January 2017).
15. To give just a few examples, the 'Blue Bra' is represented and disseminated in the political cartoons of the Brazilian artist Carlos Latuff; in the pieces of textile art created by the Jordanian designer Naser Al-Khalylah and in the political video posters disseminated online by the anonymous artist collective Operation Blue Bra Girl.
16. For more on this issue see Bardhan and Foss (2016).

Acknowledgments

I would like to express my gratitude first and foremost to Mihaela Mihai for her insightful comments and suggestions. I am also indebted to the many scholars who commented on this piece at the ECPR Pisa Joint Session 2016 and to Katerina Kralova.

Disclosure statement

No potential conflict of interest was reported by the author.

Funding

This article has received funding from the Charles University under the Primus grant (PRIMUS/HUM/12) and Research Center No.9

ORCID

Maria Alina Asavei http://orcid.org/0000-0002-4252-8044

References

Adorno, T. (1983). *Prisms*. Cambridge: MIT Press.
Adorno, T. (2012). *Critical models: Interventions and catchwords*. New York: Columbia University Press.

Altinay, A. G., & Petö., A. (2016). *Gendered wars, gendered memories: Feminist conversations on war, genocide and political violence*. London: Routledge.
Arendt, H. (1973). *The origins of totalitarianism*. London: Harcourt, Brace, Jovanovich.
Arendt, H. (2003). *Responsibility and judgment*. New York: Schocken Books.
Asavei, M. A. (2014). Collectivism. In M. Kelly (Ed.), *Oxford encyclopedia of aesthetics* (pp. 89–95). Oxford: Oxford University Press.
Assmann, A. (2004). Four formats of memory: From individual to collective constructions of the past. In C. Emden & D. Midgley (Eds.), *Cultural memory and historical consciousness in the German speaking word since 1500* (pp. 19–39). Bern: Peter Lang.
Assmann, A. (2006). Memory, individual and collective. In R. E. Goodin (Ed.), *The Oxford handbook of political science* (pp. 210–227). Oxford: Oxford University Press.
Baines, J. (1985). Color terminology and color classification: ancient egyptian color terminology and polychromy. *American Anthropologist, 87*(2), 282-297. doi:10.1525/aa.1985.87.issue-2
Bardhan, S., & Foss, K. (2016). *Revolutionary graffiti and Cairene women: Performing agency through gaze aversion*. Retrieved January 10, 2017, from https://cjdept.unm.edu/research/recent/docs/revolutionary-graffiti-and-cairene-women-performing-agency-through-gaze-aversion.pdf
Beech, D. (2008). Include me out. *Art Monthly, 315*(3), 1–4.
Bell, C., & O'Rourke, C. (2007). Does feminism need a theory of transitional justice? An introductory essay. *International Journal of Transitional Justice, 1*, 23–44.
Bishop, C. (2006). The social turn: Collaboration and its discontents. *Artforum International, 44*, 178–183.
Boal, A. (1985). *Theatre of the oppressed*. New York: Theatre Communication Group.
Bottici, C., & Challand, B. (2001). *The politics of imagination*. Oxon: Birkbeck Law Press.
Bytyci, F. (2015). Stadium of skirts targets stigma attached to victims of wartime rape. *Reuters* [online], June 12. Retrieved September 17, 2017, from http://www.reuters.com/article/us-kosovo-rape-exhibition/stadium-of-skirts-targets-stigma-attached-to-victims-of-wartime-rape-idUSKBN0OS1KB20150612
Figueroa, Y. (2015). Reparations as transformations: Radical literary (re)-imaginings of futurities through decolonial love. *Decolonization: Indigeneity, Education & Society, 4*(1), 41–58.
Garcia, J. (2005). *The watercolor Bible: A painter's complete guide*. Ohio: North Light Books.
Garrett, D. (2011). *Kant's model of the mind: The concept of imagination before Kant* [online]. Los Angeles: California State University. Retrieved March 10, 2016, from http://web.calstatela.edu/faculty/jgarret/560/notes-kant.pdf
Gubar, S. (2003). *Poetry after auschwitz: remembering what one never new*. Bloomington: Indiana University Press.
Gurewitsch, B. (1998). *Mothers, sisters, resisters: Oral histories of women who survived the Holocaust*. Tuscaloosa: University of Alabama Press.
Halbwachs, M. (1992). *On collective memory*. Chicago: University of Chicago Press.
Hirsh, M. (2008). The generation of postmemory. *Poetics Today, 29*(1), 103–128.
Hobbes, T. (1909). *Leviathan*. Oxford: Clarendon Press.
Ibsch, E. (2004). *Die shoab erzablt: zeugnis und experiment in der literatur*. Tubingen: Max Niemeyer Verlag.
Kant, I. (1987). *The critique of judgment*. Indianapolis: Hackett.
Keightley, E., & Pickering, M. (2012). *The mnemonic imagination: Remembering as creative practice*. London: Palgrave Macmillan.

Kester, G. (2004). *Conversation pieces: Community and communication in modern art*. Berkeley: University of California Press.
Kind, A., & Kung, P. (2016). *Knowledge through imagination*. Oxford: Oxford University Press.
Lanzmann, C. (1994). Holocauste, la représentation impossible. *Le Monde*, March 3. column1.
Levy, L., & Sznaider, N. (2002). Memory unbound: The Holocaust and the formation of cosmopolitan memory. *European Journal of Social Theory*, 5(1), 87–105.
Lopez, R. (2015). The (re)collection of memory after mass atrocity and the dilemma for transitional justice. *NYU Journal of International Law and Politics*, 47(4), 800–852.
Martin, E. (2006). Re-reading Adorno: The "after-Auschwitz" aporia. *Forum – Postgraduate Journal of Culture and Arts* [online], 2 (Spring). Retrieved March 2, 2016, from http://www.forumjournal.org/article/viewFile/556/841
Naidu, E. (2004). *Symbolic reparations: A fractured opportunity* [online]. Retrieved June 19, 2017, from http://www.csvr.org.za/docs/livingmemory/symbolicreparations.pdf
Önol, I., & Kohn, K. (2015). Collaborative archives: Connecting histories. In *Women mobilizing memory* [online]. Retrieved July 17, 2017, from http://notloire.net/wp-content/uploads/2015/11/WMMCatalogue_Collaborative-Archives.pdf
Osiel, M. (1997). *Mass atrocity, collective memory and the law*. New Brunswick, NJ: Transaction Publishers.
Paterson, P. (2017). *Pedagogy and theatre of the oppressed* [online]. Retrieved June 10, 2017, from http://ptoweb.org/aboutpto/a-brief-biography-of-augusto-boal/
Popescu, I. D. (2015). Introduction: Memory and imagination in the post-witness era. In D. I. Popescu & T. Schult (Eds.), *Revisiting Holocaust representations in the post-witness era* (pp. 1–7). London: Palgrave Macmillan.
Rigney, A. (2016). Cultural memory studies: Mediation, narrative and the aesthetic. In A. L. Tota & T. Hagen (Eds.), *Routledge international book of memory studies* (pp. 65–77). London: Routledge.
Saidel, R., & Medgepeth, S. (2010). Judy Chicago lead the way in artistically portraying sexual violence against women during the Holocaust. *Forward* [online], October 13. Retrieved April 14, 2016, from http://forward.com/culture/132148/judy-chicago-led-the-way-in-artistically-portrayin/
Salem, S. (2015). Creating spaces for dissent: The role of social media in 2011 Egyptian Revolution. In D. Trottier & C. Fuchs (Eds.), *Social media, politics and the state: Protests, revolutions, riots, crime and policing in the age of Facebook, Tweeter and YouTube* (pp. 171–189). New York: Routledge.
Schöllhammer, G. (2011). Sanja Ivekovic's counter-monument to the Luxembourg war memorial »Gëlle Fra«" [online]. Retrieved June 29, 2017, from https://www.moma.org/interactives/exhibitions/2011/sanjaivekovic/essays/GS%20Rosa%20of%20Luxembourg.pdf
Sharlach, L. (2000). Rape as genocide: Bangladesh, the Former Yugoslavia and Rwanda. *New Political Science*, 22(1), 89–102.
Simić, O., & Volcic, Z. (2014). In the land of wartime rape: Bosnia, cinema and reparation. *Griffith Journal of Law and Human Dignity*, 2(2), 377–401.
Sontag, S. (2003). *Regarding the pain of others*. New York: Picador.
Soueif, A. (2011). Image of unknown woman beaten by Egypt's military echoes around the world. *The Guardian* [online], December 18. Retrieved April 15, 2017, from http://www.theguardian.com/commentisfree/2011/dec/18/egypt-military-beating-female-protester-tahrir-square

Tierney, N. (1994). *Imagination and ethical ideal*. New York: Sunny Press.

Tran, M. (2015). Dresses on washing lines pay tribute to Kosovo survivors of sexual violence. *The Guardian* [online], June 11. Retrieved September 20, 2017, from https://www.theguardian.com/world/2015/jun/11/kosovo-sexual-violence-survivors-art-dresses

Waxman, Z. (2007). Unheard testimony, untold stories: The representations of women holocaust experiences. *Women's History Review, 12*(4), 661–677.

Whitfield, S. (2007). The holocaust: remembrances, reflections, revisions. *Religion Compass, 1*(1), 190-202. doi:10.1111/reco.2007.1.issue-1

Wiesel, E. (1989). Art and the Holocaust: Trivializing memory. *The New York Times* [online], June 11. Retrieved March 2, 2016, from http://www.nytimes.com/1989/06/11/movies/art-and-the-holocaust-trivializing-memory.html?pagewanted=all

Winter, J. (2006). *Remembering war: The Great War between memory and history in the Twentieth Century*. New Haven: Yale University Press.

Zelizer, B. (1999). Holocaust photography then and now. In B. Brennen & H. Hardt (Eds.), *Picturing the past: Media history and photography* (pp. 98–122). Urbana: University of Illinois Press.

Zelizer, B. (2001). *Visual culture and the Holocaust*. New Jersey: Rutgers.

Index

9/11 (terrorist attacks) 92, 93, 94, 95, 98

Abu Ghraib 38, 93
abuses 11, 28, 29, 31, 32, 38, 39; Abu Ghraib 38, 93; prisons 54–55, 56–57, 58–59, 61
accountability 10, 11, 29
Adorno, T. 129, 131
Ahmed, S. 34–35, 38, 39
Alexander, M. 55–56, 60
Alston, C. 79
America *see* United States
amnesties 5, 109, 110
anarcho-pacifism 66–67, 68, 69, 74
animal cruelty 91, 95, 97
Animal Farm (Orwell, 1945) 4, 87, 96, 97, 98, 99
animals 1, 4, 60, 87, 90, 91, 94–95, 96, 97, 98
animal suffering 87, 95, 96, 97, 98
animating guilt 41–42
anti-Semitism 37, 38; France 17, 18–19
anti-war veterans 3, 28, 38–39, 40, 41, 42
apartheid, South Africa 5, 29, 108, 109–111, 112; Pass Laws 111, 113
Arendt, H. 2, 3, 28, 30–34, 35–36, 37–38, 41, 43, 50, 59, 73, 87
art 69–70, 77, 78, 79, 80, 122, 124–125
Art Biennale, Venice 5, 102–103, 104, 106; *Faces and Phases* 5–6, 103, 108, 114–116, 117–118, 119; *The Journey* 5, 103, 108, 109–111, 118; South Africa 103, 104, 106, 107–108, 111, 117, 118; *For thirty years next to his heart* 5, 103, 108, 111, 112–114, 118
artistic memory work 123, 125, 126, 127–128, 129, 131, 134–136; *Blue Bra* stencil 6, 133–134; *Double Jeopardy* 129–130; *Thinking of You* 6, 131–133, 134; *Women Mobilizing Memory* 130–131

artistic practices 115, 122, 124–125, 132
artistic representation 5, 103–105, 106, 119, 135
artworks 1, 3, 5, 6, 103, 106, 108, 135; collaborative 122, 123; *Faces and Phases* 5–6, 103, 108, 114–116, 117–118, 119; *The Journey* 5, 103, 108, 109–111, 118; participatory 122, 123, 124, 125, 126, 135; *For thirty years next to his heart* 5, 103, 108, 111, 112–114, 118
Asavei, M. A. 5, 6
assimilation 2, 28, 33, 34, 36
atrocities 3, 28, 30–32, 33, 38, 39, 43, 73
Attentisme 14–15
authoritarianism 8, 98, 99

Bamm, P. 32
banality of evil 73
Bardhan, S. 134
Beech, D. 122
beneficiaries 11, 29, 38
Biko, S. 5, 108, 109, 110, 111, 118
Bitzer (*Hard Times* character) 88, 89
black queer identities 6, 114–115, 118–119
blameworthiness 10, 11
Bloom, P. 87
Blue Bra stencil (Egypt, 2011) 6, 133–134
Boal, A. 6, 128
Bondelzwort Commission Report (1923) 33
Booth, W. C. 88, 89, 93–94
Brassett, J. 77
Burger, R. 125
bystanders 3, 11, 14–15, 29, 38, 40

Césaire, A. 47
Chakarvarti, S. 35
Chaplin, C. 2, 28, 34, 36–37, 38

INDEX

Chicago, J. 123, 129, 130, 131; *Double Jeopardy* 129–130
Christianity and Patriotism (Tolstoy, 1894) 72
Christoyannopoulos, A. 3, 4, 5
Cohen, T. 87
Coles, R. 87
collaborationism, France 16, 17
collaborative artworks 122, 123
collaborators 2, 8–9, 11, 14, 15, 16, 17
collective action 11, 13
collective memories 6, 123–124, 125–126, 132, 134, 135, 136
colonial imaginaries 3, 48, 49–50
colonial institutions 48, 49–50
colonialism 1, 47–48, 49–50, 51, 52
comic pariahs 37, 38, 39, 42
compassion 87
complicity 2, 3, 8, 9–12, 14, 15, 20, 80
conquistadores, Spain 47–48, 50
conscious pariah 34, 37–38
Cook County court system, Chicago 57
criminal justice 3, 47, 52
criminal justice imaginaries 3, 56–57, 58, 59
criminals 53, 55–57, 60; *see also* incarceration; prisons
Critchley, S. 75
critical thinking 33, 40
cruel humour 28, 41
cruelty 4–5, 6, 86–87, 94–95, 98, 99

defamiliarisation 6, 67, 68, 69, 70–71, 72, 78–80; empathy 77–78, 87, 88; hierarchies 76–77, 78; implicitly concede 75–76, 78, 80; *ostranenie* 4, 67; routine perceptions 73–74, 78, 80
de Goede, M. 74, 77
dehumanization 3, 13, 39, 78, 90, 91, 94, 95
de Man, P. 96
denial 28, 30–31, 33, 34
Denner, M. A. 69, 70, 74
denunciations 16, 18–19
desensitisation 27, 31, 33, 39–40, 43
de Sepúlveda, J. G. 48–49
detachment 33, 43
dissent 38, 77
dissidents 15, 16
Dole, J. 60–61
dompas (passbook), South Africa 5, 111, 112–114, 118
Double Jeopardy (Chicago, 1993) 129–130
Dougherty, K. 42
Dussel, E. 3, 47, 51

Egyptian revolution 133–134
Eichmann, A. 2, 30, 31, 32, 33, 87
Elizabeth Costello (Coetzee, 2004) 87, 89–92, 95, 97, 98
emotional desensitization 27, 31, 33, 39–40, 43
emotional detachment 33, 43
emotional indifference 27, 29, 30–31, 42–43
emotion deadening 27, 28, 30, 41 move to above emotional? No because its letter by letter
empathy 77–78, 87, 88
employment, German Occupied France 16, 17–18
Encyclopedic Palace, The (Gioni, 2013) 107–108
English law 53

Faces and Phases 2006-2013 (Muholi) 5–6, 103, 108, 114–116, 117–118, 119
Fanon, F. 47
Fernandez, D. 71
Fletcher, A. 96
flogging 70, 75
Foss, K. 134
France: anti-Semitism 17, 18–19; German Occupation 16–20; *maquis* 15–16

Gandhi, M. 67, 69, 79
Garnsey, E. 5, 6
General Commissariat for Jewish Questions, Vichy France 17, 18
German Occupation (France, 1940–1944) 16–20
Golden Rule 77–78
Gordon, A. 41
guilt 10, 39, 41–42

Hamilton, L. 58, 61
hate crimes, South Africa 5–6, 115
haunting laughter 41, 42
Heep, U. (*David Copperfield* character) 89
Hegel, G. W. 49
Heine, H. 2, 4, 28, 34, 35, 36, 37
heroes 3, 4, 40, 41, 42
hierarchies 76–77, 78
Hobbes, T. 49, 52
Holocaust 35, 90–91, 128–130
homophobic violence, South Africa *see* hate crimes, South Africa
Honig, B. 34
hope 9, 10, 12, 13, 14, 15
human rights institutions 29
human rights violations 9, 29, 57

human worth 11
humiliation 39
humour 4, 33, 34–35, 37, 38–39, 40, 42, 75–76, 77

identification 4, 6, 86–88, 89, 90, 92
ignorance 2, 4–5, 90–91
Imaginary Fact: Contemporary South African Art and the Archive, Art Biennale, Venice 107, 108
imagination 1, 2, 3, 6, 7, 9, 10, 12–13, 15, 50–51, 59, 87, 126–127; identification 86, 87, 88, 90; memories 128, 129; mnemonic 126, 127; tragic 28, 29, 30, 42–43
implicitly concede 75–76, 78, 80
incarceration 3, 46, 47, 51, 53, 54, 56–57, 59–61; United States 1, 46, 52, 53
indifference 27, 29, 30–31, 42–43
indigenous Americans 47–49, 50
indigenous people 47–49, 50, 51
individual complicity 10, 12
individualism 1–2
institutionalised violence 1, 5, 30–32, 47, 61, 71
instructive imagination 127
intent 11
intersubjective relationality 9
Iraq Veterans Against the War (IVAW) 38, 39, 40, 42
ironic humour 35, 75, 77

Johnson, K. R. 58–59
Joll, Colonel (*Waiting for the Barbarians* character) 92–93, 94, 95, 98, 99
Journey, The (Koloane, 1998) 5, 103, 108, 109–111, 118

Kafka, F. 34
Keightley, E. 126, 127
Kester, G. 125
killjoy 35, 38, 39
Kind, A. 126
Kingdom of God Is within You, The (Tolstoy, 1893) 71–72, 73
Kinross prison, Michigan 58
Knapp, L. 67
Koloane, D. 108, 111, 118, 119; *The Journey* 5, 103, 108, 109–111, 118
Koselleck, R. 125
Kosovo Women Network 132
Kung, P. 126

Langer, L. L. 35
laughter 28, 34–35, 38, 39, 41, 42, 75, 77

Lazare, B. 34, 37–38
LeBron, C. J. 42
Leebaw, A. 2, 3, 4, 5
legal accountability 10, 11
Levy, L. 127
Lifton, R. J. 39, 41
literature 4–5, 88–89, 122
living ghosts 41
Locke, J. 49, 52
Lott, E. J. 38
lustration laws, Eastern Europe 8–9

McGregor, J. 87
McGregor, T. 87
McLean, H. 71
Madres de Plaza de Mayo, Argentina 15
Major (*Animal Farm* character) 97
maquis, France 15–16
Mar, R. A. 88
Mashatile, P. 107, 117
mass incarceration *see* incarceration
mass violence *see* violence
Medgepeth, S. 130
memories 2, 6, 9, 12, 13, 14, 123, 126–127, 128, 129, 134; collective 6, 123–124, 125–126, 132, 134, 135, 136; traumatic 128, 130–131
Mignolo, W. 48
Mihai, M. 1–2
milice, Vichy France 17, 18
military occupation 8, 16–20
mnemonic imagination 126, 127
modern capitalism 53
modern states 52
moral guilt 10
moral judgement 40
moral-legal philosophy 10–11
Muholi, Z. 108, 115, 118, 119; *Faces and Phases* 5–6, 103, 108, 114–116, 117–118, 119
Mulhall, S. 89
My Lai atrocities, Vietnam 38

national imaginaries 5, 6
Native Americans 50
Nazis 90–91, 129–130
Ngesi, N. J. 111, 112, 113
Nguyen, V. T. 41
Nietzsche, F. 87
Nussbaum, M. 87, 88, 89

Oatley, K. 88
O'Brien, T. 40, 41
Odysseos, L. 77

Orwell, G. 96–97, 98; *Animal Farm* 4, 87, 96, 97, 98, 99
ostranenie (остранение) 4, 67
otherness 51

pacifism 16, 18, 66–67, 79
Paine, T. 38
pariah humour 2–3, 6, 28, 34, 35, 36, 37, 38, 42–43
participants 38–39
participatory artworks 122, 123, 124, 125, 126, 135
Pârvulescu, I. 14
passive compliance 14–15
Pass Laws, South Africa 111, 113
Paterson, P. 128
Pavlo, W. 56
perceptions 73–74, 78, 79, 80
perpetrators 15, 29, 80, 88
persecution 39
Pétain, General 16, 17
Peterson, J. B. 88
Pickering, M. 126, 127
Pitkin, H. F. 34
political reconciliation 27, 28, 29
political representation 5, 103–105, 106–107, 118, 119
political repression 6, 8, 14, 15
political violence 1, 2, 5, 6, 14, 27, 74, 79–80
positionality 9, 12, 14, 17, 20
posthumanism 95–96
post-memory 124
power relations 11
prisons 3; abuses 54–55, 56–57, 58–59, 61; *Resurrection* 70, 71

Quijano, A. 3, 47

race 50
racism 37, 39
rape 124, 129–130, 131, 132; *see also* sexual violence
reconciliation 2, 27, 28, 29, 30, 32–33
reflexivity 11
representation 103, 104, 105; artistic 5, 103–105, 106, 119, 135; political 5, 103–105, 106–107, 118, 119
repressive political regimes 6, 8, 14, 15
resignation 32, 33
resistance 2, 9, 10, 12, 14, 15–16, 28, 32, 33, 77
responsibility 29, 30, 31–32, 38, 39, 40
Resurrection (Tolstoy, 1899) 70, 71
revolutions 97–98, 133–134

righteous violence 47, 48, 50, 52
Rigney, A. 125
Rodriguez, R. 3, 47
Rogin, M. 38
Romania (1945–1989) 14
Rorty, R. 88
routine perceptions 73–74, 78, 80
Russia 4, 68–69

Saidel, R. 130
satire 75–76
Saward, M. 106, 118
Schiff, J. L. 3, 4, 5
Schmidt, A. 32
secret police informers, Eastern Europe 8–9
security 52–54, 58, 98
sensus communis 125
sexual violence 1, 123, 124, 129–130, 131–132, 133, 135
shame 29, 38, 40, 41, 42
Shklovsky, V. 4, 67, 69, 70, 74, 78
Sitze, A. 33
slavery, United States 47
Smuts, J. 33
social embeddedness 12–13
social imaginaries 1, 3, 6, 47, 48, 50–51, 53
social trust 15
Socrates 35
solidarity 4, 6, 9, 14, 15, 19, 30, 38, 88
Sontag, S. 125
South Africa 5–6, 103, 107, 108, 116–117, 119; apartheid 5, 29, 108, 109–111, 112, 113; Art Biennale, Venice 103, 104, 106, 107–108, 111, 117, 118; Bondelzwort Commission Report 33; *Faces and Phases* 5–6, 103, 108, 114–116, 117–118, 119; hate crimes 5–6, 115; *The Journey* 5, 103, 108, 109–111, 118; *For thirty years next to his heart* 5, 103, 108, 111, 112–114, 118
spect-actors 6, 7, 125, 127, 128, 132, 133
state-organised violence 46, 51, 52, 68–69, 71–72, 73
Stateville Correctional Center, Illinois 57
static guilt 41
Stern, A. (*Waiting for the Barbarians* character) 91, 92, 97, 98
Stone-Mediatore, S. 3
storytelling 3, 29, 30, 32, 39, 40, 41, 42
subjectification 11, 14
superiority 34, 51
symbolic reparations 122, 124, 133, 135

sympathetic identifications 4, 87–89, 91, 93, 96–97, 99
sympathetic imaginations 86–87, 95–96
systemic violence 2, 3, 9, 42, 80
systemic wrongdoing 8, 9, 14
Sznaider, N. 127

temporality 9, 10
testimonies 6–7; *see also* storytelling
'the Indian' 48–49, 51
therapeutic closure 29
therapeutic reconciliation 29
Thinking of You (Xhafa-Mripa, 2015) 6, 131–133, 134
For thirty years next to his heart (Williamson, 1990) 5, 103, 108, 111, 112–114, 118
Todorov, T. 51
Tolstoy, L. 4–5, 66–67, 68–69, 70–71, 72–73, 74, 76, 77, 78, 79, 80; Christianity and Patriotism 72; *The Kingdom of God Is within You* 71–72, 73; *Resurrection* 70, 71
torture 92–95, 98; Abu Ghraib 38, 93
totalitarianism 8
tough-on-crime security 53–54, 56, 60
tragic imagination 28, 29, 30, 42–43
tragic narrative 30
tragic reconciliation 29–30
tragic unreconciliation 28, 33, 42–43
transcendent imagination 127
transgressive humour *see* humour
transgressive laughter *see* laughter
transitional justice institutions 29, 30
traumatic memories 128, 130–131
Trump, D. 85–86, 97, 98
trust 9, 13
Truth and Reconciliation Commission (TRC), South Africa 5, 29, 109, 110
truth commissions 29, 33
Tutu, D. 29

United States 3, 46, 55–56, 85–86; incarceration 1, 46, 52, 53; prisons 52, 54–55, 57, 58–59, 60, 61; slavery 47; tough-on-crime security 53–54
unreconciliation 30, 32, 38, 39, 43

Van Cleve, N. G. 57
Vaughn Correctional Center 58
Venice Biennale *see* Art Biennale, Venice
veterans 38, 39, 41, 42; anti-war 3, 28, 38–39, 40, 41, 42

Vichy France 1, 2, 8, 9, 16–20; anti-Semitism 18–19; women 18, 19, 20
victims 1, 6, 29
Vietnam Veterans Against the War (VVAW) 38, 39, 40, 41
Vietnam War 40, 41
violations *see* abuses; human rights violations
violence 1, 3, 4–5, 11, 98–99, 128; incarceration 59–60; institutionalised 1, 5, 30–32, 47, 61, 71; political 1, 2, 5, 6, 14, 27, 74, 79–80; against women 6, 122, 123, 124, 127, 129–130, 131, 133–136;
prisons 54–55, 56–57, 58–59, 61; righteous 47, 48, 50, 52; sexual 1, 123, 124, 129–130, 131–132, 133, 135; state-organised 46, 51, 52, 68–69, 71–72, 73; systemic 2, 3, 9, 80
visual activism 115, 116, 118
visual art 5, 6; *see also* artistic memory work; artworks
VVAW *see* Vietnam Veterans Against the War (VVAW)

Waiting for the Barbarians (Coetzee, 1980) 4, 87, 89–93, 94, 95, 97, 98, 99
war 2, 3, 6, 80
war ghosts 40–41
Waxman, Z. 130
willed ignorance 2, 90–91
Williamson, S. 108, 118, 119; *For thirty years next to his heart* 5, 103, 108, 111, 112–114, 118
Winter Soldier hearings (1971) 28, 38, 39
winter soldiers 3, 28, 38, 40
'witchcraft' laws 53
women 1, 130–131, 132; Holocaust 129–130; sexual violence 1, 123, 124, 129–130, 131–132, 133, 135; Vichy France 18, 19, 20; violence against 6, 122, 123, 124, 127, 129–130, 131, 133–136
Women Mobilizing Memory: Collaborative Archives, Connective Histories (2015) 130–131
wrongdoing 8, 9, 10–11, 14, 15

Xhafa-Mripa, A. 131; *Thinking of You* 6, 131–133, 134
Xingwana, L. 116

Young, I. M. 87, 88